Social History of Women and
Gender in the Modern Middle East

The

Phillis Wheatley
Collection

MPC Women's Programs
New Book Library

THE SOCIAL HISTORY OF THE MODERN MIDDLE EAST

Series Editor: Edmund Burke III

This series seeks to provide a forum for historically grounded studies on the Middle East in a broad, interdisciplinary context. New research has challenged tacit acceptance about how the Middle East came to modernity and has enlarged our understanding of the complex changes in the region over time and their impact on people and popular culture. By focusing on the nuances of everyday life and the experiences of nonelites—women, workers, peasants, and minorities—stereotypes about what it means to be Arab and Islamic can be challenged and broken down. Far from being a "history with the politics left out," a social history of the Middle East provides a way of reinterpreting the political history of the region, including the development of nationalism and the so-called Islamic revival.

BOOKS IN THIS SERIES

A Social History of Women and Gender in the Modern Middle East, *edited by Margaret L. Meriwether and Judith E. Tucker*

The Social History of Labor in the Middle East, *edited by Ellis Jay Goldberg*

FORTHCOMING

The Social History of Class in the Middle East, *edited by Peter Sluglett*

Social History of Women and Gender in the Modern Middle East

edited by
Margaret L. Meriwether
Judith E. Tucker

Westview Press
A Member of the Perseus Books Group

The Social History of the Modern Middle East

Copyright © 1999 by Westview Press, A Member of the Perseus Books Group

Published in 1999 in the United States of America by Westview Press, 5500 Central Avenue, Boulder, Colorado 80301-2877, and in the United Kingdom by Westview Press, 12 Hid's Copse Road, Cumnor Hill, Oxford OX2 9JJ

Library of Congress Cataloging-in-Publication Data
Social history of women and gender in the modern Middle East / edited
   by Margaret L. Meriwether, Judith E. Tucker.
      p.   cm. — (Social history of the modern Middle East)
   Includes bibliographical references and index.
   ISBN 0-8133-2100-X (hardcover). — ISBN 0-8133-2101-8
(pbk.)
      1. Women—Middle East—History.   2. Women—Middle East—Social
conditions.   3. Sex role—Middle East—History.   4. Feminism—Middle
East.   I. Meriwether, Margaret L.   II. Tucker, Judith E.
III. Series.
HQ1726.5.S63   1999
305.4'0956—dc21   99-17105
                                                                                       CIP
The paper used in this publication meets the requirements of the American National Standard
for Permanence of Paper for Printed Library Materials Z39.48-1984.

10   9   8   7   6   5   4   3   2   1

Contents

Foreword

Over the past decades, important new perspectives on the modern Middle East have emerged due to new sources and new questions as well as the changing historical context. Old paradigms, rooted in modernization theory and the rise of nationalism in the region, are gradually giving way to more complex understandings grounded in social and cultural history. From a field preoccupied with the state and elite groups, recent studies of the Middle East have begun to incorporate the experiences of nonelite women, workers, peasants, ethnic minorities, and tribespeople. While this evolution is still continuing, already the outlines of a new social history of the region are visible.

In this moment of intellectual transition, a series devoted to the social history of the Middle East has much to contribute. The Westview Press series The Social History of the Modern Middle East seeks to provide a focus for historically grounded social science research on the Middle East. Rather than seeing in narrow disciplinary terms, this series views the region using a broad interdisciplinary space within the social sciences, a zone of convergence between anthropology, politics, sociology, women's studies, and history. It seeks to stimulate and focus methodological reflection and scholarship on topics of importance to the Middle Eastern field and to make more widely available the work of a new generation of researchers. Books in the series are designed to supplement courses at the upper division and graduate levels not only in modern Middle Eastern history, but also in anthropology, politics, sociology, and women's studies.

Research on the social history of the Middle East since 1750 has tended to proceed unevenly across the region, with scholars who focus on similar topics in different countries often unaware of one another's work. Work on the Middle East has also been relatively poorly integrated into broader trends affecting the disciplines of the Middle East field. Several reasons may be adduced in explanation. In part, the particular linguistic demands of the field have encouraged specialization in one cultural area or even one country. In addition, scholarly debates tend to take place in hard-to-find specialized journals, and their findings are slow to make their way into the mainstream. As a result, new research on workers, women and the family, and urbanism has been slow to find its way into textbooks.

To facilitate the wider dissemination of new work on Middle Eastern culture and society, volumes in the Social History of the Modern Middle East series will draw together work that crosses disciplinary lines and subregional traditions of scholarship. Under the general editorship of Edmund Burke, III (Professor of History at the University of California, Santa Cruz), volumes have been commissioned on the social history of labor, women and the family, and Middle Eastern urbanism. Others are under consideration. Edited by established scholars, each book will consist of six to nine original essays that will allow readers to follow recent findings on particular topics. Books will survey the region broadly, from the Maghrib to the Hindu Kush. Each will contain chapters on Turkey, Egypt, and Iran, the three most populous states in the region; coverage of other states will vary, depending upon the availability of scholarship. All are works of original scholarship that demonstrate the value of particular approaches as well as provide convenient summaries of the state of research on important topics.

Although the study of women and gender in the Middle East emerged in the 1980s as a major area of research, the history of women has been slower to emerge. Inspired by feminism, the hidden history of women in the Middle East has come gradually to light. Utilizing new sources and asking new questions of old sources, historians of women have made notable contributions to the history of women and the family in the Middle East. In the process they have had an important impact on how the social history of the region, previously resistant to the importance of gender, has been conceptualized. No longer is it possible to make blanket assumptions about the social, religious, political, and economic roles of women. Increasingly, the new research has exposed the ways in which women's fates, even while constrained by a common patriarchal framework, differed from one another according to their ethnic, religious, and social backgrounds (among others). The second volume in this series, *The Social History of Women and Gender in the Modern Middle East*, co-edited by Margaret L. Meriwether and Judith E. Tucker, provides a broad survey of recent work on the subject.

This book provides an assessment of recent work on Middle Eastern women's history from a number of different theoretical perspectives. The introduction by the co-editors summarizes the state of research and suggests some possible frameworks for writing the history of Middle Eastern women. It also contains a useful bibliography of recent works on the history of women in the Middle East that should be of use to beginners as well as more experienced scholars.

The book includes chapters on gender, work, and handicraft production in colonial North Africa by Julia Clancy-Smith; on the historiography of women, the state, and the family by Mervat F. Hatem; on the emergence of women's movements in the Middle East in the period 1900–1940 by Ellen L. Fleischmann; on Islamic family law—legal texts and social practices— by Annelies Moors; and on gender and religion in the Middle East and South Asia by Mary Elaine Hegland. Taken as a whole, they provide the reader with an informative summary of the state of play of the literature on this topic and suggest areas for future research.

Margaret Meriwether is associate professor of history at Denison University. She is the author of the forthcoming book *The Kin Who Count: Family and Society in Ottoman Aleppo 1770–1840* (University of Texas Press, 1999).

Judith Tucker is professor of history at Georgetown University. She is the author of *In the House of the Law: Gender and Islamic Law in Ottoman Syria and Palestine* (University of California Press, 1998), *Women in Nineteenth-Century Egypt* (Cambridge University Press, 1991), and the editor of *Arab Women: Old Boundaries, New Frontiers* (Indiana University Press, 1993).

Edmund Burke, III
Series Editor

Introduction

Margaret L. Meriwether
Judith E. Tucker

$\mathcal{M}$iddle Eastern women have long been a subject of great fascination to outsiders. The veiled and oppressed Middle Eastern woman, the victim of a misogynist religion, has been one of the most enduring images of the region in the minds of the general public. Travelers, missionaries, colonial administrators, and diplomats who have spent time in the region have often perpetuated the accepted image. So too have scholars steeped in the Orientalist tradition. Over the past twenty years, however, the study of Middle Eastern women has claimed the attention of scholars who have questioned the traditional wisdom. Inspired by the great progress in women's studies outside the Middle East, these scholars have produced a plethora of works on women and gender in the region. Impressionistically we would guess that more has been written on women and gender in the past twenty years than on any other subject in Middle Eastern studies; since the early 1990s the program of the Middle East Studies Association annual meeting has included numerous panels on this topic. Using new theoretical frameworks, innovative methodological approaches, and nontraditional sources, scholars have made great progress in shedding light on complex and controversial issues, amid the challenges of an environment in which the "woman question" remains a highly charged political and cultural issue.

The prolific output and generally high quality of the scholarship on Middle Eastern women can be attributed in part to the interdisciplinary nature of this endeavor. Those of us who are historians are very dependent on the work of anthropologists, sociologists, and others for figuring out how to uncover and interpret the past of previously "silent" groups. Increasingly, social scientists are concerned with questions of change and with placing their findings about contemporary society in a historical context. Nevertheless, efforts to learn about women's lives in the past have been slower to develop than have studies of women in the contemporary Middle East, although they have gained considerable momentum in the past ten years, as discussed below. As a result, a lack of historical perspective is a not uncommon problem with much of what is written about women. There is a tendency to assume changelessness, at least for any period before the nineteenth century, and to read into the past social and cultural patterns that did not exist. This lack of historical perspective, partly grounded in our limited knowledge of women and gender, is compounded by the lack of visibility of the work that has been done. One of the obstacles that has limited the "mainstreaming" of this research has been the fragmented state of the literature. Apart from a few important monographs, much of it is found in journal articles and edited volumes, only a couple of which deal specifically with women's history. Therefore there is a need to draw attention to and synthesize the historical research that has been done, to show how this research has already begun to modify our understanding of the past, and to point out the importance of and further direction for research in this field.

This volume is intended to help accomplish these goals by bringing together in a single volume chapters that highlight the research that has been done on the history of Middle Eastern women in the nineteenth and twentieth centuries. Each chapter deals with a major theme in this research and is written by a scholar who is actively engaged in research on that theme. The chapters do not constitute a review of the literature per se or an attempt to synthesize all the research that has been done on a particular topic. Rather, their point of departure is the research interests of the individual authors, placing these interests in the context of other work that has been done, making comparisons across the different regions of the Middle East, and highlighting ongoing debates and key issues as well as gaps in the literature. They also include starter bibliographies for those who wish to pursue particular topics further. This volume then is designed to be a starting point for those who wish to get a sense of the field: teachers wishing to incorporate gender issues into survey courses or topical seminars on Middle Eastern history; students at both the undergraduate and graduate level searching for research topics; and Middle East specialists who are not historians or are not directly involved in women's studies. It is also meant to be accessible to nonspecialists. It seems that little of the research on women and the family in the Middle East has reached scholars of other regions. Stereotypes of women and misunderstandings of gender issues often seem as pervasive among Western feminists and women's studies scholars as among the general public. It is important that they be made aware of developments in the study of women and gender in the Middle East.

The State of Historical Study of Middle East Women

The history of women and gender in the Middle East context is still a developing scholarly field, characterized by divergence in method and motivation. Some serious research on women's history in the region has been done using the older approaches of women worthies and compensatory political history as well as newer methods in social history and the study of dominant and contesting gender discourse. We need to look at these four areas where the project of writing women's history has been pursued in order to understand differences in agenda and the major controversies in the field.

Women Worthies

The expression "women worthies" refers to the history of notable women, women who have played a role that is visible (although often neglected in history writing) in public activities. The "worthies" genre has usually taken the form of biographical studies of famous women or the retelling of well-known historical events with new recognition of the part played by individual women. This is still the most common approach to women's history in the Middle East and one with a long indigenous history. The biographies of the Prophet's wives and other notable women of the early Muslim community represented a hagiographic genre aimed at providing models of behavior for later Muslims. They also constituted a genre that perhaps unwittingly attested to the importance of women, as public political actors and sources of spiritual inspiration, in the early Muslim community. Women also figured in the biographical dictionaries *(tabaqat)* that were produced over the course of the Islamic centuries. These dictionaries featured biographies of contemporary individuals who were important, usually in terms of their religious learning or local prominence. Some of these dictionaries included significant numbers of women, particularly in the pre-Ottoman years.[1]

These biographical studies allow us to research the part that famous women played as, for example, in the retelling of the events of early Islam with attention to the role of women in Leila Ahmed's *Women and Gender in Islam* (1992) or a review of Islamic history focusing on elite women who wielded real political power in Fatima Mernissi's *The Forgotten Queens of Islam* (1993). The study of these notable women has also led to a total reassessment of the exercise of power in at least one case: Leslie Peirce's *The Imperial Harem* (1993), a study of the elite women of the Ottoman imperial harem, contests the standard version of dynastic power in the empire. The importance of the household institution and the mothers (in particular) but also the wives, daughters, and concubines of the reigning monarch in the making of policy at the highest levels of the empire changes the way we must think about Ottoman politics. Mary Ann Fay's research (1996, 1997) on the elite women of households in Mamluk Egypt highlights their central importance to the reproduction of political power in the Mamluk or neo-Mamluk system.

This kind of history writing has sought to set the record straight. At times, the inclusion of women has forced a change in the way we think about the structure of power as in the studies of the imperial harem. It has also contributed to present debates on the position of the indigenous tradition on women's roles in public politics and public space. Above all, these studies have made the point that women are as fully capable of wielding power and exercising authority as men. The feminist critics of the women worthies genre, on the other hand, focus on its elite bias and the dangers of glorifying the past activities of an elite, when a more democratic and egalitarian vision of society is seen as critical to any social progress in the modern world.

Political and Institutional History

A second approach has been to write the histories of women's political movements and activities, whether they were feminist (i.e., focused on the achievement of women's rights) or nationalist. Feminist movements are very much part of the modern history of the Middle East and are often integrally linked to the history of nationalist struggle. The history of women's movements is most developed in Egypt: We have a history of the early women's press by Beth Baron (1994), a history of the Egyptian Feminist Union and Huda Sha'rawi by Margot Badran (1995), and a biography of Doria Shafik, the Egyptian feminist who founded the Bint al-Nil Union, by Cynthia Nelson (1996). Such works are often written in an institutional history style that reconstructs the events, leadership, and activities of the subject organization while allowing us to follow the evolution of feminist thought as it developed in practice. Surely the institutional history of women's movements has been very important for a present sense of continuity; the documentation of past feminist activity legitimates present activity. There is also a sense that one can learn from past mistakes. As current women's movements in the Middle East struggle to define the proper relationship between Western feminism and Middle East feminism, the history of the early Egyptian movement can be instructive. For example, the Egyptian Feminist Union initially modeled itself and its goals on European feminism, with all the resultant problems of class bias and the difficulties of dealing with the relationship between gender oppression and national oppression. Close study of the Egyptian feminist movement usually helps to make the case for the need to develop a truly indigenous feminism.

The political and institutional approach also looks at women's activities in movements that were not ostensibly feminist. Most important has been the participation of women in the nationalist movements so central to the modern history of the Middle East. This is, perhaps, the most developed approach to Palestinian history: There are a number of studies of women and Palestinian nationalism (Julie Peteet 1991; Rosemary Sayigh 1993) and one comprehensive examination of the Palestinian women's movement in the period of the British Mandate by Ellen Fleischmann (1996). Iran has also been fairly well covered thanks to Parvin Paidar's history of women and politics in the twentieth century (1995). Again, most of these studies seek to restore women to history, to document their role. This approach is not only additive, however. When we look at women's activities at the popular level, we often discover new dimensions of the national struggle. The ways in which the family, for example, has been mobilized and transformed in the service of nationalism is an issue just beginning to be explored. The study of female participation at the popular level also helps us grasp the contemporary situation. Much of the writing on the women in the Palestinian *intifada* in recent years seems to assume that Palestinian women had never, before the 1980s, played any significant role in the nationalist movement: Women's current participation fell out of the sky. Such historical myopia does a disservice to the women of the past and also closes off that past with all its possible lessons for us.

The most controversial issue that arises in the realm of political history concerns the relationship between feminism and nationalism or, put differently, the complex relation of gender, nation, class, and race. Our understanding of this complex set of issues is being advanced by new work on the part of younger scholars who are examining the creation of the new woman as an integral part of the development of national identity in the Middle East: Two recent doctoral dissertations by Lisa Pollard (1997) and Mona Russell (1998) examine this phenomenon in the context of nineteenth- and early-twentieth-century Egypt. The problematic ways in which some Western feminists have approached the issue of feminism and nationalism are still, however, a topic of debate. No one clear answer has emerged to suggest how to order these layers or put an end to the feminist-nationalist tension; we have, instead, a multiplicity of voices and experiences.

Social and Economic History

Both the women worthies and the political history approaches often raise new questions about, for instance, the nature of political power or the location of political activity (it can happen in the harem or the home as easily as in the court or parliament). But, in general, these approaches seek to add women to history, not question the fundamental bases of history writing. Social and economic historians also have sought to add women to history. Social and economic historians have easily moved, in their study of the lives of people, be they peasants, workers, merchants, or slaves, to include the women who formed the majority of past populations. These approaches have looked at women in the Middle East as economic actors and as members of communities, families, and classes. By constituting history as including the life patterns, thoughts, and activities of the ordinary person, social and economic history opened up a world of new dimensions far from the arenas of traditional political history (Meriwether 1999; Quataert 1993; Tucker 1985).

In the context of Middle East history, this work can be revolutionary insofar as it shatters the myth of the Muslim woman's passivity and isolation in some kind of secluded, unchanging traditional world. When people study specific times and places, such as lower Egypt (Tucker 1985), Aleppo (Meriwether 1999), or Anatolian towns (Quataert 1993) in the nineteenth century, they discover that women were well integrated into the economy of the time. We find a good deal of specialization by gender, but women were very much part of the economic life of their communities as craftswomen, petty traders, and providers of various services, and therefore very much affected by the changes resulting from European penetration.

And the significance is not just the obvious female contribution to basic economic processes. The lines between family, community, and a public sphere of politics and power are blurred, quite obviously so in premodern society. A marriage, for example, may be a political or economic alliance: The key to many developments in political history might be found in a history of strategic marriages and the associated exchanges of property. At this point, however, we do not have enough material on the social history of women and men alike, much less on family history, a particularly underdeveloped field in the Middle East context. Scholars have been slow to follow up on the pathbreaking work of Alan Duben and Cem Behar in *Istanbul Households* (1991). Recently, however, there are hopeful signs of renewed interest in approaching family history with close attention to the concerns of gender history: Margaret Meriwether (1999), Beshara Doumani (1998), and Kenneth Cuno (1995, 1998) are doing work in family history in Aleppo, the Arab East, and Egypt respectively, research that promises to bring this field into some systematic focus for the first time. This is still, perhaps, the most underresearched area of Middle East history, and an obvious place for encouraging research. There is a wealth of materials, particularly for the Ottoman period for which we have the rich resources of the Islamic court records, extant for most major Arab and Turkish towns.

The field of social and economic history is not particularly prone to controversies; we see widespread agreement among historians on the inclusion of women. The only major question concerns the import of that inclusion: Is there a new awareness of the many ways in which society is gendered as a result of such inclusion? The answer varies widely depending on the historian.

Cultural History and Gender Discourse

There is strong current interest in the final approach, that of the study of cultural history and particularly gender discourse, which is probably the fastest evolving field in women's history in the Middle East. The study of discourse on gender attends to the ways in which the dominant culture in a particular place and time has defined maleness and femaleness as points of opposition, of difference, with the male in a position of power and domination. There is clear resonance in the Middle East: Historians want to understand how the male-privileging "Islamic" discourse on male and female has evolved; to be able to recognize it when they see it; and, if they have feminist goals, to be able to struggle against it. We also must pay attention to the subversive discourses, that is, the ways in which people attempt to undermine and contest the discourse of power.

There is a sense of immediacy in the context of much of the Middle East today where an "Islamist discourse" is evoked to define women's roles and power in ways that are often confining and restrictive. We find an intriguing intersection of the present Islamist discourse on a monolithic and immutable Islam that dictates certain gender roles with an Orientalist discourse that also stresses the unchanging and, in its version, oppressive gender system imposed by Islamic law and thought. Fatima Mernissi (1991) raised a call several years ago for feminist scholars to engage in serious study of the Islamic tradition, not to leave the representation and interpretation of this tradition entirely in the hands of those who would emphasize its more conservative and even antifeminist side. Several historians have responded with studies of the Islamic tradition that attempt to revisit the question of Islam and gender based on investigations of the ways that tradition was understood in particular Muslim contexts. The work of Barbara Stowasser (1994) on the images of women in the Qur'an and Denise Spellberg (1994) on the legacy of 'A'isha are two fine examples of how close historical examination of the development of Islamic views on gender reveals a variety and complexity of understandings that cannot be reduced to simple misogynistic or patriarchal positions.

Historical studies of Islamic law, as both legal thought and practice, also have contributed to greater nuance in our approach to the Islamic tradition. A number of historians have turned their attention to legal sources, particularly to Islamic court records, not just as repositories of social and economic data but also as keys to understanding how gendered discourses of power were inscribed in the law. Careful analysis of the details and language of court records can shed light on the ways in which an Islamic discourse on gendered rights and social obligations was being elaborated and actualized through judicial processes. Most of these studies look to the Ottoman period because of the wealth of available court records for many cities and towns in the empire. The court records have been employed in this way in the context of seventeenth-century Anatolia (Peirce 1997b), nineteenth-century Damascus (al-Qattan 1996), and nineteenth-century Jaffa and Haifa (Agmon 1996). The study of other kinds of jurisprudential literature such as *fiqh* and fatwas perhaps even better suited to the exploration of legal discourse has emerged more slowly, but there are a few new monographs (Spectorsky 1993; Tucker 1998).

Overall, the study of Islamic legal discourse is an attempt to historicize and concretize discussion of Islam and gender, to investigate the dominant discourse on gender as represented in Islamic writings in a particular time and place. We can study both the writings of the muftis (Muslim jurisprudents who represent the thinking of Muslim intellectuals on gender) and the activities of the Islamic courts (in which ordinary persons both display their understanding of the legal discourse on gender and, in some instances, contest it) as this area of historical research continues to grow.

Not all Middle East feminists agree that this is a research priority. Some argue that to engage with the "Islamic" discourse on gender is a mistake: We are dealing here with a gender system that cannot be rehabilitated, and feminists risk wasting their time and effort, as well as the integrity of their vision, if they pursue the strategy of debating the Islamist interpretation of gender in Islam. They are also doomed to lose the argument because the al-Azhar–trained conservative Islamic scholar will always have the last say on topics construed as religious.

The Writing of Women's History in the Middle East

Although many historians of women's issues active in the West are of Middle Eastern origin, in the region itself the situation is somewhat different. Perhaps the most striking aspect of the women's history field is the virtual absence, until quite recently, of serious historical study of women, an absence of apparently small concern to most women researchers and activists. This phenomenon may come as a surprise to most historians of Europe and North America. The importance of the biennial Berkshire conference on women's history, the centrality of history to many women's studies programs, the ambitious research activities that have challenged many standard interpretations of Western history all attest to the fact that the study of gendered history is viewed as basic to feminism, to women's present and future. Without reclaiming and rewriting the past, we cannot fashion a vision for the future.

Why is a focus on gendered history apparently viewed differently in the Middle East? Women scholars and activists (often one and the same in the Middle East context) generally agree that not much historical writing on women is available, especially outside the boundaries of the women worthies genre. Correcting this situation, however, has clearly not been a research priority, even among feminists, for a number of possible reasons.[2]

First, there is a feeling that we need to let well enough alone. To study Middle Eastern women's history is to risk dredging up a past that is better forgotten. Often women want to make a clean break with a past of women's oppression born of tradition and look to a future for women that will be so different that the past holds few lessons. The idea that the modern woman must turn her back on the past still has its supporters.

Second, women are concerned that the history they know and can know tends to be the history of activities of elite women. In the modern period, these are the women who were active in philanthropic and nationalist organizations, many of whom left records in the form of memoirs and family papers. Again, this is not a past they want to build on, a pattern they want to perpetuate. Indeed, they want to leave it behind, having no wish to enshrine elite leadership, and instead highlight the more varied backgrounds of women's leadership today and empower all women.

The third reason for downplaying women's history has often been voiced in relation to the specific Palestinian case, but it is certainly applicable to other localities as well. The history of the Palestinian people was "co-opted" by the national movement; all history has been written from the point of view of the national struggle narrowly defined. There is no room for gendered history in the meganarrative of colonial oppressor and colonized oppressed, two monolithic categories that do not allow for gender difference.

The fourth reason came as a predictable consequence of the first three: There are very few women historians in the Middle East in general, and the field continues to have trouble attracting women scholars, a problem that is exacerbated by poor research facilities particularly in the social sciences and humanities fields.

New voices are being heard in the region now, in areas as diverse as Morocco, Egypt, and Palestine, that are making the case that historical research on women and gender in Islam or the Middle East will not necessarily ensnare women in past social relations or validate some sort of unchanging tradition: On the contrary, they argue that it is through the study of women's past as well as of the history of relations between men and women and gendered society that we can deepen our understanding of the present and fashion strategies for the future. In fact, in the current debates on culture, tradition, and authenticity, Middle Eastern feminists need to be armed with historical studies that can help them contest conservative and misogynist versions of Islamic history.

Women and Gender in the Middle East Before 1800

This volume focuses on women and gender in the *modern* Middle East, and its underlying assumption is that women's lives and gender relations have changed in fundamental ways with the historical transformations of the Middle East in the past two hundred years. The authors of the individual chapters are sensitive to the differences in the nature and degree of change as a result of differences in class, region, and specific historical context, as well as to some of the underlying similarities in the lives of these women. They are also aware of the danger of ignoring important continuities that persisted in the face of change or even as a strategy for adapting to change. Nor do they assume that change is necessarily unilinear or progressive. Any scholar trying to analyze the extent, nature, direction, and significance of change, as it affected women's lives in the nineteenth and twentieth centuries, is, however, faced with a major challenge: our limited knowledge of this topic before 1800. This can result in a tendency to fall back on generalizations that fail to contextualize women's experiences and gender dynamics and that draw sharp dichotomies between modern and premodern eras. This historical myopia, as evident above, can produce misleading analyses and conclusions.

Fortunately, the history of Middle Eastern women before 1800 is beginning to get the attention it deserves. The works by Spellberg, Peirce, and Ahmed mentioned in the previous section, as well as three edited volumes dealing specifically with the history of Middle Eastern women, two of which focus primarily on the premodern and early modern periods, attest to the new level of interest in these earlier eras (Keddie and Baron 1991; Sonbol 1996; Zilfi 1997). Much of this work focuses on Ottoman women. Court records, fatwas, *sikayet,* and proverbs are all being used by historians to gain insights into and a level of detail about women's everyday lives and the workings of the gender system unavailable for other times and places before the modern era. Enough has been done now to provide the rudiments of a historiographical framework and a background for these studies of women and gender in the modern era.

Gender, Property, and Power

If there is one underlying theme common to much of the diverse research on women in the Ottoman Empire, it is an emphasis on "a wide field of action that was available to women in the period despite an inherited gender system that prescribed women's subordination to men" (Zilfi 1997, 5). Social relationships, especially gender and family relationships, were not fixed by a monolithic Islamic cultural system but rather were negotiated among various actors, including women. These relationships varied according to context and as a result were flexible and dynamic. This wide field of action was not just a product of loopholes in the law, the exigencies of everyday life, or chance, but was directly connected to certain structural features and institutional arrangements in the Ottoman state and society. These included the institutional flexibility, especially in the judicial system that interpreted and applied the *shari'a* but also in other agencies of the state, that reflected an underlying concern about ensuring the rights of the vulnerable and providing some basic standard of justice. Equally important were women's own efforts to use the strategies and resources (social and cultural as well as economic) available to them as they tried to establish some control over their own lives and the situations around them. This is not to deny the reality of a dominant patriarchal ideology, or the constraints on women's choices and agency and women's subordination to males in important symbolic and actual ways. Still, it underscores the need to contextualize this system and recognize the degree to which gender relations were subject to negotiation and even contested. Women were already pushing against gender boundaries long before the changes of the nineteenth century.

We probably know more about women as economic actors than about any other aspect of their lives during the Ottoman period. This is largely because of the importance of the religious court archives as sources for the study of women and gender. These are to a large extent documents about property, and through them women's access to property emerges. Women's involvement in work, particularly in handicraft and artisanal production and in agricultural labor, is less apparent from these sources. Because women were rarely part of the formal and male-centered structures of production such as the craft corporations, whose activities were regulated by the state, the invisibility of their contributions to production is a problem for this period as it is for the nineteenth and twentieth centuries (see Chapter 1).

In these sources, women appear as economic actors, as they bought and sold property, inherited and bequeathed wealth, established *waqf*s, borrowed and lent money, and at times even served as holders of *timar* and usufruct rights on *miri* land, as tax farmers and in business partnerships. Their access to wealth was originated through inheritance, dower, and beneficiary rights in religious endowments; once they acquired property, many assumed an active role in managing and investing this wealth. Moreover, their agency was apparent in their willingness to claim their rights to property and contest any infringements of these rights. The many studies on women and property document women's economic activities and the extent of their integration into local economies, and perform the necessary task of correcting the historical record (see, e.g., Faroqhi 1986; Marcus 1984; Meriwether 1993).

At the same time, this research on women and property is moving beyond simply restoring women to Ottoman history. We are accumulating enough data from different parts of the empire and different centuries of Ottoman rule to address some comparative and theoretical issues. There is no doubt of the gendered nature of work; in many places women were the spinners and men were the weavers, for example. Access to property was also gendered; females did not have control over the amount of wealth or property that men did, except on rare occasions, and they were sometimes denied access to certain kinds of resources, such as land or commercial properties. They also had to be vigilant in protecting their rights and make use of the judicial system when necessary.

As we learn more about women and property, potentially significant differences emerge in different parts of the empire. For example, upper-class women in Cairo were tax farmers, upper-class women in Aleppo were not (Fay 1997; Meriwether 1999). In some places, women frequently owned commercial properties, whereas in others they owned only houses. Inheritance practices also varied significantly in ways that particularly affected women. In Ottoman cities, where female rights to inheritance were theoretically observed, the type and amount of property involved, the timing of the distribution of estates, and whether a woman claimed or did not claim her inheritance all had an impact on just what these inheritance rights meant.

Exploring the relationship between gender and property can further our understanding of the dynamics of the local economy. At the same time it can help us better understand the implications of this access to property for women. Did access to and control of wealth in itself translate into greater autonomy or authority for women? Did access to wealth provide women with some leverage and bargaining power in their everyday lives? Could at least some women use this access to wealth to alter gender boundaries? The answers to these questions depend in part on the extent and nature of this wealth and the opportunities or constraints inherent in particular economic conditions.

Yet another variable that affected the relationship between gender and property was the nature of the state. The link between control of economic resources, access to power, and the nature of the Ottoman state is pursued in a number of studies on Ottoman women, from the royal family on down. Access to power for women was not only dependent on class position and the ability to mobilize resources but also on the structure of the state and the distribution of state power. It is the connection between the position of women and the decentralization of the empire in the postclassical period that has particularly drawn the attention of historians.

The preeminent study of Ottoman women and power is Leslie Peirce's *The Imperial Harem* (1993). As indicated above, this study of royal women is not only about "women worthies" and a corrective to the generally negative view held by historians of the "sultanate of women," but has also forced us to revise our understanding of Ottoman politics and the exercise of sovereignty. In the seventeenth century, the mothers of the Ottoman sultans, as well as other women in the royal family, were accused by certain factions in the Ottoman ruling class of usurping power and undermining the Ottoman state, an accusation that was picked up by later historians. The critique of these royal women by their political opponents was part of a discourse on gender that was a metaphor for their dissatisfaction with other political and social changes. Peirce sets this discourse against other evidence supporting the institutionalization of women's roles within the imperial household, societal expectations about their exercise of sovereignty, and the widespread sense of the legitimacy of the roles that these royal women played. Their exercise of sovereignty, whether through preparing their sons to be sultans, acting as regents, corresponding with other rulers, or engaging in pious and charitable acts, was fully expected by society.

Much of the discussion of gender and state outside the palace and away from the center has focused on women of the provincial elites and the relationship between the diffusion of state power in the postclassical period, the emergence of provincial households as the center of power, and the politics of the household. According to Mary Ann Fay, "Historically, women seem to have had more autonomy and/or power and generally higher status in societies where power was located in households rather than in more formal mechanisms and structures of the centralized, bureaucratized state" (1997, 33). The lack of separation between affairs of state and the affairs of the household, the household acting as the physical center of political activities, and women's role in perpetuating the power of the household reinforced the link between the politics of households and female empowerment. In seventeenth- and eighteenth-century Egypt, women were critical to the perpetuation of Mamluk households, as wives and concubines and as conveyors of property and status. The power they could exercise was both a cause and an effect of the considerable resources they controlled— whether tax farms, religious endowments, land, or residential and commercial properties—and their own independent patronage networks (Fay 1997; Marsot 1995; Hathaway 1997). Similarly, in Mosul the formation of the Jalili households in the early decades of the eighteenth century redrew the political, religious, and spatial map of the city. The women of the Jalili households were involved in the process of consolidating the political dominance of these households, most notably in their involvement in building large religious and commercial complexes (Khoury 1997). In other parts of the empire, notable households were less powerful and state power more effective, and the women in these households were less able to exercise the degree of influence or control comparable resources than their sisters in places like Cairo and Mosul. Even in these circumstances, however, notable women were important in repairing family fortunes as household heads in the absence of their husbands or as widows, and in representing the family in official and public capacities (Faroqhi 1997; Meriwether 1999).

Outside elite households, women did not have access to formal and informal networks of power in the way upper-class women did. Nevertheless, an important source of empowerment for them was their ability to voice grievances or claim rights before legal and political authorities. The *shari'a* courts provided such a forum at the local level (see below), and numerous scholars have documented women's use of the court for these purposes. In addition to courts, other channels to state officials were available. Beginning in the seventeenth century, the subject population of the empire was given the right to petition the imperial council, part of an effort by the state to stem official corruption and abuse. Nonelite women, often from distant parts of the empire, took advantage of this petitioning process; about 8 percent of these petitions were from women (Zarinebaf-Shahr 1997, 258). These actions would not have been possible without both an institutional framework and an ethos that was open to such petitions. More significantly, they reveal women's knowledge of how the system worked and their exercise of agency in using that system to their advantage: "Presenting a petition to the authorities in the capital was impossible without the organizing skills and access to resources far beyond those needed to apply to the local kadi" (Faroqhi 1997, 27). Clearly there were women who had these skills and took advantage of the opportunity to take matters to the highest authorities.

Gender, Law, and Religion

The historical evidence on women and gender in the Ottoman period is so rich because women throughout the empire made extensive use of the courts, for everything from registering the sale of a piece of property to suing brothers for illegally depriving them of valuable landholdings. Women would not have turned to the courts as much as they did if they did not believe that the use of the courts was an effective way to protect their interests. Using the courts to claim rights and to register and thus give legal weight to important transactions gave women important leverage in negotiating the familial and social relationships in which their lives were embedded.

Women's use of the courts and the availability of these records presents us with a rich archive of how gender issues were understood, interpreted, and enforced by Ottoman jurists. In Chapter 4 of this volume, Annelies Moors discusses the major shift in approach to the study of Islamic law and the resulting emphasis on the flexible, pragmatic, and dynamic nature of the law. Research on Ottoman court records as well as other legal litera- ture such as the fatwas has played a role in revisionist thinking about the nature of the Islamic legal system.

The flexible and pragmatic nature of Islamic law was apparent in the way in which court officials and legal scholars dealt with issues brought forward by women who used the courts. While never questioning a gender system that enshrined male dominance, *qadi*s and muftis nevertheless in- terpreted the law in ways that often worked for women. Women used the courts as way of negotiating, testing, and even pushing gender boundaries. The legal system worked for them by modifying and limiting male privi- lege, at least to some extent. The way the law could work for women can be illustrated by a brief look at some of the recent research on marriage and divorce, two areas of Islamic law that appear to be fundamental to the inequality in the gender system.

Gender inequality was embedded in Islamic marriage law through ad- vantages given to men, such as their right to an easy divorce, their right to have more than one wife, and their absolute authority over their wives. The control and subordination of women was also reflected in the limitations on women's rights to choose a spouse and end a marriage.

Yet recent research on marriage, which has focused less on legal texts and more on social practices and the way the legal system has dealt with marriage questions, has shown that women had ways of redressing this im- balance. Not only could a husband's authority be modified by his wife's connected ties to her natal family, but many women used the courts to gain some control over choice of spouse, payment of the dower, and guardian- ship of children, for example. Some took advantage of the option of im- posing conditions in marriage contracts, such as restricting the husband's right to take another wife or choosing the place of residence. The judges' rulings on marriage issues reflected the wide range of interpretation possi- ble within the law and often worked to the advantage of women (Abdal- Rehim 1996; Hanna 1996; Meriwether 1999; Tucker 1998).

The ending of a marriage also reflected the inequality between men and women. Under Islamic law, men have the right to unilateral repudiation of a marriage for any reason; women's rights to initiate divorce are very lim- ited and involve a financial penalty. Yet research on divorce has shown that Ottoman women had more opportunities to get out of an unwanted mar- riage than previously thought. Judith Tucker (1991) found that legal sepa- rations and annulments, which did not involve the financial penalty that fe- male-initiated divorce *(khul')* could entail, were used in Nablus. The conditions that many women attached to marriage contracts in Cairo during this time were also insurance that they could divorce without penalty if these conditions were not met (Abdal-Rehim 1996). Moreover, women made use of the law to avoid some of the financial penalties associated with divorce. Madeline Zilfi noted that even in *talaq* divorce, women often went to court to register and claim the financial compensations that they were entitled to receive, so that they would have the means to enforce payment. She also noted the strategies that women used to avoid the financial penalties of *khul'* divorces (1997). In fact, women were initiating divorces in record numbers in eighteenth-century Istanbul, to the point that it became a matter of great concern to some male observers. Zilfi concludes that "to the extent that the right to initiate divorce validated the notion that women, too, deserved to be satisfied in their mates, it can be thought to have enhanced women's status" (1997, 295).

In the context of the *shari'a,* gender boundaries were flexible and subject to negotiation, and many women took advantage of this. The flexibility of gender boundaries was also apparent in other aspects of women's lives usually associated with female subordination, namely segregation and veiling. These were not mandated by Islamic law but were matters of social convention given sanction in religious and legal discourse. For example, in eighteenth-century Mosul, upper-class women remained largely confined to their homes, but middle- and lower-class women had considerable mobility within their quarters, and working-class women moved freely in the central areas of the city. Dina Khoury concludes that attitudes "exhibited a flexibility which mitigated the tensions that existed between the prescriptive literature on women's visibility in public spaces, and the actual practice of lower-class women" (1997, 118). European observers in many Ottoman cities commented on women attending picnics and other leisure-time activities and visiting tombs. In Istanbul during the Tulip era (1718–1730), women were seen much more frequently in public. Although the conservative backlash that linked declining moral standards as reflected in the "immodest" behavior of women with political misconduct and imperial decline was successful in limiting women's mobility after 1730, the eagerness of women to take advantage of the new openness of society during this time reflected their receptiveness to change and perhaps an impatience with the restrictions imposed on their mobility (Zilfi 1996).

Women's mobility and access to public space varied according to class, region, and time period. But even for upper-class women, whose mobility was most limited, there was a sense in which they were very visible in public space. Women of means, from the royal family to the provincial middle class, were active as founders and overseers of religious endowments. As a result, their names, if not the women themselves, were highly visible in their association with major religious buildings. In eighteenth-century Mosul, for example, upper-class women played a major role in the process of reshaping sacred space through their patronage of large religious complexes (Khoury 1997). This was a public expression of their piety, which had religious, symbolic, and sometimes political connotations.

Women's involvement with religious endowments raises the issue of their relationship to religion in yet another way: their involvement in religious ritual. Although much of women's religious life took place in the home, as has been true in more recent times (see Chapter 5), and is therefore difficult for historians to examine, women did take part in public rituals as well, at least in some places and periods. In eighteenth-century Mosul, for example, women were frequent visitors to tombs and took part in public Ashura rituals (Khoury 1997). Women were more regularly involved in Sufi rituals, as patronesses of Sufi *zawiyas*, as participants in Sufi rituals, and as actual members of institutionalized Sufi orders in some cases. It was in the less orthodox forms of religious expression that they were more welcome (Clancy-Smith 1991). At the same time, women were not absent from the ranks of religious scholars. Some achieved sufficient reputation to be included in biographical collections (Roded 1994). Ottoman women from *ulama* families were more widely educated in the religious sciences than has usually been recognized (Berkey 1991).

It is within this context of an early modern society that offered women more autonomy and ways of achieving some control over their own lives that the changes of the modern era must be seen.

Women and Gender in the Modern Middle East

The papers in this volume range over fairly wide territory as they address different dimensions of women's lives in the modern Middle East, including issues of women's work and contributions to production, the impact of modern state policy on women and the family, the various uses and abuses of Islamic law, the ability of women themselves to mobilize and organize on their own behalf, and the ways in which women have understood Islam and its implications for a gendered society. The academic backgrounds of the authors are as diverse as the topics: We have two historians (Julia Clancy-Smith and Ellen Fleischmann), two anthropologists (Mary Elaine Hegland and Annelies Moors), and one political scientist (Mervat Hatem) among our contributors. Despite this variety of topics and approaches, the authors often find themselves grappling with surprisingly similar problems, all of which appear to be common concerns for those who study Middle Eastern women today.

A first widely shared concern is the problem of definition. What exactly is a Middle Eastern woman? Does such a category make any analytic sense or does it invariably do violence to the subject it hopes to serve? On the one hand, our authors trace signal historical developments that affected much of the region in similar ways, such as the impact of colonialism and integration into a world market that Clancy-Smith argues shaped so much of the economic trajectory of the region and invariably women's work roles and economic power. Similarly, the rise of modern Middle Eastern states with comparable educational, legal, and social policies led to certain gendered views of society that took only a limited number of forms: Both Hatem and Moors stress the rather narrow parameters within which the modern state has constructed the official views of gender, which have such an impact on policies affecting women. The prominence of Islam, whether in Shi'i or Sunni form, as a dominant ideology with certain implications for women is another factor that crosses national borders in the region and beyond, as Hegland demonstrates in her discussion of Iran and Pakistan. And finally, women in the region have recognized certain affinities and natural alliances among themselves, as Fleischmann observes, which they were to draw upon as they built their women's movements.

But this sense of regional unity easily collapses in the face of the careful consideration all authors give to the specific contexts of different women's lives. We soon learn that the enormous diversity of the region eludes facile generalization. Women's work patterns may have been affected in most places by the play of international capital, but Clancy-Smith is quick to note that other factors including local traditions, processes of uneven development, and varying colonial strategies could produce differences in the amount and nature of women's work even within the same country. Nor did the rise of the modern state carry the same consequences from country to country: Questions of gender and national identity could be constructed very differently. As Moors points out, women may be the badge of tradition for one state and the symbol of modernity for another, with parallel variations of state policies. Hegland's discussion of religion also points out some of the ways in which what Islam has to say about gender can differ in various contexts; the Islam of opposition movements, for example, has often given women more freedom of movement than the Islam of established state legitimacy. Women's own sense of transregional affinity, which led to certain historical alliances, can also be fragile as diverging interests and contexts come into play. Fleischmann points out that the relationship between women's movements and national struggles invariably took different forms as the timing and eventual fate of the nationalist struggle varied from place to place.

So our authors refer to "Middle Eastern women" only in the most guarded of terms. They construct this category for analytic purposes, allowing us to comprehend some of the ways in which large structural events and ideological trends intersected with gender definitions in the region, but their accounts are full of the nuance that accompanies the grounding of their discussion of women in the concrete and specific.

A second problem our authors all confront is the difficulty of approaching the topic of Middle Eastern women with ideas of gender and feminism shaped by their experiences outside the region. We have traveled far from the naïveté of earlier studies of women and gender that subscribed to the notion of clear universal standards of gender equity that could be applied across the board. Although all our authors reject the idea that the West sets the standard for gender relations and provides a model for judging gendered societies elsewhere, they are not so quick to throw out the goal of gender equity altogether, suggesting instead that we explore the different forms the road to gender equity might take. Certainly the importance of context, and particularly political context, is always paramount. In her discussion of feminisms in the Middle East, Fleischmann points out that feminism has both particular and universal aspects. The history of women's movements reflects particular contexts and concerns that only sometimes resonate with universal goals: Feminists from the region have been able to make common cause on occasion with their sisters elsewhere around issues of female empowerment, but their struggles in a context of national and racial oppression inevitably influence their priorities and strategies. The policies of some of the states in the region that seek to promote national identity and development through the cultivation of "state feminism" also provide specific challenges, as Hatem explains. Women may welcome the contributions of state feminism in terms of advances toward formal gender equity, but they may also suffer from the limitations such policies impose on their autonomy.

Probably the area of greatest debate is that of Islam and feminist theory. Islam is nowhere portrayed as a monolithic and oppressive gender system that provides the master definition of women in the region. On the contrary, Hegland's discussion of Muslim women finds them working within the confines of the Islamic tradition to carve out female space and even female power. Although such activity is often read as a form of necessary accommodation or even "accommodating protest," Hegland describes the variety of women's voices that can be found under the Islamic umbrella. Moors discusses the wide range of approaches to Islamic law. The law does not present us with a unitary system of gendered oppression but rather offers an array of gendered rights and social obligations that can provide women with some distinct possibilities.

A third, and final, problem that challenges all our authors is the extent to which the study of women in the region draws them inexorably into a rethinking of some of the grand narratives that have informed scholarly views of the region in general, and women's history in particular. Clancy-Smith's exploration of women's work leads her to reexamine the classic definition of work as something that takes place in the public sphere. On the contrary, such a definition fits very poorly with the historical development of production in North Africa and the rest of the region; it is only when we completely revise this notion that we are able to comprehend not only the full extent and nature of women's work, but signal developments in work patterns in the region in general. Fleischmann's chapter takes on the grand narrative of nationalism, which privileges visible male activity and formal politics at the expense of understanding the many ways in which women were involved in the national struggle. The binary opposition of the nationalist narrative that only recognizes the contradiction between the oppressed and the oppressor at the level of national independence does not allow us to explore the many ways in which women and gender issues were centrally involved in the history of nationalism as actors and as symbols, as Fleischmann's discussion of the "new woman" suggests. Hatem addresses the problematic of the master narrative directly through her critique of the modernization paradigm in its many guises. The limitations of this paradigm, which underlies much of the writing on the region, is nowhere more apparent than in studies of women and gender: The traditional/modern dichotomy freezes women in a narrow representational mode.

Perhaps the master narratives of Islam have proved the most difficult to unseat. In the study of Islamic law we are confronted with the idea that legal history is the history of legal scholars and texts rather than lived experience. Indeed, it is only since the late 1980s that new studies, as Moors points out, have attempted to bring society into the picture. Work on women and gender is making central contributions to a revisionist school, as Moors's discussion of women's pursuit of legal strategies illustrates. Hegland confronts another powerful master narrative, that of Islam as victimizing women, and stresses the variety of interpretations and debates that surround the subject of women and gender in Islam. She is particularly interested in the ways in which women's own actions, by virtue of various strategies, belie notions of a simple and uniform Islamic patriarchy. For all our authors, the study of women and gender issues has helped to stretch and contest the standard frameworks of Middle East studies and encourage the rethinking of paradigms and approaches in the field.

Notes

1. See Roded 1994 for a survey and discussion of women in biographical dictionaries.

2. The following remarks are based on conversations with women scholars at the Women's Studies Centre in Beit Hanina and the Women's Studies Program at Birzeit University, Palestine, and on discussions with members of the Women and Memory Forum in Cairo.

References

Abdal-Rehim and Abdal-Rahman. 1996. "The Family and Gender Laws in Egypt During the Ottoman Period." In *Women, Family, and Divorce Laws in Islamic History*, ed. Amira E. Sonbol. Syracuse, N.Y.: Syracuse University Press.

Agmon, Iris. 1996. "Muslim Women in Court According to the *Sijill* of Late Ottoman Jaffa and Haifa: Some Methodological Notes." In *Women, Family, and Divorce Laws in Islamic History*, ed. Amira E. Sonbol. Syracuse, N.Y.: Syracuse University Press.

Ahmed, Leila. 1992. *Women and Gender in Islam: Historical Roots of a Modern Debate*. New Haven: Yale University Press.

Badran, Margot. 1995. *Feminists, Islam, and Nation: Gender and the Making of Modern Egypt*. Princeton: Princeton University Press.

Baron, Beth. 1994. *The Women's Awakening in Egypt: Culture, Society, and the Press*. New Haven: Yale University Press.

Berkey, Jonathan P. 1991. "Women and Islamic Education in the Mamluk Period." In *Women in Middle Eastern History: Shifting Boundaries in Sex and Gender*, ed. Nikki Keddie and Beth Baron. New Haven: Yale University Press.

Clancy-Smith, Julia. 1991. "The House of Zainab: Female Authority and Saintly Succession in Colonial Algeria." In *Women in Middle Eastern History: Shifting Boundaries in Sex and Gender*, ed. Nikki Keddie and Beth Baron. New Haven: Yale University Press.

Cuno, Kenneth. 1995. "Joint Family Households and Rural Notables in Nineteenth-Century Egypt." *International Journal of Middle East Studies* 27: 485–502.

_____. 1998. "A Tale of Two Villages: Family, Property, and Economic Activity in Rural Egypt in the 1840s." In *Agriculture in Egypt from Ancient Times to the Modern Era*, ed. Eugene Rogan and Alan Bowman. Oxford: Oxford University Press.

Doumani, Beshara. 1998. "Endowing Family: Waqf, Property Devolution, and Gender in Greater Syria, 1800–1860." *Comparative Studies in Society and History* 40: 3–41.

Duben, Alan, and Cem Behar. 1991. *Istanbul Households: Marriage, Family, and Fertility, 1880–1940*. Cambridge: Cambridge University Press.

Faroqhi, Suraiya. 1986. *Men of Modest Substance: House Owners and House Property in Seventeenth-Century Ankara and Kayseri*. Cambridge: Cambridge University Press.

_____. 1997. "Crime, Women, and Wealth in the Eighteenth-Century Anatolian Countryside." In *Women in the Ottoman Empire: Middle Eastern Women in the Early Modern Era*, ed. Madeline C. Zilfi. Leiden: E. J. Brill.

Fay, Mary Ann. 1996. "The Ties That Bound: Women and Households in Eighteenth-Century Egypt." In *Women, Family, and Divorce Laws in Islamic History*, ed. Amira E. Sonbol. Syracuse, N.Y.: Syracuse University Press.

_____. 1997. "Women and Waqf: Property, Power, and the Domain of Gender in Eighteenth-Century Egypt." In *Women in the Ottoman Empire: Middle Eastern Women in the Early Modern Era*, ed. Madeline C. Zilfi. Leiden: E. J. Brill.

Fleischmann, Ellen. 1996. "The Nation and Its 'New' Women: Feminism, Nationalism, Colonialism, and the Palestinian Women's Movement, 1920–1948." Ph.D. dissertation, Georgetown University.

Hanna, Nelly. 1996. "Marriage Among Merchant Families in Seventeenth-Century Cairo." In *Women, Family, and Divorce Laws in Islamic History,* ed. Amira E. Sonbol. Syracuse, N.Y.: Syracuse University Press.

Hathaway, Jane. 1997. *The Politics of Households in Ottoman Egypt.* Cambridge: Cambridge University Press.

Ivanona, Svetlana. 1996. "The Divorce Between Zubaida Hatun and Esseid Osman Aga: Women in the Eighteenth-Century Shari'a Court of Rumelia." In *Women, Family, and Divorce Laws in Islamic History,* ed. Amira E. Sonbol. Syracuse, N.Y.: Syracuse University Press.

Keddie, Nikki, and Beth Baron, eds. 1991. *Women in Middle Eastern History: Shifting Boundaries in Sex and Gender.* New Haven: Yale University Press.

Khoury, Dina. 1996. "Drawing Boundaries and Defining Space: Women and Space in Ottoman Iraq." In *Women, Family, and Divorce Laws in Islamic History,* ed. Amira E. Sonbol. Syracuse, N.Y.: Syracuse University Press.

_____. 1997. "Slippers at the Entrance or Behind Closed Doors: Domestic Spaces for Mosuli Women." In *Women in the Ottoman Empire: Middle Eastern Women in the Early Modern Era,* ed. Madeline C. Zilfi. Leiden: E. J. Brill.

Letters from Memory. 1998. Cairo: Women and Memory Forum.

Marcus, Abraham. 1984. "Men, Women, and Property: Dealers in Real Estate in Eighteenth-Century Aleppo." *Journal of the Economic and Social History of the Orient* 26: 138–163.

Marsot, Afaf. 1995. *Women and Men in Late Eighteenth-Century Egypt.* Austin: University of Texas Press.

Meriwether, Margaret L. 1993. "Women and Economic Change in Nineteenth-Century Syria: The Case of Aleppo." In *Arab Women: Old Boundaries, New Frontiers,* ed. Judith E. Tucker. Bloomington: Indiana University Press.

_____. 1999. *The Kin Who Count: Family and Society in Ottoman Aleppo.* Austin: University of Texas Press.

Mernissi, Fatima. 1991. *The Veil and the Male Elite: A Feminist Interpretation of Women's Rights in Islam.* Reading, Mass.: Addison-Wesley.

_____. 1993. *The Forgotten Queens of Islam.* Minneapolis: University of Minnesota Press.

Nelson, Cynthia. 1996. *Doria Shafik, Egyptian Feminist.* Gainesville: University Press of Florida.

Paidar, Parvin. 1995. *Women and the Political Process in Twentieth-Century Iran.* Cambridge: Cambridge University Press.

Palestinian Women: A Status Report. 1997. Birzeit: Birzeit University Press.

Peirce, Leslie. 1993. *The Imperial Harem: Women and Sovereignty in the Ottoman Empire.* New York: Oxford University Press.

_____. 1997a. "Seniority, Sexuality, and Social Order: The Vocabulary of Gender in Early Modern Ottoman Society." In *Women in the Ottoman Empire: Middle Eastern Women in the Early Modern Era,* ed. Madeline C. Zilfi. Leiden: E. J. Brill.

_____. 1997b. "'She Is Trouble and I Will Divorce Her': Orality, Honor, and Divorce in the Ottoman Court of 'Aintab." In *Women in the Medieval Islamic World: Power, Patronage, Piety,* ed. Gavin Hambly. Cambridge: Cambridge University Press.

Peteet, Julie. 1991. *Gender in Crisis: Women and the Palestinian Resistance Movement.* New York: Columbia University Press.

Pollard, Lisa. 1997. "Nurturing the Nation: The Family Politics of the 1919 Revolution." Ph.D. dissertation, University of California at Berkeley.

Al-Qattan, Najwa. 1996. "Textual Differentiation in the Damascus *Sijill:* Religious Discrimination or Politics of Gender?" In *Women, Family, and Divorce Laws in Islamic History,* ed. Amira E. Sonbol. Syracuse, N.Y.: Syracuse University Press.

Quataert, Donald. 1993. *Ottoman Manufacturing in the Age of the Industrial Revolution.* Cambridge: Cambridge University Press.

Roded, Ruth. 1990. "Great Mosques, *Zawiya*s, and Neighborhood Mosques: Popular Beneficiaries of *Waqf* Endowments in Eighteenth- and Nineteenth-Century Aleppo." *Journal of the American Oriental Society* 110: 33–38.

_____. 1994. *Women in Islamic Biographical Collections.* Boulder: Lynne Rienner.

Russell, Mona. 1998. "Creating the New Woman: Consumerism, Education, and National Identity in Egypt, 1863–1922." Ph.D. dissertation, Georgetown University.

Sayigh, Rosemary. 1993. "Palestinian Women and Politics in Lebanon." In *Arab Women: Old Boundaries, New Frontiers,* ed. Judith E. Tucker. Bloomington: Indiana University Press.

Sonbol, Amira E., ed. 1996. *Women, Family, and Divorce Laws in Islamic History.* Syracuse, N.Y.: Syracuse University Press.

Spectorsky, Susan A. 1993. *Chapters on Marriage and Divorce: Responses of Ibn Hanbal and Ibn Rahwayh.* Austin: University of Texas Press.

Spellberg, Denise. 1994. *Politics, Gender, and the Islamic Past: The Legacy of 'A'isha bint Abi Bakr.* New York: Columbia University Press.

Stowasser, Barbara. 1994. *Women in the Qur'an: Traditions and Interpretations.* Oxford: Oxford University Press.

Tucker, Judith E. 1985. *Women in Nineteenth-Century Egypt.* Cambridge: Cambridge University Press.

_____. 1988. "Marriage and Family in Nablus, 1720–1856: Towards a History of Arab Marriage." *Journal of Family History* 13: 165–179.

_____. 1991. "Ties That Bound: Women and Family in Eighteenth- and Nineteenth-Century Nablus." In *Women in Middle Eastern History: Shifting Boundaries in Sex and Gender,* ed. Nikki Keddie and Beth Baron. New Haven: Yale University Press.

_____. 1998. *In the House of the Law: Gender and Islamic Law in Ottoman Syria and Palestine.* Berkeley: University of California Press.

Tucker, Judith E., ed. 1993. *Arab Women: Old Boundaries, New Frontiers.* Bloomington: Indiana University Press.

Zarinebaf-Shahr, Fariba. 1997. "Ottoman Women and the Tradition of Seeking Justice in the Eighteenth Century." In *Women in the Ottoman Empire: Middle Eastern Women in the Early Modern Era,* ed. Madeline C. Zilfi. Leiden: E. J. Brill.

Zilfi, Madeline C. 1996. "Women and Society in the Tulip Era." In *Women, Family, and Divorce Laws in Islamic History,* ed. Amira E. Sonbol. Syracuse, N.Y.: Syracuse University Press.

_____. 1997. "'We Don't Get Along': Women and *Hul* Divorce in the Eighteenth Century." In *Women in the Ottoman Empire: Middle Eastern Women in the Early Modern Era,* ed. Madeline C. Zilfi. Leiden: E. J. Brill.

Zilfi, Madeline C., ed. 1997. *Women in the Ottoman Empire: Middle Eastern Women in the Early Modern Era.* Leiden: E. J. Brill.

A Woman Without Her Distaff: Gender, Work, and Handicraft Production in Colonial North Africa*

Julia Clancy-Smith

A man without his plow, a woman without her distaff, are given to boredom and laziness.

—*Algerian proverb from Tlemcen*[1]

Oh, sheep of Hafsia, your wool is for the wedding blanket woven by irreproachable women.

—*Tunisian shearing chant*[2]

𝓘n the course of the nineteenth century, states and local economies in the Middle East and North Africa were increasingly, if unevenly, drawn into world market networks that were largely centered in western Europe and North America. Male and female producers in cities and the countryside, and in societies from Morocco to Iran, were thus ensnared by much wider economic forces over which they often exerted little control. These processes ultimately unleashed transformations deeply affecting all levels of

---

*The author wishes to thank Sherry Vatter and Margaret L. Meriwether for their helpful comments on earlier versions of this chapter. Steve Lloyd also deserves my gratitude for kindly providing me with difficult-to-obtain handicraft journals as well as slides of Tunisian textiles.

social organization—from the redistribution of wealth and power, the emergence of new classes, and fundamental alterations in the gendered division of labor to the appearance of novel consumer tastes.[3] As Leonard Helfgott observed in his history of the Iranian carpet: "Changes in the production, movement, and the use of objects, from the workplace to the marketplace to the final point of consumption, mirror the modern world's social and historical development."[4] Given the enormous diversity of peoples and cultures within the Middle East, however, these changes affected certain sociocultural groups and specific geographical areas at different times and in varying ways.

Those states that fell under direct European rule, especially settler colonialism, in the past century tended to be most intensely influenced by the new global relationships of production and distribution. Nowhere was this

This photo of a popular souk in the Moroccan city of Fez suggests the influence of the world market. The stack of plastic tubs and other industrial containers in the foreground adjacent to the young boy are imported from Asia; in the past, baskets woven by rural women would have been sold in the market and used for carrying or storage. (Photo by Julia Clancy-Smith, taken in 1991.)

more true than in nineteenth-century North Africa where the "New European Imperialism" and the "Scramble for Africa" began as early as 1830. Invading Algeria that year, France had made the country an eternal piece of French territory on the African continent by 1848; adjacent Tunisia was added to the French empire in 1881 and Morocco by 1912. Nevertheless, many of the transformations in the relationships of production seen in colonial North Africa can be detected in other parts of the Middle East. For example, although Egypt was not formally occupied by Great Britain until 1882, the Egyptian economy, linked to the world market mainly through the mechanism of cotton production, began to show signs of being a colonial economy as early as 1850.[5]

This essay explores the impact that colonialism had upon women and work in North Africa, principally Algeria and Tunisia, from roughly 1850 until the eve of decolonialization in the post–World War II era. Here, work will principally be defined and understood as manufacturing enterprises, particularly handicrafts fashioned by women, whether exclusively for household consumption or for both domestic use and commercialization in markets. Handicraft production by indigenous female artisans represents a crucial site of scholarly inquiry because of the key position that textiles, pottery, and other items played in both the household economy and in translocal economic relationships. Moreover, the household must be viewed as a complex mediating institution that linked individual and collective production and consumption to the larger political economy of the village, city, region, or state.[6] Finally, until well into the twentieth century, North Africa was overwhelmingly rural; the vast majority of the population lived in villages or were members of pastoral-nomadic communities. Rural women, whether sedentary or transhumant, produced a multitude of commodities—tents, all clothing and bed linens, mats, rugs, sacks for the storage or transport of grains, cooking utensils, and so on. Without these products, the fruit of female labor, the clan could not survive. Raw materials came from diverse sources—wool from flocks, goat and camel hair, sparta grass, clay, and, in the oases, palm fronds from date-palm trees.[7]

However, it should be remembered that North African women have always played a significant role in the service sectors of the region's economies, acting as religious agents, healers, marriage brokers, midwives, laundresses, cooks, prostitutes, servants, musicians, and entertainers—in addition to toiling long and hard as agriculturists, pastoralists, and traders.[8] In some places, female producers labored to make items tied to warfare and group security. For example, in the nineteenth century, gunpowder was manufactured by the village women of the Khrumir tribe of the Algerian-Tunisian border area, resulting, according to one European observer, in "good quality gunpowder."[9] Finally, many of the manufacturing and service-sector activities carried out by women were intimately connected to the cultural and symbolic life of the group, whether in the Middle East or North Africa.

Despite the critical importance of women's productive and reproductive functions to the very nature of political economy, these functions have long suffered, and still suffer, from the invisibility factor. For sociocultural reasons, female production was vastly underreported, when it was noted at all.[10] For example, detailed investigations of handicraft production, particularly textiles, scrutinize at great length the articles produced, yet often fail to talk about the producers, many of whom were women.[11] Indeed, the social vocabulary available to speak about "women at work" had either not yet been articulated or was misleading.[12] This stems from the fact that feminine handicraft and manufacturing activities shaded off into service-sector activities, often performed in a domestic setting or in addition to daily family chores. Classic definitions of production inevitably associated it with something called the "public sphere," a culturally defined workplace and space informed mainly by the experience of industrializing Europe.[13]

Further exacerbating the invisibility problem, women were systematically denied the status of "artisans" in many colonial studies undertaken chiefly by European men.[14] Yet, as will be seen below, females in precolonial and colonial Algeria and Tunisia not only achieved recognition as artisans but also instructed apprentices, for which they were remunerated. In addition, the very rhythms of daily work, whether weaving or pottery making, were frequently governed by seasonal factors, which in turn were often culturally determined. Paradoxically, it was the very fact that women artisans performed their crafts together with a multiplicity of other activities— economic, symbolic, or otherwise—that caused their labor to be socially demeaned or marginalized.[15]

Of course, women's work cannot be separated from men's productive and exchange activities; household economies strove to achieve a balanced mix of male-female production and consumption. In many parts of the nineteenth-century Middle East, male artisans and handicraft-sector laborers suffered the devastating impact of competition from European-made, factory-produced commodities before their female counterparts did.[16] Forced to emigrate or to seek other kinds of work, these men's experiences with the vagaries of rapidly shifting labor markets could not but affect women as well. At times, these shifts open up new wage-earning opportunities for women; at others, women's work too was adversely affected.[17]

How North Africa's encounters with the twin forces of European colonialism and world market integration, together with other related processes such as tourism, migration, and new tastes and preferences, transformed female handicraft production is the subject of this essay.

Making Algeria French, c. 1830–1930

Algeria was the first Arab state to fall under European colonial rule, in 1830.[18] The subsequent four decades of brutal military pacification, accompanied by dislocations in local economies, large-scale Muslim flight from the country, and the immigration of European settlers, destroyed or undermined the traditional handicraft sector as well as its mainstay, agriculture. In addition, the gradual demise of the pastoral-nomadic economy, which provided the raw materials needed for handicrafts and manufacturing, brought ruin to village and town producers by the late nineteenth century.[19] The nature and extent of the destruction varied in time and space, however. Generally, the communities and regions least directly touched by the colonial enterprise—the Sahara and the mountains of the Kabylia and Awras—were those whose artisans, male and female, were able to preserve their craft and associated traditions.[20]

Yet by the end of the century, even producers residing and working in areas removed from the principal nodes of French settler colonialism were increasingly influenced by new tastes, materials, and techniques. Dramatic shifts in traditional market structures, networks, and patron-clients relations, as well as changing patterns of consumption in the middle to upper ranks of Algerian Muslim society, deprived many artisans of outlets and customers.[21] To these were added the disruptions of rebellion and warfare. For example, World War I, with its massive mobilization of North African men serving under France's flag, unwittingly delivered the coup de grâce to the indigenous production of clothing. Obliged to wear European uniforms, North African soldiers acquired new tastes in attire; the traditional apparel worn by North African males and produced by weavers and tailors were much less in demand after 1918.[22]

Thus, by World War I, if not earlier, the introduction of capitalism, land seizures from the tribes, or urban real estate speculation had brought about the impoverishment of the indigenous population, which in turn either destroyed or seriously compromised North African handicraft production. Only in the interwar period did the nature and extent of these changes become the subject of systematic inquiry by colonial governments intent upon formulating new policies to help artisans and guilds. But by then it was almost too late; the handicraft sector was nearly moribund in Algeria, while in Morocco and Tunisia it was in the throes of a deep crisis.[23] It was no accident that the traditional handicraft sector in Morocco, the last North African nation colonized by France, endured long after Algeria's had suffered nearly irreversible decline. Ironically, many of the historical sources for artisans and traditional manufactures during this period were generated by colonial officials who—unbeknownst to them—were presiding over the demise of the very activities they sought to save or resurrect.[24]

The lavish 1930 celebration, exalting France's century-long domination of Algeria, marked a turning point in colonial awareness of the disastrous state of the Maghreb's age-old arts and handicrafts. Numerous missions were organized to reinvigorate this sector of the economy as well as the "natives'" cultural patrimony, which in any case had long since been appropriated by *la mère patrie*.[25] The concerted colonial effort to revive—or reinvent—traditional handicrafts for both men and women in North Africa was an explicitly political project, which, however, masqueraded behind the more respectable veil of cultural *sauvegarde*. For some colonial apologists, the need to create a cult of historical memory for Europeans calling French Algeria home demanded that the traditional arts not be lost to vulgar modernization.[26]

A major conundrum was determining what exactly constituted the "authentic" and the "traditional" in indigenous artistic production. Upon closer examination, some colonial specialists noted that the "traditional" embroideries of urban Algerian women turned out to have been influenced by colors, patterns, and dyes from Europe. Most officials, however, were more worried by disturbing demographic increases among the North Africans as well as by outbursts of organized nationalist protest in the cities, where male unemployment in the traditional manufacturing sectors was very high; resurrecting the artisanal sector and its artisans might avert economic and, therefore, political disasters.[27]

In some cases, colonial inquiries into the deteriorating state of the indigenous carpet industry made North African women the targets of blame. According to Jean Blottière in his 1930 study, the intrinsic value of native carpets had declined because carpet production had been "left to the maladroit inspiration of ignorant women with no taste and this industry from the artistic point of view [was] in full decadence by the beginning of the last century. Nevertheless, it [would be] easy to resuscitate the Algerian carpet industry by infusing it with fresh blood."[28] Other studies scarcely mentioned women as producers of numerous commodities both for domestic use and consumption as well as for distribution in markets.[29]

Two principal elements were regarded as crucial for work and production to be valued and thus recognized. First, the work in question had to attain a certain degree of institutionalization; it had to be performed in a nondomestic setting—that of guilds or artisans' associations. And second, the productive activity had to be full-time and remunerated in monetary fashion. This definition, inspired by a rigidly gendered notion of what constituted professionalization, either obscured female producers or downgraded the importance of their work.[30] Finally, colonial writers undertaking scientific inquiries into the indigenous handicraft sector often exculpated France's role in that sector's decline by claiming that artistic production in Algeria was already in "profound decadence" prior to

1830.[31] According to this view, one of the many benefits that French rule had brought was the cultural resurrection of native artisanal production after centuries of neglect under Turkish-Arab misrule. Wrote Blottière triumphantly in 1930: "The renaissance of the Algerian carpet is now an accomplished fact."[32]

Algerian Women and Handicraft Production: Resurrection or Reinvention?

For fin de siècle Europeans residing in the colonies or in Europe, two of the most visible cultural markers of oriental civilization were its women and its handicrafts or artisanal products, particularly carpets. As the nineteenth century gave way to the twentieth, these markers were increasingly on display and available to Western consumers and audiences. In colonial Algeria, the photographer's studio spawned a visual trade in women; photographs cum obscene postcards featuring Algerian prostitutes in inviting poses and postures rendered the Arab Muslim woman accessible to European male spectators.[33] Oriental women and carpets were among the most popular exhibitions at that peculiarly characteristic institution of late-nineteenth-century Europe—the world's fair or "exposition universelle."[34] Indeed, the interior of an urban Arab North African dwelling and a more modest Berber village home were recreated in Paris for onlookers. Despite the effort to faithfully recreate the Tunisian artisans' workshop at the 1900 exposition in Paris, however, one singular element was missing—female handicraft workers.[35]

Marguerite Bel: Saving the Algerian Female Artisan

One of the first colonial writers to sound the alarm regarding female handicraft workers during the interwar period was Marguerite A. Bel, who had two advantages over other French functionaries. First, she was a woman and had access to domestic and other female spaces not normally open to her male counterparts. And second, Bel held the post of inspector of artistic and professional instruction for the native girls' schools, which were mainly nonacademic institutions. In response to the growing alarm over the declining quality and quantity of Algerian handicrafts as well as to pressures from French social reformers to educate females, French administrators recruited Algerian girls and women as pupils for the colonial trade schools, or *écoles-ouvriers*. These schools, which also offered basic home economics courses, sought to teach or retrain females in the "indigenous minor arts," particularly embroidery and weaving.[36] Many of them also sought to market the finished products; a percentage of the earnings was usually retained by individual female producers.

In 1939, Bel published an important study based upon her years of experience with female artisans in the cities and countryside.[37] This study is especially valuable for the visual evidence it provides from the first decades of the twentieth century, since it contains photos of women working together in a colonial atelier for embroidery and rug production in Oran as well as illustrations of female Kabyle potters laboring in their villages.[38] One of Bel's main objectives was to contest the colonial male hierarchy's charges that Algerian women either were to blame for the degraded level of arts and handicrafts or were nonproductive members of society.[39]

Unlike many other authors, Bel clearly recognized the factors bringing ruin to Algeria's handicraft industry; tourism, world market forces, and trade agreements with neighboring Morocco were the main culprits. According to Bel, in Algeria both indigenous and European merchants imported handicrafts from either Morocco or the East, despite the fact that similar products were available locally. Above all, Moroccan products flooded Algerian markets because official stamping of origin was not required, except for rugs. Until about 1926, although imported goods were of competitive quality, some Algerian producers, male and female, managed to survive.[40]

Then came the world economic crisis, which deeply affected Algeria beginning in 1931. By 1936–1937, Tlemcen's ancient artisanal industry was virtually destroyed. In addition, increasing European tourism to Algeria, and the concomitant demand for cheap "native" souvenirs, lowered the quality of artisanal products in the country because producers were forced to cater to the tourist trade for lack of alternative outlets. In addition, since World War I, both city and countryside in Algeria had suffered a second commercial invasion—that of inexpensive but shoddy manufactures not only from Europe but also from Japan; these competed with higher-priced yet superior local products.[41] One of the main conduits of foreign penetration and competition was the railroad, which had sent its iron tentacles far and wide in Algeria between 1880 and 1914, opening up previously semi-isolated areas.[42]

Traditional artisans in Algeria were only able to fend off competition from abroad by using low-quality raw materials. For example, male artisans north of Tlemcen had long woven straw hats worn in western Algeria and eastern Morocco; for decorating the hats, *garance,* a natural red dye used since at least Roman times, had been employed. However, in order to compete with cheaper manufactured hats, the weavers were forced to use inferior, though less expensive, artificial dyes that produced garish colors. These same processes adversely affected female artisans in many productive domains as well.[43] A second problem was that as Algeria's economy became exclusively tied to that of France and then to the world market, older intraregional and interregional patterns of trade and exchange were undermined.

Microspecializations in handcrafted consumer items—carpets with special patterns, mats, pottery, lace—had existed for centuries and been developed by both male and female artisans; only vestiges of these still remained in force by the time Bel was writing. Indeed, it was the existence of these regional variations in textiles and other kinds of products that had undergirded significant commercial relations throughout Algeria and the Maghreb until the nineteenth century. For example, certain types of wool working were associated either with the countryside or with cities in the interior such as Tlemcen, Mascara, and Al Kalaa; and with the Mzab region. Berber women from specific tribes or villages were known to be the most accomplished potters, and their wares were eagerly sought in markets or by clients.[44]

Bel's study constitutes a precious historical record that both inventories what remained of traditional feminine handicraft organization and output and catalogues the inroads made into this sector by the colonial economy. She divides her study of women into an urban versus rural dichotomy (i.e., *arts ruraux, arts citadins*), which, she argues, "particularly applies to female production since rural women and urban women represent two worlds and ways of life, almost two opposing civilizations."[45] In Bel's view, urban women of the upper ranks of indigenous Algerian society were the most exposed to changing tastes and fashions coming from outside the country: "These women are eager to purchase new things, whether they come from Europe or from the East."[46] Although there is some element of truth in this, particularly since the European colonial presence was highly concentrated in the cities along the coast, the statement needs qualification. By the interwar period, if not before, the tastes and preferences of the urban areas had penetrated even the most remote villages and tribes. Moreover, the rural-to-urban migratory impulse within colonial Algeria was already well advanced by then, bringing country people into the *bidonvilles,* or squatter quarters, surrounding the large cities, especially the capital.[47] A more accurate division would be one informed by an analysis of class or social ranking as well as by urban and rural distinctions, keeping in mind that the village and town often shaded off into one another.

Feminine Handicraft Production in Urban Areas

Traditionally, city women in Algeria tended to produce luxury items using expensive raw materials, such as linen and silk with precious metals spun into thread, which were more readily available in urban areas. In addition, cities boasted a native bourgeoisie able to purchase or acquire luxury items for household use; their status demanded that they embellish their homes with these items, although the ranks of the elite had been greatly thinned by colonialism. Moreover, there existed a sort of cultural geography of urban feminine handicraft production; cities on, or enjoying close ties to, the Mediterranean displayed similarities in the types of products made. There, Algerian females principally worked in embroidery and lace; the tools of their trade were their needles, although different cities specialized in different commodities. This kind of female artisanal production was more prevalent in cities located in the region between Algiers and Tunisia than in western Algeria.[48]

For example, women in Constantine were renowned for their lamé embroidery using gold or silver thread worked upon fine silk cloth. Moreover, Constantine conserved longer than any other locality the tradition of embroidery richly worked with gold, silver, and silk thread. The reasons for this are not difficult to discern. This city in the interior was not as dramatically influenced by the French colonial presence and maintained its historical, intimate ties with Tunis and the eastern Arab world, areas that continued to produce the raw materials needed for this craft. In terms of motifs and materials employed, the embroidery worked by women from the eastern coast of Algeria (from Djidjelli to Bône) resembled that produced by women in the Levant—in Syria and the Balkans—as well as the Moroccan embroidery of Salé. In contrast, the cities of the Mzab, lost in the central Algerian desert, also boasted their own feminine artistic traditions with peculiar embroidery patterns and colors generally not found elsewhere.[49] It is doubtful that urban bourgeois women marketed their finished pieces (unless the family had fallen into particularly hard times) since these were intended exclusively for domestic use and served as an index of a girl's or woman's "worth" to the clan and to any prospective suitors.

The existence of widely varying regional differences in embroidery techniques, and in the finished products, raises a fundamental question: How were these traditions preserved from generation to generation? In the beginning of the nineteenth century, lamé and other types of luxury embroidery were taught to young girls of the bourgeois classes by *mu'allimat* (i.e., *maitresses-brodeuses*) or by women particularly skilled in needlework. They were often from higher social ranks and enjoyed local reputations as gentlewomen. This last attribute was especially important, because these women also instructed their young pupils in a wide array of domestic arts. Thus, an embroidery session was not "just an embroidery lesson" but a communal pedagogical exercise inculcating wider social and educational values.[50]

Not only were these embroidery pieces for public contemplation, but they represented sources of prestige and status—of social identity—for both teacher and pupil. The finished items, made with as much artistic skill as possible, particularly if destined for a trousseau, were often displayed during marriage ceremonies. Family, guests, and visitors could view the embroidery pieces, which furnished proof of the excellence of instruction that

This photo from the late nineteenth century captures Algerian women in a tradi-tional house in the Algiers medina working on embroidery frames. Their work may well have been overseen by a mu'allima *or female instructor in domestic arts and handicrafts. (Photo courtesy of the Library of Congress.)*

the *mu'allima* provided to her pupils. In addition, when the female ap-prentice had become accomplished with her needle and in her craft, an achievement that demanded much time practicing and improving her art, she gained a new identity and peer recognition. She embroidered her name and the date of completion on her piece; in Bône and elsewhere the girl put her name in both French and Arabic in the upper-left-hand corner of the fabric.[51] In some places, the female instructor had the right to sell in the market some of her pupils' pieces, such sales representing part of her re-muneration from the girls' parents.[52]

Thus, that embroidery work was performed within the confines of the household or domestic space under the watchful eye of a gentlewoman-instructor does not necessarily mean that such work lacked institutional-ization, standardized techniques, or recognized levels of quality. Rather, these factors operated according to different sociocultural norms. Whereas embroidery appears to have been an exclusively female industry, the same was not true of lace production in Algeria. Here the traditional gendered division of labor was most evident in work techniques. Some male artisans produced lace, yet did so in a fashion that clearly delineated male from female spheres. Female lace makers worked their needles from the edge of the lace product inward toward the interior, whereas male producers manipulated their needles from the interior of the piece toward the outside, away from the body.[53]

Between City and Countryside

Of the natural fibers employed in North Africa, wool was the most commonly used by all classes. Unlike the urban-based lace and luxury embroidery handicrafts, the wool industry and its products tended to be associated with the countryside and was often organized as a dispersed rural industry. Algerian towns whose inhabitants enjoyed close relations with nearby village and pastoral nomad communities frequently were renowned as weaving and spinning centers. At the time of the French conquest, only one city, Al Kalaa (between Belizane and Mascara), was engaged in the large-scale production of knotted rugs. These represented an important item of trade with the cities of central and western Algeria and contributed greatly to the urban economy. Characterized by highly original decorative elements—yellow, blue, and green motifs set against a dun-colored background—and by special production techniques, the knotted rug industry of Al Kalaa was gradually destroyed by European imports. The use of artificial dyes and the demands of tourism caused this type of labor-intensive rug to completely disappear from household looms and markets by the beginning of the twentieth century. Colonial intervention led to the establishment of state-run carpet factories, which recruited Algerian women as wage laborers for very low salaries, and some of Al Kalaa's women worked at these factory looms.[54] However, by the interwar period, they produced, in Bel's view, "tawdry articles such as the rubbish sold to Europeans who don't know any better."[55]

In Tlemcen, a city with especially strong ties to its agricultural hinterland, the class nature of wool production comes clearly into focus. There, work in wool was traditionally regarded as an honorable profession by those social ranks classified as members of the petite bourgeoisie. City women washed, carded, and spun the wool needed by female weavers to produce blankets and coverings. As late as the 1930s, Tlemcen counted at least 120 domestic ateliers devoted to weaving woolen household items. During the annual three-month period when most marriages were celebrated and the social demand for bed linens and other trousseau items peaked, the amount of spun wool utilized by Tlemcen's weavers per day was estimated at about one ton. Here, the seasonal nature of semitraditional female textile production for the household or for clients becomes evident. Under the French regime, the mass production of rugs for export was also introduced to Tlemcen. Female workers, often village or pastoral women driven into the cities by rural impoverishment, prepared spun wool for use in carpet workshops, which mainly employed semiskilled young girls or unmarried women barely paid survival wages.[56]

All over Algeria, rural-to-urban population movements had brought the village into the city by World War I. In Mascara, Saida, and Algiers, village women who had migrated due to deteriorating rural conditions took up the production of wool cloaks, veils, and shawls; their products were often of poor quality due to the use of cheaper and thus inferior raw materials and to their lack of training. Such had not always been the situation in the western city of Mascara; in the middle of the nineteenth century, Mascara enjoyed a reputation as a producer of fine woolen articles of apparel. In 1858, a European traveler in the region observed that "Mascara is famous as a supplier of burnouses and haiks manufactured by Arab women, having no rival but Tunis."[57]

Rural Female Artisans

Thus far, I have mainly concentrated on city and town female production. Yet, as mentioned above, the vast majority of North African women worked and lived their lives in villages, whether small hamlets or semi-sedentarized pastoral nomadic communities. Of the myriad activities performed by rural women, preparing the wool (or goat hair) and weaving it into various commodities represented one of the most important for the household. Indeed, among pastoral peoples, the very "house" that sheltered family members—the black tent—was woven by tribal women.[58] At certain times of the year, every home, hut, or tent boasted a weaving loom. Wool preparation and weaving in the traditional economy of Algeria demonstrate three significant dimensions of women's work—the seasonal nature of such work, the interdependence of sedentary and pastoral peoples, and the highly ritualized nature of the long, complex processes involved in textile production.

The rhythms of working in wool fluctuated in accordance with the agrarian cycle. In the spring, sheep shearing took place. Subsequently, village or tribal women made use of the long, hot days of early summer to wash and dry the wool; cleaning the raw wool was an arduous task often involving a number of labor-intensive processes.[59] Late summer and early autumn were devoted to combing, carding, and spinning the wool. All of these activities, wherever they were carried out, were deeply invested with rituals and cultural protocols. Special prayers and invocations were recited by women as they labored to wash and clean the wool. Combing, carding, and spinning, frequently done in a group, also had their own set of ritual conventions, some designed to ward off evil spirits, the jinn.[60] Thus, seasonal, ritual, and work cycles all meshed. In winter, the gardens and fields demanded less attention; more time was available for the weaving of cloth for domestic consumption. Once again, family needs were met first by female textile producers, who lavished the most care on these items; woven pieces destined for sale or barter to strangers tended to be mediocre and less finished in quality.[61]

However, this was not the case when women made woven textiles on demand for special clients; in these instances female artisans expended great effort to fashion high-quality commodities. Frequently, the client was a member of a certain pastoral-nomadic tribe that had, over the centuries, established patterns of economic exchange with specific villagers. The nomadic client provided raw wool from flocks to skilled sedentary female weavers to produce clothing—hooded cloaks for men, or women's attire—finer in quality than those items produced by the cruder tent looms. In general, the woven products of sedentary weavers tended to be distinguished by more sophisticated techniques and better raw materials, whereas nomadic textiles employed wool mixed with goat or camel hair. In addition to supplying raw wool to village artisans, the pastoralists found a market among sedentary communities for their storage sacks, decorated grain sacks for horses, saddle blankets, and so on. And certain pastoral weavers made flat-weave rugs or raised-wool rugs, whose techniques of production were unknown to village women.[62]

The importance of sedentary-nomadic mutualism in the traditional economy and social order is best seen in the Kabylia region of northern Algeria.[63] Here, local resource structures demanded exchanges between complementary ways of life. The typical Kabyle farming family claimed only a tiny plot of steep land unsuited to raising sheep. Raw wool for female weavers could only be procured in markets or directly from nomadic herders. Since raw wool was a costly item in the Kabyle family budget, the Berber women of the region developed over generations highly skilled techniques in spinning and weaving, which economized the wool industry. Kabyle women wove some of the finest handcrafted items found in Algeria—shawls, blankets, and bridal dresses.[64]

Potters and Pottery: The Case of the Kabylia

Due to their relative isolation vis-à-vis residents of Algeria's Europeanized cities, rural female producers retained some of the decorative traditions and techniques known throughout the country prior to 1830. In addition, although pottery making, basket weaving, and textile production were principally female activities in the countryside, a certain degree of regional or local specialization, shaped by custom and by the availability of raw materials, distinguished female from male production and created a gendered division of labor. Certain village or tribal women had, over the centuries, developed specific skills and techniques. Just as significantly, they had achieved social recognition of their craft, whose methods were handed down from mother to daughter and often kept a closely guarded secret. As a result, these women produced for networks of clients who desired particularly fine handicraft items.

Pottery making provides an example of this system. Historically, pottery of various types and qualities was produced in Algeria by sedentary female potters. The annual migratory movements of pastoral peoples precluded the potter's craft in the tribe; thus, woven baskets served the same function as pottery. Village women made clay plates, pots, water jars, and storage containers. As mentioned above, Berber women in the Kabylia region were regarded as the most skilled potters in Algeria. This contrasts with Tunisia, where the best clay pottery for domestic use was produced exclusively by male potters on the island of Djerba. Women in Djerba were excluded from any dimension of the pottery-making process—whether the preparation of

This photo shows piles of handmade pottery and clay amphorae in the marketplace of Houmt Souk, the largest town on the Tunisian island of Djerba. In contrast to other regions of North Africa, potters in Djerba were exclusively male; females were excluded from all phases of production. (Photo by Julia Clancy-Smith, taken in 1983.)

the clay or the fashioning and firing of the pots.[65] Nevertheless, female potters in other areas of Tunisia did work clay to fashion a wide range of articles for either the household or the market.

The Kabylia is a region scarce in natural resources such as wood, but rich in some places in deposits of high-grade clay.[66] Moreover, climatic extremes prevail in this rugged mountainous area, from brutally hot summers to extremely cold winters. These factors influenced both the techniques employed by female potters and the rhythms of work. For Kabyle women, pottery making was a seasonal activity because wood-burning ovens were not employed for firing. Combustible material was scarce and therefore expensive in the Kabylia. In the springtime, the female potter worked the clay and set the pots out to dry, since temperatures at that time were ideal; winters were too cold for drying and the intense heat of summer tended to crack the drying pots.[67]

The case of the Berber female potters also illustrates a pattern seen in other artisanal industries—that of producing both for the household and for the market. During the spring pottery season, the family's needs were met first—damaged clay pots and other items were replaced by new ones. Afterward, female potters sold or bartered their surplus products to village consumers. The nature of the woman's relationship with the market varied, however, in accordance with gender norms limiting her physical displacement and contact with males outside the kinship grouping. If the market was in close proximity to her village, the potter could dispose of her wares without a male intermediary. Pottery destined for sale in a distant village or market was sold by the clan's menfolk. As late as the 1930s, this female manufacturing activity was still modestly flourishing, at least in the Kabylia and Nedroma.[68]

In addition to excelling at pottery making, women also enjoyed a reputation for making especially fine woven baskets and mats. In the high Valley of the Tafna (near Tlemcen in western Algeria), notably the large villages of Tafessera and Tleta, the female basket weavers were considered "veritable artisans in working alfa grass."[69] As with potting, local resources and the seasons determined the nature of the industry and its temporal occurrence. In the springtime, village women ascended the nearby mountains to cut the soft stalks of alfa grass before they hardened. Prior to weaving the baskets, the stalks had to be processed over a very hot fire. Some of the prepared stalks were immediately worked into intricate basketry; the rest were stored for later use, particularly during the winter months when the burden of gardening and other female activities was reduced, permitting the women more time to make additional baskets.[70]

Another important rural female industry was that of woven mat production. In traditional North African homes, mats were used to cover the floors of living spaces, whether houses or tents, as well as the floors of mosques and religious buildings. For those of modest means, woven mats represented the only "luxury" items gracing their otherwise simple dwellings. In the homes of more prosperous people, mats cushioned rugs or mattresses, protecting them from the cold tile or earthen floor. Once again, as was the case with Kabyle female potters, regional specializations existed that conferred status upon and brought income to women mat weavers from certain Algerian villages. As late as the interwar period, the mats woven by rural women in the Valley of the Tafna and in Belezma were eagerly sought all over Algeria due to their reputation for durability and fineness.[71] The issue of female specialization and social recognition raises the question of how women artisans distinguished their own products from those of other regions.

In effect, the colors and decorative elements employed for woven mats operated as "signatures," or markers of provenance and of degrees of quality—in much the same way that brand names operate today. For example, the women of the tribes of Banu Snous and Banu Abu Sa'id (also in the Valley of the Tafna) wove high-quality mats and "signed" them by weaving dyed wool into the geometric decorations. Those of inferior quality were colored simply with a red dye obtained from the madder root. Women from other regions produced vivid multicolored mats; the most richly colored mats were found in eastern and central Algeria, woven in greens, blacks, reds, and blues obtained from natural dyes.[72] However, the introduction of cheaper, inferior artificial dyes at the end of the nineteenth century meant that natural colors, costlier and more time-consuming to obtain, gradually were replaced by chemicals. By the middle of the twentieth century, the highly developed art of producing natural dyes, which demanded great skill on the part of female and male artisans, had been entirely lost.[73] Female artisans were being reduced to the status of unskilled or semiskilled workers, dependent upon the market for obtaining materials.

The techniques used to produce woven mats were identical to those for weaving cloth except that processed sparta grass served as the raw material; the mats were woven like rugs, generally on a horizontal loom.[74] Although the origin of the particular type of horizontal loom used for weaving mats in Tunisia and Algeria remains uncertain, some scholars believe that it was introduced to North Africa in the sixteenth century.[75] Significant here is the fact that female (and male) handicraft workers in the "traditional" social order were open to new techniques and better ways of doing things. This runs counter to the French colonial belief that precolonial Algerian manufacturing enterprises and artisans either were frozen in a rigid, timeless observance of tradition or were in a progressive decline that began with the seventh-century Arab-Islamic conquests.

If the Kabyle weaver was particularly appreciated, all of the female weavers in rural Algeria, whether sedentary or pastoralist, Arab or Berber, claimed their own unique work techniques, decorative designs, and specializations. Once again, these qualities operated as subtle "artistic signatures" of the geographic origins of an item and thus of the identity of its female producer. Therefore, these finished textiles were far from mute; they spoke in a multitude of voices about communal values, relationships, and aesthetics. By the time that Bel was conducting her study, the more elaborate traditional female costumes woven in the Kabylia were a thing of the past. Many of the techniques used in weaving these dresses had nearly died out due to lack of demand, impoverishment, and changes in clothing styles. Catholic and Protestant missionaries in the Kabylia worked to rescue what remained of this traditional art form by finding commercial outlets for female weavers' products among resident Europeans. For example, a school for girls in the village of Ait Hisham instructed pupils in how to refashion their textile production to suit modern Western tastes.[76]

This photo shows young Moroccan girls weaving carpets for sale in the tourist industry of Fez. The "sweatshop" in which they labor is situated in an ancient palace formerly belonging to notables and located in the heart of the Fez medina. The palace now functions as a tourist trap. (Photo by Julia Clancy-Smith, taken in 1991.)

In the cities of Algeria, where wage labor and a female proletariat emerged after 1900, producing handicrafts for many women was less remunerative than working as a servant in the pay of a European family.[77] Indeed, as the historian Charles-Robert Ageron observed: "A feminine wage-laboring class emerged at the beginning of the twentieth century: 1,520 women in 1902; 7,533 in 1905; 21,397 in 1911; 25,821 in 1924; but we are very poorly informed about the exact nature of their employment."[78]

Many of the same forces, both internal and external, were at work in neighboring Tunisia, despite the fact that Tunisia was only incorporated into the French empire at the end of the nineteenth century. Nevertheless, since handicraft production endured longer in Tunisia than in Algeria, documentation about the precolonial period there is more abundant.

Tunisia: Male and Female Producers
in City, Town, and Countryside

Until the advent of the French Protectorate in 1881 and the consequent modernization of the Tunisian economy and upsurge in tourism, one of the most significant transformations in Tunisia's artisanal sector occurred in the early seventeenth century. The final expulsion of Andalusian Muslims and Jews from Iberia, and their relocation in the Maghreb, dramatically increased the pool of skilled artisans in Tunisia, which in turn stimulated craft industries in the country. Local guilds not only expanded in number but also underwent reorganization. As was true elsewhere in North Africa and the Middle East, guild members chose heads *(amins)*, one of whose many duties was to ensure the quality of the products they manufactured.[79] Although the guilds were an urban and male phenomenon, women, and at times the entire family, also participated actively in craft activities in the workshop. Also in the cities and towns, the preparation of natural fibers— wool, silk, cotton, and linen—was often a female activity. As in Algeria, Tunisian women produced woven blankets, items of clothing, and carpets as well as fine lace, embroidery, and knotted rugs.[80]

Since women's urban craft work was institutionalized in ways different from that of their male counterparts, documentation of their participation in such work is sparser. Predictably, we tend to catch glimpses of how production was socially organized when some transgression had occurred— when women were confronted with the hard realities of patriarchy. Each neighborhood in nineteenth-century Tunis boasted a *dar al-mu'allima,* or residence workshop, where girls from the quarter were sent on a regular basis to be schooled in the domestic arts.[81] In her work on women, gender, and marginality in Tunis, Dalenda Largueche relates the case of a woman identified simply as "F. Z.," who was from a respectable, but middling, family in the capital and a recognized *mu'allima*. Because of F. Z.'s reputation as a skilled artisan, her home doubled as a place of instruction for women and girls who came to learn the arts of embroidery and sewing. However, F. Z.'s husband did not approve of such constant comings and goings. He even went so far as to suggest that F. Z. had established immoral relations with a male neighbor, concealing these relations through her teaching endeavors. The husband, therefore, decided to forbid F. Z. to pursue her métier. Not wishing to give up her status as a *mu'allima* and her group of women apprentices, F. Z. refused to obey her husband's injunction. Her husband then took her before a Muslim judge, and she was sent to *Dar Joued* (a house of female correction) until she mended her ways.[82]

While providing but a brief glimpse into the daily life of an urban craftswoman, F. Z.'s story is suggestive. It tells us that some females achieved recognition in the culturally meaningful and economically remunerative activities of sewing and embroidery and that women gathered to receive instruction. F. Z.'s initial decision to oppose her husband's interdiction on continuing her profession indicates how important that status was to her.

However, the bulk of the population in nineteenth-century Tunisia lived either in villages or hamlets or were members of nomadic or seminomadic tribes. Here, specialization in production was less pronounced than in the city or town. Fiber processing was female work—washing, carding, and spinning as well as preparing wool or goat and camel hair. Rural women in precolonial Tunisia kept bees for honey and wax and also raised silkworms.[83] In addition, women produced a wide array of products, such as pottery and baskets, and wove nearly all the items needed for the household and for the pastoral economy in general—blankets, mats, rugs, and *flij*, the long, thin strips of woven material from which sacks, tents, and cushions were made on a horizontal loom.[84]

Although many of the articles made in the city as well as the countryside were for domestic consumption, some were distributed in markets or produced on command for clients. The centrality of woven textiles to local economies and to the precolonial Tunisian state is demonstrated by the intersection of taxation and cloth production. Traditionally, the weavers of the Djerid (a region of oases in the southwest), both male and female, produced especially fine textiles of wool mixed with silk thread. The products were so highly esteemed that these oases were taxed in kind by Tunisian rulers. Each year, a *mahalla* (tax-collecting expedition) was sent from Tunis to the Djerid; weavers were expected to deliver up so many lengths of finished luxury textiles to state agents as tribute in kind.[85] For much of the nineteenth century, European travelers in Tunisia reported on the flourishing state of manufacturing throughout the country—cloth production, jewelry, ceramics, leather goods, and so on. In 1845 a British diplomat visiting the Djerid noted that: "They make many burnous [i.e., hooded cloaks] at Tozeur and every house presents the industrious sight of the needle or shuttle moving quickly."[86] However, this situation would gradually change after midcentury as continual political unrest in neighboring Algeria began to influence commercial, economic, and manufacturing relationships across the border in Tunisia.

Relative to Algeria and Morocco, Tunisia had a higher proportion of sedentary inhabitants and more densely settled urban areas. In the farming suburbs attached to cities such as Tunis, Kairouan, Sousse, Gabes, and Sfax, local artisans "tended to imitate the urban guilds."[87] Thus, urban versus rural dichotomies, particularly for Mediterranean Tunisia, are not instructive. In myriad small towns and villages, women contributed to the manufacturing sector by preparing fibers for weaving, although in some regions the looms were worked exclusively by men. In other places, such as the Medjerda River valley, the Djerid, the coastal Sahel, and in the southeast, weaving tended to be monopolized by women.[88] The manufacture of *shashiya*s (red cylindrical wool caps worn by males) was centered in Tunis and its hinterland villages, revealing that work techniques and organizational patterns did not stop at the walls of Tunisian cities but spilled over into the surrounding countryside, affecting both male and female labor and the household.

Nineteenth-century *shashiya* production also provides one of the most fruitful areas of study of the gendered division of work in precolonial Tunisia. Because *shashiya*s were exported to Muslim countries around the Mediterranean, their manufacture was an economically vital sector of the traditional artisanal economy; in the early part of the nineteenth century, there were some 150 Tunisian establishments linked in one way or another with their production and distribution. Producing finished caps was a long, involved process that drew upon male and female workers both in the capital and in adjacent areas.[89] The earlier stages of wool preparation appear to have been uniquely female activities that took place in villages just outside of Tunis. There, the wool was cleaned, sorted, graded, and soaked in olive oil to soften it before spinning. Spinning the treated wool was also an exclusively female activity, taking place once again in the village in what constituted a form of the "putting out" system. Then the spun wool was distributed by male entrepreneurs to women in the small town of Ariana (now a suburb of Tunis) for knitting; here the tradition of knitting was "transmitted from mother to daughter."[90]

This work demanded uncommon skills on the part of the women, for the wool had to be knitted in an extremely tight fashion; even a slight imperfection reduced the quality and thus the final market price of the cap. We are least informed about this phase of *shashiya* production because of its feminine and semirural nature. Yet here once again a certain group of female workers—the women of Ariana—had developed recognized skills in knitting so that they held an informal "monopoly" over this stage of the manufacturing process.

The subsequent steps involved in producing a finished *shashiya*—and they were legion—were exclusively male activities.[91] A special souk in Tunis sold the caps to retailers for distribution to the rest of the country, to the Maghreb, and to other Islamic lands. This protocapitalist industry was an important generator of revenues until the import of cheaper, European-manufactured *shashiya*s began to undermine the superior Tunisian product in about 1850. (In today's Tunisia, the *shashiya* industry is virtually moribund due to lack of demand, although the numerous European tourists crowding the souks of the Tunis medina might purchase a few as souvenirs.)

In addition to its reputation for manufacturing particularly fine red caps, Tunisia has long been famous for its knotted carpets. Here too the intersection of the gendered division of labor and regional specializations is apparent. In the past, thick-pile carpets *(qtifa)*, time-consuming and expensive to make, were the exclusive domain of male weavers from pastoral-nomadic communities. These were only produced on command, and only elites could afford them.[92] Nevertheless, another kind of knotted carpet with a short pile was, and still is, woven by females, particularly in the interior city of Kairouan, an important religious center. A vertical loom *(mensej)* was employed for these carpets; this type of loom, found all over North Africa, was also used for weaving clothing, blankets, and other items.[93] One of the Kairouani carpets still produced today apparently had its origins in a short-pile Anatolian carpet first introduced into Ottoman-ruled Tunisia in the seventeenth or eighteenth century. The acquired taste for Anatolian carpets in Tunisia among female weavers and the general public alike has, in the popular mind, been attributed to a woman. Imtraud Reswick elaborates: "According to legend ... the first Kairouani carpets were woven c. 1830 by Kamla, the daughter of a Turkish governor of Kairouan. Other important families followed Kamla's example, and some of these early Kairouan [carpets] were donated to the Sidi Saheb Mosque in Kairouan and are preserved in museums."[94] The popularity of Kamla's carpets—if the story is true—did not stop at Kairouan's gates. Sometime around 1870, a widow from that city moved to the Mediterranean town of Bizerte and introduced the techniques of Kairouani carpet weaving to that region; as a result, "families who could afford to buy the wool soon followed her example."[95] The significance here is once again the fact that the "traditional" artisanal sector, dominated by female producers, was not tradition bound. Rather, novel styles and techniques of manufacturing continually enriched a well-established industry whose origins go back to medieval times if not earlier. Moreover, it was women, in their roles as both producers and consumers, who were instrumental in introducing new types of commodities and new ways of doing things to Tunisian society.

For Kairouan's inhabitants, the production of carpets was an important economic and commercial activity; it was also an essentially domestic industry. Families purchased raw wool from local pastoral-nomadic clients, who raised flocks of sheep in the semiarid plains around the city. The women of each kinship grouping were responsible not only for the preparation of the wool—washing, cleaning, and spinning—but also for weaving the carpets. However, dyeing remained a basically male operation, at least in Kairouan. Professional dyers labored in open-air workshops, using natural pigments obtained from either plants or animals. As for the various designs employed, each family had its own particular motifs, which were handed down from generation to generation and which identified the carpet and its kin-based weavers.[96] Women laboring at the loom expended enormous amounts of time to produce a finished piece. A very small carpet—for example, a prayer rug—demanded at least fifteen days; the larger carpets might take up to three or four months to produce.[97] The extended period of time required for a female weaver to complete a carpet was a direct consequence of the fact that she had to balance her time before the loom with numerous household tasks and other productive activities. Finally, in Kairouan, the female-dominated industry of weaving had an important matrimonial dimension: A "skilled weaver easily found a husband," since she could be counted on to add to the household's income.[98]

Until the time of the French Protectorate, the carpets of Kairouan were regarded as luxury items that only upper-class Tunisian families could afford to purchase; the female weavers tended to be of respectable but modest social origins. After 1881, European demand for the carpets soared, stimulating production for sale both in Tunisia and abroad in Europe. Increased demand, however, led to a deterioration in quality, as the female weavers attempted to shorten production time and as cheaper, inferior chemical dyes replaced natural colors.[99] As was the case in both Algeria and Morocco, the colonial regime intervened to salvage the "traditional" industry by imposing "modern" institutional supports and quality control standards.[100]

From Artisan to Wage Laborer, c. 1881–1956

Even before the 1881 imposition of the French Protectorate upon Tunisia, the economy, both urban and rural, was being penetrated by forces not only from Europe but also from neighboring Algeria. The thriving contraband traffic among European countries bordering the Mediterranean and Tunisia had, by the middle of the nineteenth century, introduced cotton and silk textiles from Manchester, Lyon, and even India.[101] If smuggling dumped proscribed European manufactures into North Africa, the global underground economy also furnished the Algerians with the primary material of militant resistance to France—firearms and gunpowder. Thus, the gradual demise of the textile industry in parts of North Africa was directly tied to political and military upheavals in Algeria, which reinforced world market forces.[102]

Around 1900, French colonial officials sounded the alarm about the declining state of the urban male silk-weaving industry, which had originated in Tunisia during the ninth or tenth century. According to Ernest Fallot, silk weaving occupied some 1,000 looms in the country and, with its ancillary industries such as dyeing and spinning, provided employment to some 4,000 persons, including women working mainly at home. The finished silk products had long been commercialized in markets in both Algeria and Tripolitania and furnished important revenues to the Tunisian state. Moreover, the production of wool blankets and covers known as *farashiya* or *battaniya,* woven by male and female weavers in the Djerid, in Gabes, and on the island of Djerba, had also fallen into a "profound decadence."[103] In explaining the dwindling fortunes of one of the most critical traditional sectors of the Tunisian economy, Fallot laid the blame squarely on "European competition which had introduced into Tunisia's markets, [textile] products that were similar to local productions but less costly."[104] Even the well-meaning efforts of colonial officials in Tunisia to shore up the indigenous weaving industry by introducing the Jacquard loom to the male weavers of Tunis, who were organized into guilds or corporations, failed miserably.[105]

Global Crises and Their Local Impact

Industrialization in Tunisia did not occur on a massive scale until the last years of the protectorate. Yet imports of machine-produced goods from France and elsewhere in Europe, combined with changing tastes and styles, particularly among the French-educated Tunisian elite in the capital, led to the steady deterioration of the traditional manufacturing sectors. This became glaringly apparent in the interwar period.[106] The global recession of the early 1930s struck even those Tunisian communities located some distance from the main centers of colonial exploitation in the country's northern regions. A French administrator in the Djerid reported in 1931:

> Weaving is no longer done here; the commerce in blankets and wool burnous is paralyzed by the present [economic] crisis. In the [Djerid's] houses there are numerous looms, some 5,000 in Tozeur, 4,000 in Nefta; since the price of raw materials has greatly increased, a number of work shops no longer function

since they are unable to purchase wool. These problems are not only due to the price of raw materials but also to the lack of markets for finished products.[107]

In 1932 the Office of Tunisian Arts was established by protectorate officials due to anxieties over mounting under- and unemployment among the emerging, increasingly politicized Tunisian working class, many of whose members were recruited from the decaying artisanal sector.[108] The fate of female handicraft workers was not considered of much consequence, since it was implicitly assumed that women were apolitical and that they were not truly artisans. Nevertheless, the office intervened in feminine handicraft production of Kairouani carpets and other items, with an eye to the burgeoning tourist trade. Just prior to 1956, for example, the office attempted

This photo is of the main tourist street in Nefta, an oasis in the Tunisian Djerid. The flat woven textiles hanging from the wall are klims *showing variations of the motifs characteristic of the town of Rdeyef to the north of Nefta. These were probably woven by women either at home or in a branch of the government-run National Office of the Artisanat. Although the motifs and techniques are traditional to this part of Tunisia, the dyes used are artificial, often producing garish colors. (Photo by Julia Clancy-Smith, taken in 1992.)*

to induce the female weavers of Kairouan to dramatically change the colors used—from neutral tones to polychromatic carpets whose colors "imitate the oldest and most authentic" pieces. Further, a trade fair was held each Easter in Kairouan to stimulate international demand for the carpets. Finally, the Institute of Arts and Crafts was created in the interwar period in Tunis with branches around the country to instruct indigenous males and females in traditional handicrafts.[109]

World War II, which brought Allied military forces to Tunisia to fight against the Nazi-Fascist occupation of the country, unleashed more misery for all Tunisians. Women of modest means who worked in the informal textile sector in Tunis and elsewhere were frequently among the most vulnerable. "Since the war had created supply problems, we attempted to come to the aid of the female weavers who had no more spun wool [and] the lace-makers who had no more thread."[110] This statement by a Tunisian Jew, Gladys Adda, who was active in the Tunisian Communist Party and its feminist affiliate, the Union of Women of Tunisia, indicates that indigenous women acted through formal feminist and workers' associations to come to the aid of impoverished female producers.

Nevertheless, on the eve of independence from France, the female weavers of Kairouan still numbered about 2,200, according to Jacques Revault, an expert on North African textiles. The survival of this branch of the handicraft sector was attributed to the fact that these particular carpets had become popular for wedding trousseaus among the emerging middle class in Tunisia (and they remain very much so in today's Tunisia).[111] The carpets of Kairouan furnish a singular case of modernity fueling demand and thus saving a traditional craft and its female artisans from oblivion. Observed Revault in the 1950s: "The techniques of knotting and the knowledge of the traditional motifs are handed down from mother to daughter. These motifs thus form a repertoire familiar to the weavers, who identify them after common objects they resemble."[112] In his detailed and sympathetic study from the same period, Lucien Golvin attempted to calibrate the number of women in Tunisia still working in traditional production. He gave slightly higher figures than Revault—more than 2,500 women—for weavers producing Kairouani carpets for sale; more than 4,000 lace workers still plied their trade, as did female potters whose "numbers are impossible to evaluate."[113] Altogether, more than 10,000 women (out of a population of 3.8 million) were thought to be employed in these manufacturing activities. Yet even Golvin concluded that: "These are in general the resources of the domestic [female] handicraft sector in Tunisia, which corresponds to what I would call popular art, and [is] clearly different from urban male artisans previously organized into corporations."[114]

In 1956 the former Office of Tunisian Arts acquired a new name, the National Office of the Artisanat, but its mission remained more or less the same as under the French Protectorate—the reinvention of handicrafts principally for the booming tourist industry. By the mid-1980s, Tunisia had invested heavily in tourism, which represents one of the country's most lucrative economic sectors; at least 10 percent of the total Tunisian workforce depends in one way or another upon tourism, which peddles exotic "traditional" crafts to foreign visitors.[115]

Postcolonial Postscripts

In his 1973 study of the town of Testour (in north-central Tunisia), Nicholas Hopkins found that the town's only group of organized workers was in the carpet manufacturing sector. The National Office of the Artisanat had set up a modern carpet-weaving enterprise where twenty-four young women wove rugs for sale, either in the capital (mainly to tourists) or abroad.[116]

In contrast, male-dominated production of the *qashshabiya* (a man's winter garment with a hood) was organized along lines resembling the older patterns characteristic of *shashiya* making, as discussed above. As in the past, women were involved in certain specific phases of the work but excluded from others; for example, only females prepared the wool just after the sheep-shearing season at the end of springtime. During the hot summer months, the family's women washed and cleaned raw wool along the banks of the Medjerda River. This activity was particularly cherished, since it afforded "one of the rare occasions when town women could leave their houses."[117]

The carding, spinning, and weaving of the cloth was also feminine work performed at home. However, once the cloth was prepared, it was taken to a certain shop where a male tailor, specialized in cutting the *qashshabiya*, carried on his craft, received clients, and took orders. This tailor provided employment for roughly six households; among these was a widow, two unmarried women, and three sets of mother-daughter weavers. The amount of time needed to produce enough cloth for one *qashshabiya* varied in direct proportion to the other demands upon the women's labor; alone, a weaver needed eight days to make cloth for one garment but working in pairs, only four days. Finally, since the tailor could not generally enter the houses of the female weavers (unless they were part of the kinship grouping), his wife was responsible for maintaining close contact with her husband's female "employees."[118]

The example provided by Testour seems to indicate that Tunisia's independence inverted the customary gendered division of labor—or at least introduced substantial modifications to it. At first glance, the male-controlled artisanal activity of *qashshabiya* making in Testour appears to have been "domesticated" by modernity. In contrast, under the auspices of the

These Moroccan girls work under male supervision weaving rugs and other items for sale to tourists in Fez. Although child labor laws exist in Morocco and elsewhere in North Africa, state enforcement is often lax. In addition, the girls' parents are poor and need the income from their daughters' labor for the household to survive. (Photo by Julia Clancy-Smith, taken in 1991.)

National Office of the Artisanat, Testour's female carpet weavers labored outside the home, were organized, and produced for the market, indeed for distant markets and consumers.

Although the last stages of production as well as the sale of the finished *qashshabiya* in Testour transpired outside the home, Hopkins argued that the tailor's shop was "simply an extension of the domestic economy."[119] In some respects, *qashshabiya* making represented the vestiges of a much older system of clothing production that had been under siege due to changing tastes and styles in Tunisia and elsewhere in North Africa. Some of the female weavers working for the tailor were doing so to amass enough money to purchase imported items for their trousseau; thus, they were part of a dying domestic economy and at the same time were incorporated into a national (and, one could argue, an international) wage labor economy.[120]

The women weaving carpets for the national office were scarcely artisans, for they labored under local male supervision and were paid wages for their work. The rugs they produced did not necessarily display motifs and color patterns handed down from generation to generation, from mother to daughter, and operating as "signatures" of quality and female identity. Rather, the female carpet weavers were employees of the office, which in turn had to respond to foreign demand and tastes in "native" handicrafts. Indeed, it can be asserted that "style and quality were more than matters of taste; they represented an entire social, political, and cultural order," an order whose contours were dictated by forces that lay far beyond Testour's town limits or even the borders of Tunisia or North Africa.[121]

Thus far we have dealt primarily with the political economy of female production—but what of its cultural and symbolic dimensions? Intriguing evidence of the cultural-symbolic connections among women, gender, and handicrafts is provided by Pierre Bourdieu in his study of the Kabyle people of Algeria. In the Kabylia, the weaving loom occupied a central position in the villagers' homes and in the sociosexual universe of Kabyle society. At birth, a girl-baby's umbilical cord was cut off and then "buried behind the weaving-loom."[122] Later, as the young girl approached puberty, she was "made to pass through the warp" in a ritual demonstrating the weaving loom's magical powers to ensure virginity. On her wedding day, the Kabyle bride was seated in front of the loom, facing outward. According to Bourdieu, "all of the girl's life is, as it were, summed up in the successive positions that she symbolically occupies in relation to the weaving-loom which is the symbol of male protection."[123] The Kabyle household loom, still a fixture in the main room of the household when Bourdieu carried out his study in the 1960s, nevertheless was losing its "magical" qualities and its central role in the sociocultural and symbolic universe of village life.

As discussed in this chapter, female weaving in North Africa was historically fundamental to the household as a process of production and consumption and thus as a mediating institution; yet weaving always had an equally important "mythical" component to it. The same could be said of pottery making. Brinkley Messick recently pointed out that weaving represented an "elaborate body of specialized female knowledge" and as such had a significant discursive dimension to it; in short, the rituals associated with weaving could be "read" as a gendered "subordinate discourse."[124] The transformations unleashed by European colonialism and by the penetration of world market forces in North Africa during the past century have not only turned female artisans into a modern feminine subproletariat but also created new subordinate discourses and new forms of invisibility.

Notes

1. Cited by Marguerite A. Bel and Prosper Ricard, *Le travail de laine à Tlemcen* (Algiers, 1913), 50.

2. Lucien Golvin, *Les tissages décorés d'El-Djem et de Djebeniana* (Tunis: Imprimerie Bascone et Muscat, 1949), 122.

3. On the local impact of world market forces, see Sherry Vatter's fine study, "Journeymen Textile Weavers in Nineteenth-Century Damascus: A Collective Biography," in *Struggle and Survival in the Modern Middle East,* ed. Edmund Burke III (Berkeley: University of California Press, 1993), 75–90.

4. Leonard M. Helfgott, *Ties That Bind: The Social History of the Iranian Carpet* (Washington, D.C.: The Smithsonian Institution Press, 1994), 2, in which he discusses the Iranian carpet as historical object; a similar "anthropology of things" approach to oriental carpets is adopted by Brian Spooner in his "Weavers and Dealers: The Authenticity of an Oriental Carpet," in *The Social Life of Things: Commodities in Cultural Perspective,* ed. Arjun Appadurai (Cambridge: Cambridge University Press, 1986), 195–235.

5. Judith Tucker was one of the first scholars to trace the impact that the capitalist transformation of Egypt in the past century had upon women and gender relations; Judith Tucker, *Women in Nineteenth-Century Egypt* (Cambridge: Cambridge University Press, 1985).

6. The household as mediator is the theoretical starting point for Diane Singerman's and Homa Hoodfar's edited volume, *Development, Change, and Gender in Cairo: A View from the Household* (Bloomington: Indiana University Press, 1996).

7. Lucien Golvin, *Aspects de l'artisanat en Afrique du Nord* (Paris: Presses Universitaires de France, 1957), 33–35.

8. One study of women performing service-sector functions in post-1962 Algeria is Willy Jensen's *Women Without Men: Gender and Marginality in an Algerian Town* (Leiden: E. J. Brill, 1987); on women as religious agents, see Julia Clancy-Smith, "The House of Zainab: Female Authority and Saintly Succession in Colonial Algeria," in *Women in Middle Eastern History: Shifting Boundaries in Sex and Gender,* ed. Nikki Keddie and Beth Baron (New Haven: Yale University Press, 1991), 275–291. Female musicians in Tunisia are examined in L. J. Jones, "A Sociohistorical Perspective on Tunisian Women as Professional Musicians," in *Women and Music in Cross-Cultural Perspective,* ed. Ellen Koskoff (New York: Greenwood Press, 1987), 69–84; for Egypt, see Karin van Nieuwkerk, *"A Trade Like Any Other": Female Singers and Dancers in Egypt* (Austin: University of Texas Press, 1995).

9. Paul Antichan, *La Tunisie, son passé et son avenir* (Paris: Delagrave, 1884), 221.

10. The study of women and handicraft production in colonial North Africa poses a number of problems; one of the most fundamental is that of documentation from the past. We are better informed about the urban artisanal sector, dominated by men and guilds, than village or tribal production. And the twentieth century is more richly documented than the nineteenth.

11. For example, see Augustin Berque's "Le tapis Algérien," in *Écrits sur L'Algérie,* ed. Jacques Berque (Aix-en-Provence: Édisud, 1986), 221–235.

12. Socially and culturally constructed definitions of what constitutes "work" for women in many countries and cultures today frequently exclude feminine production by devaluing it. For example, in *Money Makes Us Relatives: Women's Labor in Urban Turkey* (Austin: University of Texas Press, 1994), Jenny B. White studied female migrants from villages who lived in Istanbul and produced for the piecework industry at home as well as in workshops. She concluded that, while many women worked as much as fifty hours per week in the export sector, they denied that they truly worked. The explanation for this lies in the domestic nature and setting of women's productive activities, its kin-based organization, and male concerns with honor.

In consequence, women today are often absent from, or underreported in, studies and statistical surveys of the global modern workforce due to narrow definitions of formal-sector activities that deny recognition of female contributions. On this, see Valentine M. Moghadam, *Modernizing Women: Gender and Social Change in the Middle East* (Boulder: Lynne Rienner, 1993), 29–68; and Marnia Lazreg, "Women, Work, and Social Change in Algeria," in *Women, Employment, and the Family in the International Division of Labor,* ed. Sharon Stichter and Jane L. Parpart (New York: Macmillan, 1990), 183–197.

13. Male artisans in the traditional handicraft sectors of the Middle East and North Africa often performed productive activities in settings that combined or conflated public and domestic spaces—or, more accurately, private and public spheres bled into one another. For a discussion of the theoretical issues raised, see Erika Friedl, "Political Roles of Alabad Women: The Public-Private Dichotomy Transcended," in *Women in Middle Eastern History: Shifting Boundaries in Sex and Gender,* ed. Nikki Keddie and Beth Baron (New Haven: Yale University Press, 1991), 215–231.

14. The same had been true in France throughout the nineteenth century, where the economy was overwhelmingly dependent upon skilled handicraft manufacture and dispersed manual methods of production in which both women and men participated. Yet females workers were rarely accorded the distinction of artisan in France either; see Whitney Walton, *France at the Crystal Palace: Bourgeois Taste and Artisan Manufacture in the Nineteenth Century* (Berkeley and Los Angeles: University of California Press, 1992), 4–14.

15. In her *Women's Work: The First 20,000 Years: Women, Cloth, and Society in Early Times* (New York: Norton, 1994), Elizabeth Wayland Barber reveals the critical importance to societies in the ancient Near East and Mediterranean world of female weavers and cloth producers, an importance that was passed over in silence until very recently.

16. For a study of the decline of the Moroccan male handicraft sector, see Kenneth L. Brown, *People of Salé: Tradition and Change in a Moroccan City, 1830–1930* (Cambridge: Harvard University Press, 1976), 129–154.

17. On the interrelationship between male and female production and world market forces, see Donald Quataert, "Ottoman Women, Households, and Textile Manufacturing, 1800–1914," in *Women in Middle Eastern History: Shifting Boundaries in Sex and Gender,* ed. Nikki Keddie and Beth Baron (New Haven: Yale University Press, 1991), 161–176; and also Margaret L. Meriwether, "Women and Economic Change in Nineteenth-Century Syria: The Case of Aleppo," in *Arab*

Women: Old Boundaries, New Frontiers, ed. Judith E. Tucker (Bloomington: Indiana University Press, 1993), 65–83. For a general history, see Donald Quataert, ed., *Manufacturing in the Ottoman Empire and Turkey, 1500–1950* (Albany: State University of New York Press, 1994).

18. The most detailed treatment of colonial Algeria is Charles-Robert Ageron, *Les Algériens Musulmans et la France (1871–1919),* 2 vols. (Paris: Presses Universitaires de France, 1968). John Ruedy's *Modern Algeria: The Origins and Development of a Nation* (Bloomington: Indiana University Press, 1992) is the best English-language overview; see also David Prochaska, *Making Algeria French: Colonialism in Bône, 1870–1920* (Cambridge: Cambridge University Press, 1990); and L. Carl Brown and Matthew S. Gordon, eds., *Franco-Arab Encounters* (Beirut: American University of Beirut Press, 1996).

19. On the conquest period in colonial Algerian history, see Charles-André Julien, *Histoire de l'Algérie Contemporaine,* vol. 1 (Paris: Presses Universitaires de France, 1979); and Julia Clancy-Smith, *Rebel and Saint: Muslim Notables, Populist Protest, Colonial Encounters (Algeria and Tunisia, 1800–1904)* (Berkeley and Los Angeles: University of California Press, 1994).

20. On female work and handicrafts in the Kabylia Mountains at the end of the nineteenth century, see Fadhma Amrouche, *My Life Story: The Autobiography of a Berber Woman,* trans. Dorothy S. Blair (New Brunswick, N.J.: Rutgers University Press, 1989).

21. See Ageron, *Les Algériens Musulmans,* 2: 792–858 for a discussion of the evolution of the indigenous economy from 1890 to 1919.

22. Golvin, *Aspects,* 36.

23. Ibid., 1–7.

24. William A. Hoisington, *The Casablanca Connection: French Colonial Policy, 1936–1943* (Chapel Hill: University of North Carolina Press, 1984), 93–103, examines colonial efforts in Morocco to shore up the eroding social position of the "little people" during the interwar period, particularly for the male artisans and their corporations in Fez.

25. Yaël Simpson Fletcher, "'Irresistible Seductions': Gendered Representations of Colonial Algeria Around 1930," in *Domesticating the Empire: Race, Gender, and Family Life in French and Dutch Colonialism,* ed. Julia Clancy-Smith and Frances Gouda (Charlottesville: University Press of Virginia, 1998), 193–210.

26. James Mokhiber, "The 'Disinterested Culture' of Art and Orientalism in Colonial Algeria: Jean Alazard and His Museum, 1930," master's thesis, Johns Hopkins University, 1993; cited with permission of the author.

27. Golvin, *Aspects,* 4–5.

28. Jean Blottière, "Les Productions Algériennes," *Cahiers du Centenaire de l'Algérie* 9 (1930): 70–71.

29. Golvin, *Aspects,* 3, observed the following: "The essential distinction between the artistic production of the artisan and popular art [is that] the first is an activity almost exclusively masculine while popular art can be both masculine or feminine."

30. Quataert reaches similar conclusions in "Ottoman Women, Households, and Textile Manufacturing."

31. For example, Augustin Berque, *Art Antique et Art Musulman en Algérie* (Paris: Publications du Comité National Métropolitan du Centenaire de l'Algérie, 1930), 113, 119.

32. Blottière, *Productions*, 71.

33. Malek Alloula, *The Colonial Harem* (Minneapolis: University of Minnesota Press, 1986); and Sarah Graham-Brown, *Images of Women: The Portrayal of Women in Photography of the Middle East, 1860–1950* (New York: Columbia University Press, 1988), esp. 144–169 on working women.

34. Zeynep Çelik, *Displaying the Orient: Architecture of Islam at Nineteenth-Century World's Fairs* (Berkeley and Los Angeles: University of California Press, 1992). See also the collection of articles in the special issue of *Revue du Monde Musulman et de la Méditerranée* 73-74, nos. 3-4 (1994), devoted to "Figures de l'orientalisme en architecture."

35. In large part, this oversight was due to prevailing European ideas regarding urban Arab women as leading utterly idle, sensuous lives confined behind the locked doors of harems in North African cities; on these views, see Julia Clancy-Smith, "Islam, Gender, and Identities in the Making of French Algeria, 1830–1962," in *Domesticating the Empire: Race, Gender, and Family Life in French and Dutch Colonialism,* ed. Julia Clancy-Smith and Frances Gouda (Charlottesville: University Press of Virginia, 1998), 154–174. On elite women in harems and their daily activities, see Julia Clancy-Smith and Cynthia Metcalf, "A Visit to a Tunisian Harem," *Journal of Maghrebi Studies* 1-2, no. 1 (Spring 1993): 43–49.

36. Although the first attempt to formally instruct Algerian girls in handicrafts came as early as 1845, it was not until the interwar period that these schools were centralized and institutionalized; see Marnia Lazreg, *The Eloquence of Silence: Algerian Women in Question* (New York: Routledge, 1994), 59–79; and Ageron, *Les Algériens Musulmans,* 2: 851, for a discussion of colonial attempts in 1895 to organize native schools to teach carpet production; see also Marie Bugéja, *Nos Soeurs Musulmanes,* 2nd ed. (Algiers: Éditions France-Afrique, 1931), 84–90.

37. Marguerite A. Bel, *Les arts indigènes féminins en Algérie* (Algiers: Ouvrage publié sous les auspices du Gouvernement Générale de l'Algérie, 1939). Bel's study is not paginated; therefore I have assigned page numbers to both the text and the illustrations in accordance with *The Chicago Manual of Style,* 13th ed. (Chicago: University of Chicago Press, 1982); thus, the first section, "Les Arts Indigènes Féminins en Algérie," is paginated as 1.
In her preface, page i, Bel accords the status of artisan to Algerian female handicraft workers, yet introduces a degree of ambiguity by placing quotation marks around the word—for example, *"artisane."*

38. Ibid., iii, 30–31.

39. Ibid., 66.

40. Ibid., i–ii; and Golvin, *Aspects,* 1–7.

41. On the political responses of male handicraft workers and artisans to Japanese and European inroads into their livelihood, see Jacques Berque, *French North Africa: The Maghrib Between Two World Wars,* trans. Jean Stewart (New York: Praeger, 1967), 176–177.

42. Johan H. Meuleman, *Le Constantinois entre les deux guerres mondiales: L'évolution économiques et sociale de la population rurale* (Assen, Netherlands: Van Gorcum, 1985), 122.

43. Bel, *Les arts indigènes*, i–ii; and Charles-Robert Ageron, *Histoire de L'Algérie Contemporaine*, vol. 2, *De l'insurrection de 1871 au déclenchement de la guerre de libération (1954)* (Paris: Presses Universitaires de France, 1979), 412–418.

44. Bel, *Les arts indigènes*, 2.

45. Ibid., 1.

46. Ibid.

47. Zeynep Çelik, *Urban Forms and Colonial Confrontations: Algiers Under French Rule* (Berkeley and Los Angeles: University of California Press, 1997).

48. Bel, *Les arts indigènes*, 1–16.

49. Ibid.

50. On the institution of the *mu'allimat* in Tunis, see Souad Bakalti, "L'enseignement féminin dans le primaire au temps de la Tunisie coloniale," *Revue de l'Institut des Belles Lettres Arabes* 53, no. 166 (1990): 249–273.

51. Bel, *Les arts indigènes*, 12, 15. Comparing Bel's account from the 1930s with Susan Schaefer Davis's recent study, "Working Women in a Moroccan Village," in *Women in the Muslim World*, ed. Lois Beck and Nikki Keddie (Cambridge: Harvard University Press, 1978), 416–432, reveals significant parallels in the social status and organization of seamstress work and in female instruction of pupils. Davis points out that a seamstress-teacher does not need much capital to be successful; her two most important assets are recognized skill in sewing and a virtuous reputation.

52. Bakalti, "L'enseignement féminin," 250.

53. Bel, *Les arts indigènes*, 3.

54. Ageron, *Les Algériens Musulmans*, 2: 851, notes that by 1906 weaving rugs was hardly remunerative for Algerian women; a seventeen-kilogram rug demanded two months of work, for which the female weaver was only paid fifty francs, less than one franc per day.

55. Bel, *Les arts indigènes*, 20.

56. Ibid., n. 2; and Golvin, *Aspects*, 53–55.

57. Joseph W. Blakesley, *Four Months in Algeria, with a Visit to Carthage* (Cambridge: Cambridge University Press, 1859), 206.

58. An ethnographic description from 1936 of the tents woven by women of the Larbaa and Awlad Nail tribes of central Algeria is found in C. G. Feilberg, *La Tente Noire* (Copenhagen: I Kommission Hos Gyldendalske Boghandel, 1944), 46–53.

59. Imtraud Reswick, *Traditional Textiles of Tunisia and Related North African Weavings* (Los Angeles: Craft and Folk Art Museum, 1985), 31–34. The city-oases of the Mzab, deep in the central Sahara, which displayed characteristics of both urban and rural life, provide a case apart. Here, the initial washing of the wool was an exclusively male activity, unlike the situation that generally obtained elsewhere in Algeria and in other parts of North Africa. One of the principal reasons for the male monopoly over wool washing was the traditional domestic architecture of the Mzab, itself the result of the distribution of water resources in the area. The interior courtyards of the Mzab's houses did not have fountains, and, therefore, wash-

ing wool had to take place outside of the domestic compound in large open-air basins near the wells. This space was regarded as public and was generally the preserve of men in much the same way that the café was; for reasons of family honor and to preserve female modesty, women were excluded from the washing of the raw wool. On the Mzab, see Anne-Marie Goichon, *La vie féminine au Mzab: Etude de sociologie Musulmane* (Paris: Geuthner, 1927), 108.

60. Bel, *Les arts indigènes,* 33–36.

61. Ibid., 41.

62. Ibid.

63. On the Kabylia, see Julia Clancy-Smith, "Kabylia," in *The Oxford Encyclopedia of the Modern Islamic World,* vol. 2 (Oxford: Oxford University Press, 1995), 397–398.

64. Bel, *Les arts indigènes,* 42.

65. Ibid., 29–35; and Jean-Louis Combés and Louis André, *Les Potiers de Djerba* (Tunis: Publications du Centre des Arts et Traditions Populaires, 1967).

66. A basic introduction to Kabyle society and culture is Pierre Bourdieu's *The Algerians* (Boston: Beacon Press, 1962), 1–24.

67. Bel, *Les arts indigènes,* 29–35; and Adolphe Hanoteau and Aristide Letourneux, *La Kabylie et les coutumes kabyles,* 3 vols. (Paris: Challamel, 1872–1873).

68. Bel, *Les arts indigènes,* 29–35; and Golvin, *Aspects,* 69, 73.

69. Bel, *Les arts indigènes,* 36–37.

70. Ibid.; and Prosper Ricard, "Nattes Berbères de l'Afrique du Nord," *Hespéris* 5 (1925): 105–123.

71. Bel, *Les arts indigènes,* 38–40.

72. Ibid.

73. Reswick, *Traditional Textiles,* 43–44.

74. Ibid., 60–63; and Bel, *Les arts indigènes,* 38.

75. Reswick, *Traditional Textiles,* 60; and Ricard, "Nattes Berbères," 119.

76. Reswick, *Traditional Textiles,* 42–47; and Ageron, *Histoire,* 2: 504–506.

77. Golvin, *Aspects,* 60; and Ageron, *Les Algériens Musulmans,* 2: 849; Ageron notes that the vast majority of working Algerian women were servants for Europeans, some 4,655 at the beginning of the twentieth century.

78. Ageron, *Les Algériens Musulmans,* 2: 849.

79. Reswick, *Traditional Textiles,* 20–21; Lucette Valensi, *On the Eve of Colonialism: North Africa Before the French Conquest, 1790–1830* (New York: Africana, 1977), 36–42; and Mustapha Kraïem, *La Tunisie Précoloniale* (Tunis: Société Tunisienne de Diffusion, 1973), 2: 37–40.

80. Reswick, *Traditional Textiles,* 23–46.

81. Bakalti, "L'enseignement féminin," 249–250.

82. Dalenda Largueche, "Dar Joued ou l'oubli dans la mémoire," in *Etre Marginal au Maghreb,* ed. Fanny Colonna and Zakya Daoud (Paris: Éditions du CNRS, 1993), 188–189.

83. Hermann Puckler-Muskau, *Travels in Algeria* (London, 1839), 2: 176.

84. Reswick, *Traditional Textiles,* 21; and Kraïem, *La Tunisie,* 2: 41.

85. Lucette Valensi, *Fellahs Tunisiens: L'économie rurale et la vie des campagnes aux 18eme et 19eme siècles* (Paris: Mouton, 1977), 211.

86. James Richardson, "An Account of the Present State of Tunis," 1845, Great Britain, Public Record Office, Foreign Office, Tunisia, 102 (29).

87. Reswick, *Traditional Textiles,* 21.

88. Ibid.; see also Victor Fleury, "Les industries indigènes de la Régence," *Revue Tunisienne* 2 (1896): 175–197.

89. Lucette Valensi, "Islam et capitalisme: production et commerce des chéchias en Tunisie et en France aux XVIIIe et XIXe siècles," *Revue d'Histoire Moderne et Contemporaine* 17 (1969): 376–400.

90. Kraïem, *La Tunisie,* 2: 42–44.

91. Ibid.

92. Jacques Revault, *Designs and Patterns from North African Carpets and Textiles* (New York: Dover Publications, 1973), viii.

93. Reswick, *Traditional Textiles,* 63–65, 105.

94. Ibid., 105–106.

95. Ibid., 107.

96. Kraïem, *La Tunisie,* 2: 44–46.

97. Ibid., 45; and Reswick, *Traditional Textiles,* 105–112.

98. Golvin, *Aspects,* 187.

99. Reswick, *Traditional Textiles,* 107.

100. Ibid.; and Golvin, *Aspects,* 61–62, 65–67. See also the articles in *Cahiers des Arts et Techniques d'Afrique du Nord 5* (1959), which are devoted to efforts at renovating traditional handicrafts in North Africa.

101. On the contraband trade in both Tunisia and Algeria, see Clancy-Smith, *Rebel and Saint,* 155–167; on the impact of textiles imported from Europe via Malta on the North African economy, see E. Pellissier de Reynaud, *Description de la régence de Tunis,* vol. 16 of *Exploration Scientifique de l'Algérie* (Paris: Imprimerie Royale, 1853), 365.

102. Archives du Ministère des Affaires Étrangères, Quai d'Orsay, Paris, memoires et documents, vol. 14, de Lanessan report of 1885.

103. Ernest Fallot, *La Situation Économique de la Tunisie* (Marseilles, 1899), 12.

104. Ibid.

105. Élisée Reclus, *L'Afrique Septentrionale,* vol. 11 of *Nouvelle Géographie Universelle: La Terre et les Hommes* (Paris: Hachette, 1886), 282.

106. See the 1927 treatise by Tahar Haddad, *Les travailleurs Tunisiens et l'emergence du mouvement syndical,* trans. Abderrazak Halioui (Tunis: Maison Arabe du Livre, 1985), 22–25, in which he decries the advent of mechanization and of new tastes among Tunisian consumers, trends that he argues are to the detriment of the artisan class.

107. Archives Nationales de Tunisie, Dar el-Bey, Tunis, A-113-1, report of December 10, 1931.

108. James P. Mokhiber, a Ph.D. candidate at Johns Hopkins University, has an in-progress dissertation devoted to the Office of Tunisian Arts; see also Mustapha Kraïem, *La Classe Ouvrière Tunisienne et la Lutte de Liberation Nationale (1939–1952)* (Tunis: Presses de L'Imprimerie UGTT, 1980).

109. Golvin, *Aspects,* 67; and Great Britain Intelligence Division, *Tunisia* (Oxford: Oxford University Press, 1945), 339.

110. Habib Kazdaghli, ed., *Nisa' wa dhakira: tunisiyat fi al-hayat al-'amma* (Tunis: Éditions Média, Collection Mémoires, 1993), 63.

111. Revault, *Designs and Patterns,* viii.

112. Golvin, *Aspects,* 65.

113. Ibid., 69.

114. Ibid.

115. Figures for tourism are found in Harold D. Nelson, ed., *Tunisia: A Country Study,* 3rd ed. (Washington, D.C.: American University Foreign Area Studies, 1988), 193–194.

116. Nicholas S. Hopkins, *Testour ou la transformation des campagnes Maghrébines* (Tunis: Cérès Productions, 1983), 101.

117. Ibid., 102.

118. Ibid., 107.

119. Ibid., 103.

120. Ibid., 107.

121. Walton, *France,* 15.

122. Pierre Bourdieu, "The Berber House," in *Rules and Meanings: The Anthropology of Everyday Knowledge,* ed. Mary Douglas (New York: Penguin, 1973), 98–110.

123. Ibid., 100.

124. Brinkley Messick, "Subordinate Discourse: Women, Weaving, and Gender Relations in North Africa," *American Anthropologist* 14, no. 2 (1987): 211.

References

Bakalti, Souad. *La Femme Tunisienne au temps de la colonisation, 1881–1956.* Paris: L'Harmattan, 1996.

Bel, Marguerite A. *Les arts indigènes féminins en Algérie.* Algiers, 1939.

Clancy-Smith, Julia, and Cynthia Metcalf. "A Visit to a Tunisian Harem." *Journal of Maghrebi Studies* 1-2, 1 (Spring 1993): 43–49.

Goichon, Anne-Marie. *La vie féminine au Mzab: Etude de sociologie Musulmane.* Paris: Geuthner, 1927.

Golvin, Lucien. *Aspects de l'artisanat en Afrique du Nord.* Paris: Presses Universitaires de France, 1957.

_____. *Les tissages décorés d'El Djem et de Djebeniana.* Tunis: Imprimerie Bascone et Muscat, 1949.

Helfgott, Leonard M. *Ties That Bind: The Social History of the Iranian Carpet.* Washington, D.C.: The Smithsonian Institution Press, 1994.

Jensen, Willy. *Women Without Men: Gender and Marginality in an Algerian Town.* Leiden: E. J. Brill, 1987.

Kerrou, Mohamed, and Moncef Mhalla. "La prostitution dans la médina de Tunis au XIXe au XXe siècle." In *Etre Marginal au Maghreb,* ed. Fanny Colonna, 201–221. Paris: Alif, 1993.

Lazreg, Marnia. "Women, Work, and Social Change in Algeria." In *Women, Employment, and the Family in the International Division of Labor,* ed. Sharon Stichter and Jane L. Parpart, 183–197. New York: Macmillan, 1990.

Lobban, Richard, ed. *Middle Eastern Women and the Invisible Economy.* Gainesville: University of Florida Press, 1998.

Messick, Brinkley. "Subordinate Discourse: Women, Weaving, and Gender Relations in North Africa." *American Anthropologist* 14, no. 2 (1987): 210–225.

Quataert, Donald. "Ottoman Women, Households, and Textile Manufacturing, 1800–1914." In *Women in Middle Eastern History: Shifting Boundaries in Sex and Gender,* ed. Nikki Keddie and Beth Baron, 161–176. New Haven: Yale University Press, 1991.

Reswick, Imtraud. *Traditional Textiles of Tunisia and Related North African Weavings.* Los Angeles: Craft and Folk Art Museum, 1985.

Simon, Rachel. *Change Within Tradition Among Jewish Women in Libya.* Seattle: University of Washington Press, 1992.

Singerman, Diane, and Homa Hoodfar, eds. *Development, Change, and Gender in Cairo: A View from the Household.* Bloomington: Indiana University Press, 1996.

Vatter, Sherry. "Journeymen Textile Weavers in Nineteenth-Century Damascus: A Collective Biography." In *Struggle and Survival in the Modern Middle East,* ed. Edmund Burke III, 75–90. Berkeley: University of California Press, 1993.

White, Jenny B. *Money Makes Us Relatives: Women's Labor in Urban Turkey.* Austin: University of Texas Press, 1994.

Zouari-Bouattour, Salma. *Femme et emploi en Tunisie.* In *Femmes, culture et société au Maghreb,* ed. R. Bourquia, M. Charrad, and N. Gallagher, vol. 11, 161–179. Casablanca: Éditions Afrique-Orient, 1996.

❀ 2 ❀

Modernization, the State, and the Family in Middle East Women's Studies

Mervat F. Hatem

*I*n this survey of recent research done on gender and the state in the Middle East, I wish to explore why this literature, which is concerned with the study of the modern nation-state, has privileged the "Muslim family" as its primary focus of analysis. The answer has a great deal to do with the influence that the modernization discourse has had on the interpretation of the changes taking place in these societies, including changes in gender roles and relations. First, I wish to briefly outline how Middle East political science has conceptualized the relationships among modernization, the state, and the family. Because this discipline has generally exhibited a lack of interest in gender studies, most of the works reviewed here on gender and the state have been produced by sociologists, anthropologists, and historians working within the theoretical framework of Middle East women's studies. Both fields share a common view of the state and its role in the modernization of society. Women's studies has extended these views to a discussion of the family. Despite their efforts to problematize the concept of the traditional Muslim family, women's studies scholars have retained the belief that the family represents the primary arena against which the state's modernizing policies are to be tested. The historical and theoretical perspectives offered by both political scientists and women's studies scholars provide important contexts within which the state narratives, examined later, should be understood.

In the 1950s and 1960s, political scientists shared in the enthusiasm surrounding Daniel Lerner's *The Passing of Traditional Society*. This study optimistically predicted that society-wide changes in attitudes, communications systems, and social roles would contribute to the building of modern societies in place of traditional Islamic ones.[1] When emerging societies did not develop participatory political systems, political scientists were not discouraged. They emphasized the fact that the new military regimes and one-party states were playing a developmental and modernizing role as representatives of the "new middle class."[2]

In these theoretical formulations, gender emerged as a peripheral part of the discussion about the transition from tradition to modernity. Lerner marginally used it as one more marker of traditional versus modern society. He suggested that the former was less capable on its own to significantly change gender relations and roles. In the Arab world, a culture of male vanity prevailed, leading men to jealously segregate women and exclude them from participation in public life. As a result, the Western media, especially films and illustrated magazines, served as an important source of gendered messages and images that educated middle-class women relied on in their quest for new conceptions of gender relations.[3]

In a similar vein, Manfred Halpern offered a brief examination of how the pressures of modernization have undermined the strength of the patriarchal family in the Middle East. As peasants moved from the countryside to the cities, women in traditional families were to be liberated by their new role as wage earners. In the search for employment, women workers, who were generally paid less than men, were more successful in landing jobs. This generated new tensions between men and women and served to undermine patriarchal authority in traditional families.[4] In other words, modernization offered women liberation from the traditional patriarchal family, but not gender equality!

The 1970s brought increasing scholarly unease with the widespread faith in the modernizing mission and potential of military and authoritarian states in the Middle East. Critics of these regimes suggested that political authoritarianism and stalled economic development were the only contributions of the state policies pursued in the 1950s and 1960s. In explaining the limited success of these modernizing states, an increasing number of political scientists referred to the "resiliency of tradition" in the region—the pull of the traditional ties of family, religion, and political factionalism.[5] These factors were said to be integral to the political culture of the region, somehow managing to hold firm against a rapidly changing world. The rise of the Islamic Republic in Iran and the spread of Islamism in the region gave credence to this view. Not only did these developments mark the ascendance of traditional forces and agendas, but the popularity of their critiques of socialist and modernist states established these forces as serious challengers for political power.

These developments led to renewed interest in the study of the state in the 1980s. The new studies focused on the "modern economic and social powers" of the state, powers that made the state a strong actor in most of these societies.[6] Islamist attacks on the modern state contributed to the general view of the state as an important arena, where the political struggles between modern and traditional forces were to be settled in favor of the modernists.

Again, gender did not emerge as a key component in these discursive developments. A few analysts made passing reference to gender as an issue or a cultural artifact that distinguished the Islamist from the secularist political players. In their discussion of the role that women's associations played in this political struggle, analysts either exaggerated their symbolic importance or dismissed them altogether as having limited political relevance.[7]

In short, political scientists theorized the Middle Eastern state in terms of modernity, tradition, and the struggle between the two. As a result, the modernization discourse continued to serve as a master narrative. Within this discussion, gender served as a footnote. Although some argued that the different theoretical shifts represented changing approaches to the study of the state and political science,[8] these shifts only represented internal changes and emphases within this dominant discourse.

As mentioned earlier, most of the studies of gender and the state in the region have been produced by historians, anthropologists, and sociologists, reflecting the multidisciplinary perspectives of Middle East women's studies. The theoretical genealogy of the field, commenced in the late 1970s, reflected the continued privileging of the modernization discourse, complemented by borrowed assumptions and concepts from U.S. women's studies. The result was a greater theoretical elaboration of the relationships women developed with modernity, tradition, and the state.

As an example, let me turn to the earliest anthologies devoted to Middle East women's studies, published in the 1970s.[9] Their introductions begin with a rejection of the primacy given to the study of war, politics, and economic and religious leadership as modern/public/male concerns.[10] Their authors offer to valorize the study of women by placing familial/feminine/private concerns at the center of their research agendas. They declare the study of the "Muslim family" to be a legitimate vantage point from which to document women's interactions with the rest of society.[11]

Not only did scholars of Middle East women's studies accept the binary opposition between men and women, between the public and private arenas, but they embraced the important split between modern and traditional societies. They viewed the "Muslim/traditional family" as establishing a direct connection between women and tradition. The family provided a foundational basis for understanding women's lived experience and cultural difference. In these discussions of the traditional family, Islamic/Qur'anic ideals of gender, which inspired Islamic *shari'a* (law) and its definition of a subordinate personal status (with regard to rights in marriage, divorce, custody of children, and inheritance), were supplemented with the study of tribal and family customs (e.g., the practices of veiling and sexual segregation) as other components of "Islamic traditions."[12] In one formulation, these two cultural components of the traditional family were potentially contradictory. Whereas the Qur'anic principles posited the theoretical and legal superiority of men over women, the actual operation of tribal and family customs gave considerable latitude and authority to women.[13]

As defined above, traditional societies and families provided oppositional concepts against which modern society was contrasted. Their archaic values, belief systems, and institutions represented everything that modern society was not: They were static, resistant to change, essentially unequal, lacking freedom, and prone to irrationality. Rather than reject the concept of the "traditional/Muslim family," feminists aimed to rehabilitate it by rejecting some of its widespread misconceptions and providing an empirical fit between it and the political and economic realities at hand. In these studies, the family was used to show how women were active participants in their societies, exercising power over the lives of their men and children.[14] Sexual segregation could be shown to have created a female world that was centered around the family and that provided the family with complex social networks and important bases of power.[15]

These different perspectives on the family changed our views of Islamic society and its women.[16] As part of the study of the impact that indigenous traditions had on the family, new attention was given to the study of Islamic law and social practice. In this way, the family became an analytic prism through which one could study the effects of a changing society on women. Feminist theorists also used the family to alleviate the social-class and urban biases that resulted from the emphasis put on the modern, Westernized families of middle- and upper-class women. Because most women functioned within the traditional Middle Eastern family, this was considered the relevant primary unit of analysis.

The assumed "traditional" character of working-class families contributed several problems. It implied that there was something "original" and unchanging in the lives of the women who were part of this institution.[17] Worse, traditional families were assumed to be the exact opposite of their modern counterparts. Whereas upper- and middle-class families were open to changes, working-class families were somehow less affected by them and bound to older, traditional social practices and roles.

In this way, one could still attribute gender inequality in the traditional families of the working classes exclusively to cultural, tribal, and religious traditions. It was these traditions that restricted women's access to the public domain and justified their continuing subordinate status.[18] Because of the assumed limited ability of traditional families themselves to reverse women's subordination, the modernization discourse gave the state and its modern institutions (of education, of the law, of work, and of the economy) a direct and sometimes an indirect positive role to play in changing gender power relations in Middle Eastern families and societies.[19] Some have suggested that the state's role in modernization and development provided an important engine for change. The modernization of society improved women's access to the public domain and, more importantly, changed gender relations within the family. Here, legal reform of the Islamic personal status laws (governing marriage, divorce, and custody of children) was defined as the most significant indicator of change.

The many narratives offered by Middle East women's studies on the development of the modern nation-state provided different definitions of and perspectives on modernization. Although these narratives were sufficiently distinct from one another, they relied on the same key concepts of modernity and development, tradition and Islam, and the general assumptions outlined above regarding the "Muslim family." As a result, their analytic boundaries were permeable, reaffirming my view that they belong to the same discourse. All of these narratives agreed that the equalization of gender relations and roles was a result of the general modernization of society. Most underlined the importance of state policies designating the "Muslim family" as the legal bearer of Islamic traditions. As a sign of this special importance, most narratives treated the reform of the personal status law as a litmus test for (1) the relative success or failure of modernization, (2) the "progressive" or "conservative" character of the state, and (3) the advancement of Muslim women toward gender equality.

In the next two sections of this essay, I will test the above propositions. The first section will present the narratives that studied the state in nineteenth- and early-twentieth-century Middle East societies. The second will focus on the state in the second half of the twentieth century. After reconstructing each narrative, I will try to offer a critical assessment of its views. In concluding, I will discuss the limits of the modernization discourse and the efforts to break with it.

Modernization, Gender, and the State in the Study of the Nineteenth-Century Middle East

The Nationalist Narrative

Nationalism was the basis of the oldest and most popular narrative used to analyze the new relationship among modernization, gender, and the state in the Middle East. This was a narrative of progress that viewed modernization and westernization as part of the process of building new societies. In this discussion, the subordinate role of women in the Muslim family was treated as both a cause and a symptom of societal backwardness. The influence of the West and of westernized reformers, who championed new gendered agendas, provided solutions to this problem. The reformers supported public education and employment for women. The new gendered roles and rights given to women were identified with social progress. In endorsing these changes, the nationalist movement, often in tandem with the postcolonial state, demonstrated its modernist credentials and gained political legitimacy.

As an example of this narrative, I will review one historical account of the evolution of Turkish nationalism in the nineteenth century, specifically how it contributed a modern and secular state and to new conceptions of women's citizenship rights.[20] The account begins by highlighting the emancipatory effects of the secular modern state and its "radical break with Ottoman Islam and its institutions."[21] The Turkish republic abolished the caliphate (1924) and abrogated the constitutional provision that declared Islam to be the state's religion (1928).[22] More specifically, it adopted a Turkish civil code, which was almost identical to the Swiss one, in 1927. The code formally severed all links with the *shari'a,* outlawing polygyny and giving men and women equal rights to divorce and custody.[23] As for suffrage, women were given the vote at local elections in 1930 and at national ones in 1934.[24]

The Tanzimat period (1839–1876) provides the historical roots of these dramatic changes. The reorganization of Ottoman society, through the introduction of technical, administrative, and educational reforms, was supported and approved by Great Britain. Local supporters of these reforms were members of a new class of Ottoman imperial bureaucrats. Their new, "modernized" structures excluded "craftsmen, artisans, the urban lower middle class, petty civil servants and the lower ranks of the 'ulema,'"[25] whose opposition took more Islamic forms. As a result, modernization required the balancing of Western expectations of change against the opposition of an Islamically led and inspired majority.[26]

Contrary to the unidimensional views generally attributed to these modernizers, the historical account under examination emphasized their ambivalent attitudes to change. Even while criticizing certain social institutions in Ottoman society (forced and arranged marriages, concubinage, and polygamy), the modernizers were critical of "Westernism."[27] Their views could best be described as offering a modernist Islamic perspective that was clearly instrumentalist. They used the change in gender roles to argue that their perspective contributed to a healthier society.[28]

The process of modernization included the building of new state schools for women and the training of midwives and teachers. In addition, many publications for women emerged. Women also participated in the public debate on gender.[29]

The overthrow of Abdulhamid II's autocratic regime in 1908 by the Young Turks, members of the Committee of Union and Progress, initiated the second constitutional period (1908–1918). This period witnessed intense social and ideological ferment, accelerating the proliferation of women's associations, the opening of the university to women, and the increased incorporation of women into the labor force.[30] More importantly, debates on women and the family were used by Islamist, Westernist, and Turkist writers to distinguish their views of the Turkish nation and its national projects.

The Turkist intervention in this debate on Turkish national identity bypassed the counterposing of Islam to the West. Ziya Gokalp, the key ideologue of this view, argued that the history of pre-Islamic Turkish societies offered evidence to support the existence of egalitarian families, monogamous marriages, and Turkish feminism.[31] This "golden age" inspired the 1917 family code, which established the foundation for the "National Family." Marriages were to be monogamous and based on consent. The new code stipulated the presence of a state employee alongside the two witnesses required by the *shari'a* to "provide women with greater security in the conjugal contract" and made polygyny contingent on the consent of the first wife.[32]

Even more dramatic changes followed World War I, the war of national liberation, and the proclamation of a secular Turkish republic under Mustafa Kemal Atatürk (1923). This period witnessed the development of the construct of the "new woman" as an explicit symbol of the break with the Ottoman past. This new Turkish woman became the object of paternalistic state benevolence, being granted a 4.5 percent rate of political representation in Parliament, a level not reached since then.[33] Unfortunately, the change also resulted in the loss of women's "autonomous political initiatives."[34]

To its credit, this nationalist narrative of progress was very conscious of some of the problems of the modernization discourse. Its consideration of the new paternalism, women's political underrepresentation, and women's loss of political autonomy pointed to difficulties that could not be easily reconciled with progress. Within the modernization discourse, progress was premised on the struggle for the suppression of cultural difference, which was most frequently blamed for the subordination of women. In the Turkish case, the historical solution to this problem was the public marginalization of Islam and the *shari'a*. Although the narrative was critical of some results of the switch, it is clear from its construction (the placement of the accomplishments of the republican state at the beginning of the account) that the modernist gains remain a source of national pride and difference. Turkey's repudiation of its Islamic past and its unabashed embrace of modernity entitle it to a glorified place in the modernization discourse. This privileged position renders it a prisoner of a linear narrative that relegates the critical discussion of modernity as a source of many problems facing Turkish women to secondary analytic importance.

The Marxian Narrative

The Marxian narrative offered a critique of the above positive view of modernization, providing a contrasting account of how modernization and modernist state policies disadvantaged the working class and its women. Despite its explicit critique of the modernization discourse, this narrative did not completely break with some of the ideological views of modern education and health and their contributions to the welfare of women.

As an example, I will discuss a study of the changing position of women in nineteenth-century Egypt.[35] As a starting point, this study rejected the view that "progress for women was imported from the West and basically entailed denial of indigenous tradition."[36] It emphasized the importance of understanding the indigenous structures that preceded capitalist modernization and with which it interacted. Key among these structures was the family. Egyptian men and women, not only of elite circles but also of the peasant and working classes, clearly affected and were affected by the outcomes of social and economic development.[37]

Egypt's incorporation into the European capitalist economy was facilitated by its emergence as a modern nation-state that was both interventionist and bureaucratic.[38] The absolutist state under Muhammad 'Ali and his successors, followed by the colonial state under British control after 1882, left their imprints on the lives of ordinary Egyptians and their families with their economic and political policies. The absolutist state's active regulation of production and trade hastened the economic dispossession of peasant families.[39] Equally disruptive was the drafting of peasant men and women into corvée labor and factory work. These measures indirectly weakened the family and its resources, where working-class peasant and urban women were active. Egypt's integration into the European economy was also responsible for the weakening of the guilds, especially those dealing with textiles, another area in which urban working-class women were active.[40]

The Egyptian state developed public systems of health and education under Muhammad 'Ali and Ismail. Despite their limited scope, these systems provided social services that were important to women.[41] Emphasis on public sanitation improved the quality of rural and urban life,[42] while countrywide immunization and vaccination lowered infant mortality levels.[43] Through the establishment of a school of midwives, the state attempted to educate and train professional women to service and care for other women in an activity that was central to the life of any community.[44]

In contrast, the colonial state left the responsibility for education and health to private interests. As such, it offered women only limited access to both services and slowed down the development of alternative social institutions that served their needs. Although the British cited Islamic opposition to women's access to the public sphere, the available evidence indicates that the ulema viewed female education positively, as long as gender segregation was maintained. Nineteenth-century British views were not sympathetic to the education or the training of women. These views reflected the influences of the British model of sexual segregation and its circumscribed commitment to women's professional education.[45]

Finally, the modern nation-state had a more developed capacity for repression, affecting women adversely in yet another way. It curtailed their ability to participate in acts of political revolt.[46] The frequent political rebellions in eighteenth-century Egypt served to reduce the abuse of state power and women participated actively in them. In fact, official documents of the period described peasant and urban working-class women as "very disposed to revolt."[47] This demonstrated society's acceptance of women as political actors in the public arena.

Although corvée labor, military conscription, direct taxation, and the arbitrary exercise of government power provoked rural revolts and urban uprisings in the nineteenth century,[48] the consolidation of the repressive apparatus of the new nation-state put an end to this spontaneous and informal mode of political participation. The colonial state enhanced its ability to control the subject population by developing more effective "urban and rural police, administration of swift and summary justice and reform of the prison system."[49] The result was the complete removal of women from the political arena.[50]

In this narrative, Western economic and political processes of change together with their many institutional innovations were shown to undermine the resources, traditional institutions, and forms of participation available to working-class women. Capitalist production, integration into the European economy, and the interventionist and repressive capacities of the state weakened the family, the guilds, and the neighborhood organization that enhanced women's participation in the affairs of their society. The state's improved capacity for repression ruled out any spontaneous form of political participation.

The only state institutions that were discussed positively in this very critical account of modernization were those of health and education. Despite their association with the repressive absolutist and colonial states, these institutions were criticized only with regard to their reach and their gender-specific character. If these social services effectively catered to the majority classes and women, then they would play a positive social role. This was where the nationalist and Marxian narratives met. Modern education and health were not seen as new arenas for social control-cum-regulation by the absolutist and colonial states. They continued to be represented as neutral social services that constituted a benevolent side to modernization. This part of the discussion of the state and its institutions remained captive to modernization and its ideology in what was generally a critical analysis of capitalist modernization and state formation.

Modernization, Gender, and the State in the Study of the Twentieth-Century Middle East

The Structuralist-Functionalist Narrative on State Building

According to the structuralist-functionalist narrative, modernization is a historical process that contributes to the successful development of modern nation-state structures. The political stability and consolidation of these structures in the Maghreb (Tunisia, Algeria, and Morocco) and in Iraq involved a rearrangement of their relations with kin-based communities and institutions. The successful modernization of both the state and society depended on the ability of the former to undermine the cohesion and strength of these institutions. The political equilibrium reached between kin-based institutions and the structures of the state had various consequences for women.

Let me begin with a discussion of the Maghrebi states. The starting point of one Maghrebi narrative highlighted the importance of postcolonial state policies vis-à-vis family law in the process of state building:[51] "Tunisia adopted the most far-reaching changes whereas Morocco remained the most faithful to the prevailing Islamic legislation and Algeria followed an ambivalent course."[52] Here the relationship between state formations (specifically their concern for political stability and consolidation) and gender policy offered an explanation of these differences.[53]

After independence, the relatively "new" states employed political strategies designed to co-opt, undermine, or cautiously change their "old societies."[54] In these old Maghrebi societies, kinship and the family served as a basis of social solidarity. Marriage as a means of controlling women enhanced community cohesion, also serving to cement alliances with outsiders. The Tunisian, Algerian, and Moroccan states' different routes to nation building were influenced by the cohesion of kin-based, tribal, and local communities and by the historical relationships these communities had maintained with central authorities. During the precolonial period, kin-based communities had the least autonomy in Tunisia, the greatest autonomy in Algeria, and the most antagonistic relationship with the central authority in Morocco.[55]

French colonization contributed new structures and relations. In Tunisia, the colonial state built a centralized system of administration that further weakened kin-based communities. In contrast, the French in Algeria dismembered some communities in the process of expropriating the best land while leaving others intact. As a result, kin-based collectivities served as a shield against the colonial system, thus reinforcing their internal cohesion.

In Morocco, the French used indirect administration to manipulate local structures. Consequently, tribal communities were less affected than in either Tunisia or Algeria.[56]

The struggle for national liberation highlighted another difference in the development of the postcolonial Maghrebi states. In Tunisia, the Neo Destour Party, whose influence was felt throughout the country, dominated the process of state formation at the expense of kin-based loyalties. In contrast, the Algerian war of liberation underlined the importance of ideological differences along with linkages to local and kin-based communities. In Morocco, the monarchy continued to rely on tribal communities in rural areas and used patronage to act as an arbiter among competing interests.[57]

The above factors explain why the Maghrebi states were not equally interested in altering the relationships between central authorities and kin-based communities or in reinterpreting Maliki Islamic law. They approached this shared cultural and legal heritage differently. Tunisia introduced the most dramatic changes in its Code of Personal Status, passed in 1956. According to the code, women were required to give verbal consent during the marriage ceremony for the contract to be valid. Husbands and wives were equally entitled to file for divorce, which took place in court. Finally, polygyny was abolished. The single most important effect of the code was that it strengthened the conjugal unit at the expense of the extended (traditional) patrilineal kin group.[58]

The Moroccan Code of Personal Status adhered more closely to Maliki law. A bride expressed consent through a male legal guardian. Divorce remained an exclusively male right, requiring two witnesses to be valid. Polygyny remained legal.[59] In contrast, the Algerian Family Code, passed in 1984, introduced some legal innovations, like requiring divorce to occur in court and allowing a widowed mother to assume guardianship over her children. The Algerian code, however, did not challenge the male right to either divorce or polygyny.[60]

These personal status and family codes reflected differences in state interests and consolidation strategies. In Tunisia, the best interests of the state lay in breaking the already weakened kin solidarities. In Algeria, divisions within the state leadership led to the rearrangement of kinship rules. Finally, because the monarchy in Morocco derived its power from kin-based communities, it had very little interest in changing kinship rules.

In the Iraqi case, the ascent to power of the Ba'th Arab Socialist Party in 1968 began the process of active state construction and consolidation. Ideologically, the party was committed to the emancipation of women as part of its plan to build a modern and progressive society.[61] It sought the public integration of women through expanded access to education and employment. It also introduced changes that aimed to improve women's legal position and eliminate social prejudice against them.[62]

These policies also served to undermine the opponents of the new regime and to consolidate its control over an expanding economy.[63] In response to its ideological opponents on the Left (communists), the Ba'thist government used these gender policies to politically distinguish itself and its progressive credentials. The integration of women into the new public institutions undermined any competition from the Right, such as the *al-'Asha'ir* (clans), who were identified with the power of extended patriarchal families.[64] In weakening the power of kin groups, the state was able to make women available for wage labor in a market that suffered from acute labor shortages.[65]

This attempt to distinguish the state's gender commitment from that of its opponents did not lead to the questioning of the sexual division of labor in the family. On the contrary, the Ba'thist state idealized women's familial roles.[66] The state's pronatalist policy and its eclectic ideological commitment to change led to its amendment of the Personal Status Code promulgated in 1978. For example, the amendment lowered the marriage age from sixteen to fifteen. Not only did this rule give expression to the reality of young marriages in rural Iraq but it also expressed state support for higher fertility rates.[67] The law also put an end to forced marriages by allowing a judge to overrule a guardian's disapproval. Patriarchs and male relatives who persisted in the older practices were fined and imprisoned.[68] As for polygyny, a second marriage had to be cleared by a judge and registered in court. Failure to do so was punished by imprisonment and entitled the first wife to file for divorce. In undermining the legal bases of extended patriarchal families, the code supported the nuclear family, which was more conducive to the consolidation of state power.[69]

The above discussion of the Maghrebi and Iraqi states offers a functionalist view of modern nation-state structures, stressing political stability and consolidation as the state's teleological goals. In this light, gender policy, whether radical, ambivalent, or conservative, is seen largely as part of the attempt to reach a political equilibrium between the state as a modern institution and kinship institutions as premodern ones. In this discussion, the anthropological emphasis on kinship rules and groups is politicized and used as a measure of the strength and ability of the state to consolidate its capacity to determine the social agenda.

The functionalist emphasis on stability explains the silence about how each state's attempt to redefine or not to redefine kinship rules and Islamic law served as trigger points for oppositional perspectives and forces. Because of the emphasis on the search for political equilibrium as a prized state goal, there was no interest in discussing possible sources of change or conflict outside of these state systems. Reinforcing this structuralist, functionalist tendency to see the family codes as part of a stable political reality, no critical discussion was offered of how the new rights and rules administered by the state established new forms of social control and regulation of women in place of old ones. They transformed women into new dependents of the state and the state's interpretation of the law. Despite the important changes introduced in the most innovative of these family codes (the Tunisian one), they did not challenge women's economic dependence on men in the new nuclear families, which affected their ability to make use of the equal right to divorce. Guardianship over children remained a male prerogative. In short, the modernization of the family codes as the prized goal of state policy remained outside the realm of critical discussion. Most criticism of these codes focused on their remaining traditional aspects or the fact that they did not go far enough in modernizing the family.

The Socialist Narrative

The goal of the socialist narrative was to describe the process of socialist modernization and the role that the state played in South Yemen in delivering the emancipatory promise of socialism in a traditional Muslim precapitalist order.[70] On closer examination, the developmental and gender policies pursued by the state were not that different from those followed in modern, capitalist societies.

As its starting point, this narrative discussed how gender roles in pre-1967 South Yemen represented "traditional" or "feudal" obstacles to economic and social development.[71] The customary practices and institutions (polygyny, bride price, child marriage, and female seclusion) that weighed on women also played an important role in maintaining the property and social relations of the old precapitalist order.[72] For this reason, the developmental and gendered agendas of the socialist state were intimately related. Changes in women's position would contribute to the dismantling of the old order. Conversely, development policies designed to undermine the old system were likely to have positive effects for women.

For the socialist state, the most difficult and controversial area of social reform involved loosening the impact of religion on family laws and laws of personal status. Despite the secularization of other civil laws, the family laws remained under the control of the Muslim religious code. To start the reform effort, the juridical power of the religious leaders was eroded and some of this power was passed on to the state,[73] which then proceeded to address the main sources of inequality in these traditional codes.

The constitutional reforms introduced by the state defined women as "producers" and "mothers." In encouraging women who were not engaged in production to take on a more active role, the state hoped to undermine their long-standing seclusion. It promised to protect working women and their children with paid maternity leave and the provision of child-care services.[74]

The state also passed a family law in 1974, which required the registration of marriage contracts to ensure that the new legislation was respected. It outlawed arranged marriages by requiring a woman's consent to marriage and also put an end to child marriage by setting the legal age for adulthood at sixteen for women and eighteen for men.[75] A man could only have one wife, unless she suffered from infertility or an incurable disease.[76] Both spouses shared the expenses of a marriage. All divorces were to be processed through the courts, with men and women using the same grounds to file for divorce. Finally, women's custody of children was extended to the age of ten for boys and fifteen for girls.[77]

The new law established the primacy of the monogamous family, within which the conjugal and divorce rights of men and women were equalized. Despite the equalization of divorce procedures, the law made divorce difficult for both men and women. The state's developmental policies, which were committed to strengthening the family as a productive unit, took precedence.[78] Despite occasional state intervention to punish those who violated the law, officials admitted that enforcement in the countryside was problematic due to the strength of traditional and familial loyalties.[79] State policies were silent about certain social practices like veiling and women's seclusion, in the belief that such practices would disappear over time as a result of economic changes.[80]

In the political arena, in 1977 the state granted women the right to vote and run for elections. It also sought to mobilize women through different party and popular organizations, including the women's union.[81] Women's political participation in South Yemen was similar to that in other societies; women tended to be concentrated at the base of the political system. Those in the middle ranks were assigned activities traditionally associated with women, such as social welfare work.[82] The primary occupations of the women's union were literacy campaigns and the drafting of the family law.[83] The union also helped the state to integrate women into production by providing training in conventional (sewing and typing) as well as mechanical skills.[84] This elucidation of which skills and occupations were best suited to women risked channeling women into occupations that had lower productivity and that paid lower wages. Finally, the union did not define itself as a feminist organization but as part of the state apparatus, with the goal of implementing official policies.[85]

In the conclusion of this narrative, the outcome of this very radical attempt to restructure the roles of women was described as mixed. Although more women had access to education, their numbers continued to be lower than those of men at every level. More women were employed, but they were largely doing tedious tasks in undesirable occupations with few possibilities for advancement.[86] In explaining the surprising advent of these modern forms of inequality, there was reluctance to blame the state or socialism. Instead, it was suggested that "inherent in government policies were mechanisms and occlusions which unintentionally disadvantage women."[87]

In short, the socialist-state narrative on gender retained traditionalism as an explanation of the Third World society that it sought to transform. State economic and political development was identified as socialist progress. It was not clear what was particularly "socialist" about the state, its analysis of the problem or its development policies. Although the status of women improved, the end of the narrative blamed the continuing strength of traditional familial loyalties for the slow rate of change in the countryside. More significantly, it pointed out the emergence of new forms of gender segmentation in the state's education and employment systems. In this narrative of progress, not only socialism but also the socialist state's modern institutions, which produced their own inequalities, were being undermined by tradition. Despite the importance of this very cogent critique of socialist development, the narrative stopped short of blaming the socialist state or modernization for the problems. The new asymmetries were characterized as the unintended effects or distortions of the socialist policies of the state.

State Feminism

The narrative on state feminism highlighted the modernist economic, political, and ideological strategies used by the postcolonial state to demonstrate its feminist credentials. By supporting women's formal citizenship rights, the state sought to co-opt the agenda of existing feminist groups (e.g., Egypt) to establish its political legitimacy or to develop a gender agenda that demonstrated its secular character (e.g., Turkey).

One discussion of the Egyptian case began on a comparative note.[88] As a modern strategy, state feminism was described as bearing a strong resemblance to strategies employed by the Scandinavian welfare states. As adopted by the regime of Gamal Abdel Nasser (1952–1970), it responded to the insistent demands of active feminist groups in the 1950s and presented them as part of its populist social, economic, and political platforms. On the positive side, it gave women the right to vote and to run for public office, as well as equal rights to education and employment. In exchange, the state relied on middle-class women in the systematic delivery of important social services (e.g., education and health care) to the general public. It also recruited skilled working-class women to staff its public sector.

In contrast, the states of Anwar al-Sadat (1970–1981) and Hosni Mubarak (1981–present) responded to developmental and political crises by abandoning, or refraining from the defense of, their commitment to state feminism. The adverse effects of the state's economic and political liberalization on women's employment and political participation were not corrected. More significantly, the state formed political alliances with Islamist groups in the early 1970s and the early 1980s that gave such groups the freedom to propagate conservative definitions of gender roles and relations. When the relations between these regimes and their Islamist opponents soured, both actors used the personal status laws to maneuver their way out of political crisis. The Sadat regime, to establish its secularist credentials, amended the existing law to give women the right to file for divorce when their husbands took second wives. Following Sadat's assassination, the High Constitutional Court struck these changes down, paving the way for a brief honeymoon between the new regime and its Islamist opponents.

The narrative on state feminism was also used by Turkish theorists to explain the "instigation from above" of extensive policies intended to change the status of women.[89] These reforms were embodied in the Turkish civil code, which replaced the *shari'a* and voting rights already discussed as part of the nationalist narrative. The reforms, along with Turkish women's dress standards and code of conduct, appeared on the surface to be modern, but women's relations with men and their self-definition within the family remained traditional. The result was "simulated images of modernity."[90] The state's appropriation of the women's agenda also impeded the development of an autonomous consciousness.[91] Finally, political and economic crises led to an alliance in the 1980s between the military government of Turgut Özal and the Islamist opponents of state feminism.[92] This led to the development, among women, of post-Kemalist as well as anti-Kemalist Islamist currents, which were radically different from the pre-Kemalist traditionalist stance.[93] Unfortunately, these alternative platforms continued to subordinate women's issues to the larger societal project.[94]

In the above narrative, gender is used to distinguish the modern secular state from that of its more conservative predecessors. In addition, the support of women's citizenship—which included formal and equal rights to vote, to education, and to work in Egypt; equal rights to divorce; and rights to child custody and to inheritance in Turkey—became part of a political strategy to enhance the legitimacy of the state. Women's citizenship was put in the service of the state's changing political interests. Although this secured the state's support of women's rights, it transformed gender into a political instrument. As a result, women lost control of their autonomy as a group with a specific agenda. This political status, associated with the loss of initiative and autonomy, explained the difficulty of developing a critique of the microdynamics of these modern rights and how they introduced novel mechanisms of control and social regulation. In the case of Turkey, the narrative of state feminism suggested that the new roles that women played were examples of simulated modernity, whose content was really traditional. This particular critique of modernity was double-edged. It found fault with modernization and its gendered policies, but instead of laying the blame on modernization, it blamed tradition for the failed promise of modernity. As a result, the assumptions of the modernization discourse were again in evidence. Modernity was never to blame in the discussion of gender inequality. If Turkish modernity was only a simulation of the modern social ideal, then true modernity would lead to socially and politically independent women. In the case of Egypt, state feminism was criticized for not going far enough in changing the personal status law or women's political underrepresentation. Moreover, the gains it offered to women were limited by class and in potential.

Both of these critiques of the Middle Eastern state and its modern political strategies were important but fell short of laying to rest the discussion of modernization as an abstract progressive social ideal. In the Turkish case, the problems described were attributed to the Middle Eastern application and distortion of this ideal. In the Egyptian discussion, the comparison made at the outset with Scandinavian state feminism was not revisited at the end of the narrative. As a result, the comparative discussion that hoped to lay to rest the assumption of Middle Eastern exceptionalism remained incomplete. It would have been helpful to point out that the problems with this modern political strategy (loss of autonomy, dependence on the state, political underrepresentation, and the class-specific character of state feminism) were problems that Scandinavian women also faced within systems that had a different history and culture. A comparative perspective on modernity had another advantage. It provided a basis for concrete discussions of regional applications of this strategy instead of the idealized model of modernization upon which Middle Eastern modernity was premised. This particular exercise would help distinguish some of the general problems associated with modernity from the specific ones that reflected differences in history, culture, and institutions.

The Social Narrative on the Oil-Producing States of the Arabian Gulf

The narrative on the Gulf states focused its attention on modernization as a process that was closely identified with these states' historical, political, and economic needs and specificities. It acknowledged the colonial roots of this region's modern state structures, whose histories originate with various treaties between Great Britain and the Gulf principalities and monarchies. It put emphasis, however, on how expanded oil production contributed new economic and social needs. As a result, these states emerged as indirect and often reluctant "agents of social change." One of the effects of the new social activities of the state was the controlled modernization of gender roles.

Initially, neither Great Britain nor the modern state structures paid any attention to gender or to the changing gender roles. These became state concerns in the 1950s and 1960s when expanded oil production required the building of an infrastructure that delivered roads, a bureaucracy, education, health care, employment, and housing. During this period, the state's infrastructure began its role as an agent of "social change"[95] and modernization.

In Saudi Arabia, the state adopted an ambiguous attitude to social change and modernization. On the one hand, King Faisal had to summon troops to ensure the opening of a girls' school in Buraida in 1960.[96] On the other, the state's support of education and then employment for women was very controlled by its restrictive interpretation of "the framework of Islamic values and social practices."[97] Here, adherence to the Wahabi interpretation of Islam was blamed for enforced sexual segregation in various social arenas, for the veiling of women, and for the ban on women's driving.[98] It was also viewed as a means of ensuring the continued primacy of the household as women's principal domain, which women's education and employment threatened to change.[99]

In Kuwait, the state's support of women's entry into the educational system and through it the labor market had been part of the process of modernizing the state structure.[100] Ensuring men and women equal access to education was a measure of this new dynamic.[101] More importantly, the state initiated the modernization of society through a paternalistic welfare system.[102] Women's entry into the education system contributed to modernizing both the state and society. The paternalistic welfare state also provided educated women with employment in the state sector.[103]

These dramatic changes were not matched by revisions in the patriarchal Arab ideology, which "stood in opposition to modernization."[104] Not all educated women were encouraged to work. Because those who worked were employed in the state sector, their jobs were not taken seriously. The wages earned by these professional women were not comparable to the incomes men made in trade or the private sector.[105] During the Kuwaiti experiment with representative government, political rights were only extended to some women. Finally, women's new public roles did not liberate them from patriarchal control within the household or from the traditional tasks identified with femininity. In fact, during the 1980s, women themselves became more socially conservative. Kuwaiti working women avoided employment in settings that were not sexually segregated.[106] Many educated women chose not to work. Working-class women, who used to support themselves, similarly opted to be supported by their men, whose incomes had increased. Widowed and divorced women became wards of the state. In short, the promising social beginnings of gender equality were cut short by a patriarchal Arab ideology that resisted change and initiated a new period of conservative reaction.

In contrast, Bahrain's rapid modernization was described as having eroded the patriarchal features of society.[107] As a result, women made significant progress and claimed their share of state-provided social services like education and health care, as well as finding employment in industrial and clerical jobs.[108] "Nevertheless, the religiocultural characteristics of tribalism remained intrinsic social features and are still often invoked to confirm adherence to tradition."[109] The traditional tribal orientation among the Sunni and the Shi'i populations was responsible for the backward conditions women faced in the rural areas.[110] Moreover, the "core family (patriarchal base) in the extended family structure still holds the decisions in matters of importance—for example marriage, education, and even veiling of girls."[111] Thus, Bahraini women were visible in their society but unable to influence these important decisions and development. They were excluded from the brief liberal experiment in 1975.[112] They were unable to bring pressure to change the personal status laws.[113] Although their exclusion from the liberal experiment was partly blamed on the tribal orientation among the Sunnis and the Shi'is, it was the liberal and radical men, the modernizers, who did not support them. Similarly, the modern Bahraini women either distanced themselves from the more traditional women or failed to reach them.[114]

In short, the state delivered modern education and public employment to women in Saudi Arabia, Kuwait, and Bahrain. It contributed to social change in gender relations and roles and to the modernization of these societies. The impact of the state was undermined, however, by the resilience of traditional forces, whether these took the form of Wahabi, Sunni, or Shi'i Islam; of tribalism; or of patriarchal Arab ideology. These forces of tradition were responsible for the limited success of this pattern of development. Some have suggested that modern state policies in Kuwait and Bahrain, or other modernizing forces in those countries, were not playing the progressive roles predicted by this discourse. There was no attempt, however, to relate this to the "rentier" character of the state. Because these states depend for their revenues on outside rent (income from the sale of oil), they were largely unresponsive to the demands of a public that did not fund their numerous activities. Instead of considering this type of state as a largely modern phenomenon, most analysts assume that the socially traditional character of the present Gulf societies and states represent the past of most Arab ones and that in time they will follow in the same regional modern footsteps. Those analysts who pay attention to the social specificities of these Gulf societies blame the indigenous conservative forces (Wahabism, tribalism, patriarchal ideology) for the slow pace of change. That modernization could contribute its own conservative social and political dynamic was an oxymoron within that narrative, which tended to treat rapid modernization as a desirable social good.

Conclusion

This review of the different state narratives in Middle East women's studies is intended to show how all these narratives were preoccupied with the progress of modernization in the region (which included the development of a capitalist economy, state structures, and modern ideologies and strategies) and its impact on gender roles and relations. Within this discourse, the state was generally viewed as an agent of modernization. It introduced progressive social and political changes as well as progressive social ideals, whose effects were seen in the arena of gender relations and roles. Equally important in this discussion are the roles that tradition, Islam, patriarchy, and tribalism played in explaining why a century of modernization failed to deliver its equalizing promise.

The inability of the above narratives, derived from the modernization discourse, to develop a cogent critique of modernity needs to be explained. A discourse not only determines the questions that analysts put forth but also imposes silence on others that challenge its basic view of society. Within the modernization discourse, the desirability and progressiveness of modernity is never questioned.

It is not surprising, therefore, that the critique of modernity attempted by some students of gender in the Middle East drew its inspiration from postcolonial and postmodernist discursive formulations. A collection titled *Remaking Women*, edited by Lila Abu-Lughod and published in 1998, represents the efforts of a group of students of gender in the Middle East to subject Middle Eastern modernity to thorough critical discussion. The collection's most important accomplishment is to problematize the social system endorsed by modernity, particularly its definition of gender relations. In this way, modernity can finally be seen as one of the problems facing men and women in the Middle East, and not as a panacea to past and present forms of gender inequality.

Notes

1. Daniel Lerner, *The Passing of Traditional Society* (London: Free Press of Glencoe, 1958).

2. Manfred Halpern, *The Politics of Social Change in the Middle East and North Africa* (Princeton: Princeton University Press, 1963), 58–59.

3. Lerner, *Passing of Traditional Society,* 196–199.

4. Halpern, *Politics of Social Change,* 28, 106.

5. Lisa Anderson, "Policy Making and Theory Building: American Political Science and the Islamic Middle East," in *Theory, Politics, and the Arab World,* ed. Hisham Sharabi (New York: Routledge, 1990), 63, 65.

6. Ibid., 67.

7. Mervat F. Hatem, "Political Liberalization, Gender, and the State," in *Political Liberalization and Democratization in the Arab World,* ed. Rex Brynen, Bahgat Korany, and Paul Noble (Boulder: Lynne Rienner, 1995), 187–188.

8. Anderson, "Policy Making," 54–71.

9. Elizabeth Warnock Fernea and Basima Qattan Bezirgan, introduction to *Middle Eastern Women Speak* (Austin: University of Texas Press, 1977), xvii–xxxv; and Nikki Keddie and Lois Beck, introduction to *Women in the Muslim World* (Cambridge: Harvard University Press, 1978), 1–31.

10. Keddie and Beck, *Women in the Muslim World,* 1; and Fernea and Bezirgan, *Middle Eastern Women,* xxvi.

11. Fernea and Bezirgan, *Middle Eastern Women,* xviii-xix; and Keddie and Beck, *Women in the Muslim World,* 2.

12. Fernea and Bezirgan, *Middle Eastern Women,* xix, xxiii.

13. Ibid., xix.

14. Ibid., xix.

15. Fernea and Bezirgan, *Middle Eastern Women,* xvx; and Keddie and Beck, *Women in the Muslim World,* 12, 19.

16. Keddie and Beck, *Women in the Muslim World,* 19–20.

17. Ibid., 2, 5.

18. Keddie and Beck, *Women in the Muslim World,* 8, 10; and Fernea and Bezirgan, *Middle Eastern Women,* xxi.

19. Fernea and Bezirgan, *Middle Eastern Women,* xxxiii; Keddie and Beck, *Women in the Muslim World,* 16–17.

20. As the basis for this discussion, I have relied on the nuanced and intricate work of Deniz Kandiyoti on Turkish nationalism, "The End of Empire: Islam, Nationalism, and Women in Turkey," in *Women, Islam, and the State,* ed. Deniz Kandiyoti (Philadelphia: Temple University Press, 1991), 22–47.

21. Ibid., 22.

22. Ibid.

23. Ibid., 22–23.

24. Ibid., 23.

25. Ibid., 25.

26. Ibid.

27. Ibid., 25–26.

28. Ibid., 26.

29. Ibid., 26–28.

30. Ibid., 28–30.

31. Ibid., 34–35.

32. Ibid., 36.

33. Ibid., 41.

34. Ibid.

35. As the primary example of this narrative, I will review the important work of Judith Tucker in her *Women in Nineteenth-Century Egypt* (Cambridge: Cambridge University Press, 1985).

36. Ibid., 3.
37. Ibid., 4–5.
38. Ibid., 102.
39. Ibid., 31–32.
40. Ibid., 130.
41. Ibid.
42. Ibid., 116.
43. Ibid., 117.
44. Ibid., 120.
45. Ibid., 131.
46. Ibid., chap. 4.
47. Ibid., 140.
48. Ibid., 139.
49. Ibid., 156.
50. Ibid., 163.
51. The basis for this discussion is Mounira Charrad's distinct perspective in "The State and Gender in the Maghrib," *Middle East Report* (March-April 1990): 19–23.
52. Ibid., 19.
53. Ibid., 20.
54. Ibid.
55. Ibid., 22–23.
56. Ibid., 23.
57. Ibid.
58. Ibid., 21.
59. Ibid.
60. Ibid.
61. Amal Sharqi, "The Emancipation of Iraqi Women," in *Iraq: The Contemporary State,* ed. Tim Niblock (London: Croom Helm, 1982), 77.
62. Ibid., 79.
63. Suad Joseph, "The Mobilization of Iraqi Women in the Labor Force," *Studies in Third World Societies* 16 (June 1981): 80.
64. Ibid.; and Amal Rassam, "Revolution Within the Revolution? Women and the State in Iraq," in *Iraq: The Contemporary State,* ed. Tim Niblock (London: Croom Helm, 1982), 95.
65. Joseph, "Mobilization of Iraqi Women," 80.
66. Ibid., 81–82.
67. Rassam, "Revolution," 94.
68. Ibid., 95.
69. Joseph, "Mobilization of Iraqi Women," 84.
70. This discussion of the socialist narrative is based on the account offered by Maxine Molyneux, *State Policies and the Position of Women Workers in the People's Democratic Republic of Yemen, 1967–1977* (Geneva: International Labor Office, 1982).
71. Ibid., 4.
72. Ibid.
73. Ibid.

74. Ibid., 9.

75. Ibid.

76. Ibid., 10.

77. Ibid.

78. Ibid., 11.

79. Ibid., 13.

80. Ibid., 14.

81. Ibid., 18.

82. Ibid.

83. Ibid., 19.

84. Ibid., 20.

85. Ibid., 21.

86. Ibid., 80.

87. Ibid., 82.

88. Mervat F. Hatem, "The Paradoxes of State Feminism in Egypt," in *Women and Politics Worldwide,* ed. Barbara Nelson and Najma Chowdhury (New Haven: Yale University Press, 1994), 226–242; and Mervat F. Hatem, "Economic and Political Liberalization and the Demise of State Feminism," *International Journal of Middle East Studies* 24 (August 1992): 231–251.

89. Ayse Kadioglu, "Women's Subordination in Turkey: Is Islam Really the Villain?" *Middle East Journal* 48, no. 4 (Autumn 1994): 652.

90. Ibid., 653.

91. Ibid., 652–653.

92. Ronnie Margulies and Ergin Yiddizoglu, "The Political Uses of Islam in Turkey," *Middle East Report,* no. 153 (July-August 1988): 14–16.

93. Kadioglu, "Women's Subordination," 648.

94. Ibid., 660.

95. Many of the articles that discuss the change in gender roles in Gulf societies use the phrase "social change" in their titles to describe their nature and significance. For example, Noura al-Falah, "Power and Representation: Social Change, Gender Relations, and the Education of Women in Kuwait," in *Statecraft in the Middle East: Oil, Historical Memory, and Popular Culture,* ed. Eric Davis and Nicholas Gavrielides (Miami: Florida International University Press, 1991), 149–175; May Seikaly, "Women and Social Change in Bahrain," *International Journal of Middle East Studies* 26, no. 3 (August 1994): 415–426; and Shirley Kay, "Social Change in Modern Saudi Arabia," in *State, Society, and Economy in Saudi Arabia,* ed. Tim Niblock (New York: St. Martin's Press, 1982), 171–185.

96. Kay, "Social Change in Modern Saudi Arabia," 177.

97. Louay Bahry, "The New Saudi Woman: Modernizing in an Islamic Framework," *Middle East Journal* 36, no. 4 (Autumn 1982): 502.

98. Ibid., 503; and Eleanor Abdella Doumato, "Women and the Stability of Saudi Arabia," *Middle East Report,* no. 171 (July-August 1991): 35.

99. Doumato, "Women and Stability," 36.

100. Al-Falah, "Power and Representation," 149.

101. Ibid., 158.

102. Ibid., 159.

103. Ibid., 160.

104. Ibid., 150.
105. Ibid., 161.
106. Ibid., 168–169.
107. Seikaly, "Women and Social Change," 417.
108. Ibid., 420.
109. Ibid.
110. Ibid., 422.
111. Ibid., 423.
112. Ibid., 420.
113. Ibid., 421.
114. Ibid.

References

Anderson, Lisa. "Policy Making and Theory Building: American Political Science and the Islamic Middle East." In *Theory, Politics, and the Arab World,* ed. Hisham Sharabi. New York: Routledge, 1990.

Bahry, Louay. "The New Saudi Woman: Modernizing in an Islamic Framework." *Middle East Journal* 36, no. 4 (Autumn 1982).

Charrad, Mounira. "The State and Gender in the Maghrib." *Middle East Report* (March-April 1990): 19–23.

Doumato, Eleanor Abdella. "Women and the Stability of Saudi Arabia." *Middle East Report,* no. 171 (July-August 1991).

Al-Falah, Noura. "Power and Representation: Social Change, Gender Relations, and the Education of Women in Kuwait." In *Statecraft in the Middle East: Oil, Historical Memory, and Popular Culture,* ed. Eric Davis and Nicholas Gavrielides. Miami: Florida International University Press, 1991.

Fernea, Elizabeth Warnock, and Basima Qattan Bezirgan. Introduction to *Middle Eastern Women Speak.* Austin: University of Texas Press, 1977.

Halpern, Manfred. *The Politics of Social Chance in the Middle East and North Africa.* Princeton: Princeton University Press, 1963.

Hatem, Mervat F. "Economic and Political Liberalization and the Demise of State Feminism." *International Journal of Middle East Studies* 24 (August 1992).

_____. "The Paradoxes of State Feminism in Egypt." In *Women and Politics Worldwide,* ed. Barbara Nelson and Najma Chowdhury. New Haven: Yale University Press, 1994.

_____. "Political Liberalization, Gender, and the State." In *Political Liberalization and Democratization in the Arab World,* ed. Rex Brynen, Bahgat Korany, and Paul Noble. Boulder: Lynne Rienner, 1995.

Joseph, Suad. "The Mobilization of Iraqi Women in the Labor Force." *Studies in Third World Societies* 16 (June 1981).

Kadioglu, Ayse. "Women's Subordination in Turkey: Is Islam Really the Villain?" *Middle East Journal* 48, no. 4 (Autumn 1994).

Kandiyoti, Deniz. "The End of Empire: Islam, Nationalism, and Women in Turkey." In *Women, Islam, and the State,* ed. Deniz Kandiyoti. Philadelphia: Temple University Press, 1991.

Kay, Shirley. "Social Change in Modern Saudi Arabia." In *State, Society, and Economy in Saudi Arabia,* ed. Tim Niblock. New York: St. Martin's Press, 1982.

Keddie, Nikki, and Lois Beck. Introduction to *Women in the Muslim World.* Cambridge: Harvard University Press, 1978.

Lerner, Daniel. *The Passing of Traditional Society.* London: Free Press of Glencoe, 1958.

Margulies, Ronnie, and Ergin Yiddizoglu. "The Political Uses of Islam in Turkey." *Middle East Report,* no. 153 (July-August 1988).

Molyneux, Maxine. *State Policies and the Position of Women Workers in the People's Democratic Republic of Yemen, 1967–1977.* Geneva: International Labor Office, 1982.

Rassam, Amal. "Revolution Within the Revolution? Women and the State in Iraq." In *Iraq: The Contemporary State,* ed. Tim Niblock. London: Croom Helm, 1982.

Seikaly, May. "Women and Social Change in Bahrain." *International Journal of Middle East Studies* 26, no. 3 (August 1994).

Sharqi, Amal. "The Emancipation of Iraqi Women." In *Iraq: The Contemporary State,* ed. Tim Niblock. London: Croom Helm, 1982.

Tucker, Judith. *Women in Nineteenth-Century Egypt.* Cambridge: Cambridge University Press, 1985.

3

The Other "Awakening": The Emergence of Women's Movements in the Modern Middle East, 1900–1940

Ellen L. Fleischmann

History, Politics, and Gender

In 1945, two years before her death, the noted Egyptian feminist Huda Sha'rawi was awarded the highest possible state decoration in Egypt. Leila Ahmed notes that the award

> was a measure not only of the prominence Sha'rawi had attained as leading advocate of women's rights but also of the enormous transformation Egyptian society had undergone in the first half of this century. A society in which women of Sha'rawi's (upper) class were veiled and invisible and could have no presence in the world of public and political activities had become one in which they were visible and active in the public domain, in which their activities were reported in the papers (accompanied by photographs of their unveiled faces), and in which the state and secular-minded politicians, literati and intellectuals of the day recognized women's contributions.[1]

Sha'rawi, unlike her more anonymous and unrecognized peers in other parts of the Middle East, achieved in her lifetime and beyond a high public profile in the region, ultimately embodying the quintessential historic "pioneer" of Middle Eastern feminism. We know much less about the rich history of other Middle Eastern women activists and the women's movements within which they functioned. Beginning around the turn of the twentieth century, at the same time that upper-class Egyptian women began to write about and promote greater freedoms for women, women in other parts of the Middle East also began to organize women's societies, associations, unions, and federations, which led to the formation of nascent women's movements. Although the impetus for organizing often emanated from national crises, these usually loose associations arose during the first four decades of the twentieth century to constitute various forms of indigenous feminisms. In Iran, women left their homes for the streets during the constitutional crisis of 1906–1911; similarly, Turkish women formed their first women's associations around the time of the 1908 Committee of Union and Progress (CUP) coup and the subsequent reinstitution of constitutional rule; in Egypt, women demonstrated and organized in support of the 1919 Wafdist revolution; and Palestinian women convened a national women's congress and demonstrated against British Mandatory policies in the wake of the Wailing Wall disturbances of 1929.

This essay will trace the historical trajectory of the emergence of Middle Eastern women's movements. Of course, the linguistic, historical, geographical, and cultural diversity of the region makes such an undertaking rather daunting. An entire book utilizing sources in Arabic, Turkish, and Persian would be required to do justice to the topic.[2] One may also, with justice, question the very organizing principle or unit of analysis here called "Middle Eastern women's movements." As Marnia Lazreg indicates, "the label 'Middle Eastern women' . . . reveals its unwarranted generality." The region so defined covers twenty-one countries with "few similarities and as many differences."[3] Yet women in the region—from the middle and upper classes, it should be stressed—perceived themselves as sharing a collective cultural and even political identity that transcended regional, linguistic, and religious differences. On a number of occasions, they saw and sought common cause, coming together and uniting around shared concerns. The histories of the individual women's movements are inextricably embedded within the broader context and narrative of a collective history. This essay represents a preliminary attempt to integrate some of those individual histories within that broader collective.

In exploring this history, one is immediately confronted with the question: What is the understanding of "feminism" here, particularly within the particular historical and geopolitical context of the Middle East in the first third of the twentieth century? To answer this question requires entering an ongoing and often contentious debate among feminist scholars over redefining feminism. Of pivotal interest to those who study women and gender in the Middle East are critical examinations of the complex intersections between feminism, colonialism, and nationalism being undertaken by Third World feminist scholars.[4] Until fairly recently, the history of feminism was implicitly the history of white, Western feminism, a narrative that effectively excluded the struggles of women in Asia, Africa, the Middle

East, and Latin America as well as women of color within Western societies. This narrative was based upon definitions of feminism whose primary locus of struggle was gender inequality, a focus that did not take into account the "intersections of the various systemic networks of class, race, (hetero)sexuality, and nation" that form structures of domination against which women worldwide struggle.[5] The task for Third World feminists became one of redefining feminism in a way that divests it of its Western particularity and instead constructs new meanings incorporating both its universal aspects and its "historically specific and dynamic"[6] forms in the Third World. For our purposes, the task becomes threefold: theoretically redefining feminism; broadening our understanding of the issues that fall under its rubric; and reexamining the history of feminism in order to recognize that "feminism, perhaps outside the terms and definitions as we know it today, has existed in a variety of forms" within Third World societies throughout history.[7] An important point Marnia Lazreg makes is that "to think of feminism in the singular is sociologically inappropriate."[8] We need to not only "include" Third World women but also entirely reconceptualize feminism as a plural(istic), heterogeneous set of practices with a long, rich history worldwide. Such reformulations take into account the distinct character of the Middle Eastern women's movements, which responded to political, cultural, and social conditions that were unique in some respects, yet analogous in others to the predicaments facing other women's movements.

The problem of taking a pluralistic approach to redefine feminism, however, is that it can potentially reinforce contradictions, reducing feminism to a sum of its disparate parts. Can plurality also be universal? How do we devise "a particular set of organizing principles and ideas about women" we can call feminism(s) that helps resolve these contradictions and gives us a meaningful, working understanding of the word?[9]

At the heart of these contradictions is the question of consciousness and identity. Margot Badran defines feminism as "the awareness of constraints placed upon women because of their gender and attempts to remove these constraints and to evolve a more equitable gender system involving new roles for women and new relations between men and women."[10] Although she derives this definition from "the experience of Egyptian women as feminists in the nineteenth and twentieth centuries,"[11] the definition would exclude many women's movements in the Middle East from being considered feminist. Many women activists who became involved in women's movements did not necessarily consider or call themselves feminists.[12] Here, the intricacies of the intersections between feminism, colonialism, and nationalism come into play. In many cases women were not attempting to develop "new" gender relations and social practices so much as protect them from the corrosive effects of European colonial rule, as well as from disruptive social, economic, and cultural transformations caused by other internal and regional developments. The focus of their activism was not necessarily on changing inequitable gender relations in their societies so much as on alleviating their effects on women. Activist women perceived their efforts as defending and strengthening national culture and the family against external threats.

This was particularly the case with those women's movements that focused on national struggles. At its core, nationalism highlights the issue of identity. Women were faced with the question: Gender or nation, which came first? The answer depended upon which was the primary site of attack. One "common theme" among the different ways that women have been drawn into protest activities has been that "for a critical mass within the group the situation has become intolerable and those in power have to be challenged."[13] For many women in the Middle East, it was the national situation that became "intolerable" and national identity that was threatened during the period under study. The question of gender inequity invariably was postponed or considered divisive, and the national issue seen as the priority. This was (and continues to be, in some situations) the case even among activist women, who maintained that women could not achieve "rights" when men did not have them.[14]

Yet women used their entry into public life through that "most honorable door," the nationalist struggle, to push at the boundaries that confined them and to begin to challenge cultural, social, and political norms.[15] By acting at all, they transgressed these norms; as one observer put it, nationalism had a "releasing effect" on women.[16] Through their involvement in nationalism, they developed over time an internal critique of gender relations that was sometimes muted but often implicit. This involvement could only bring to the fore the contradictions of their multiple identities as women and national subjects or citizens, not to mention other sources of identity such as religion, class, and kin relations.

A feminist consciousness or "awareness," however, was not necessarily a preexisting condition in many women who became politically active in the women's movements. Consciousness is developed through experience. The experiences of women—their very act of organizing—constituted feminism, despite a lack of explicit feminist consciousness, which sometimes did or did not develop, depending upon the specific historical circumstances.[17]

In this vein, Chela Sandoval's concept of "oppositional consciousness" seems to offer a promising redefinition of feminism that is particularly relevant to the political and historical contexts within which Middle Eastern women's movements are situated. She defines oppositional consciousness as "the ability to read the current situation of power" and to choose and adapt "the ideological form best suited to push against its configurations, a survival skill well known to oppressed peoples."[18] Chandra Talpade Mohanty makes a similar point in describing Third World feminists' "notion of agency" as one that "works . . . through the logic of opposition."[19] Thus, the women's movements constructed their political positions through an interactive process in which they identified their opposition, and defined themselves politically, in relation to those they opposed. This kind of process does not necessarily flow one way only, nor is it merely reactive; it allows for constant change and requires adaptability within fluctuating political situations. (The opposition itself—for example, colonial structures of rule—is not static, unified, and unchanging.)[20] The women's movements developed a certain flexibility, an inherent component of this concept of feminism.[21] The *dynamic* of opposition—in all its diverse forms—is the universal dimension that binds heterogeneous feminisms together under the rubric "feminism," taking account of this heterogeneity and universality simultaneously. This framework, grounded in examination of the historical experiences of Middle Eastern women's movements, helps us make sense of their diversity as well as the commonalities of their struggles, strategies, and ideologies.

Much of the literature that focuses on women's political participation in the Middle East, written primarily by sociologists, journalists, anthropologists, and political scientists, concentrates on the contemporary era.[22] The complex and variegated *history* of this involvement—its roots; the struggles of the pioneers of previous generations; the emergence, evolution, organization, ideologies, successes, and mistakes of this historical experience—has hardly been addressed by researchers.[23] A notable exception is Egypt, whose women's movement has been the subject of much study by serious scholars.[24] The earlier periods of the Iranian women's movement have also begun to attract historical interest with the recent publication of several groundbreaking works.[25] But for the most part, many movements for which we have tantalizing evidence in the way of often scattered and scarce primary sources remain unstudied; with rare exceptions, one is hard pressed to find even an article on the histories of the Palestinian, Lebanese, Syrian, and Iraqi women's movements, for example.[26]

It is one of the premises of this essay that an understanding of the historical roots of women's involvement is important not only because it informs contemporary struggles, movements, and challenges that confront them but also because these histories merit examination in and of themselves. Unlike other fields of women's history, Middle Eastern women's history is still at the fledgling stage and is thus engaged in those tasks identified as "fundamental" by Berenice Carroll more than twenty years ago: We are, at the most basic level, still working at just "construct[ing] women as historical subjects."[27] In order to do so, a large part of our work remains documenting and collecting data on women's experiences—a major and still neglected undertaking in and of itself. Retrieving Middle Eastern women's experiences from the margins to which they have long been relegated will require much time and effort. Clearly, logistical and methodological difficulties have contributed to the dearth of history about the women's movements.[28]

There are also epistemological and theoretical reasons for the lack of historical research. One is related to the meaning of "politics" and "political." Many peoples of the Middle East still retain living memories of the experience of colonial pasts. Part of a coming to terms with, and rejection of, those pasts results in the equation of "politics" with nationhood, nationalism, and the struggle for national liberation. This places definitions and meanings of "politics" squarely within the realm of the nation-state, often making no distinction between the "political" and the "nationalist."[29] Further, "politics" is a gendered concept that locates political participation solely within the usually male domain of formal political institutions or even the less formally designated resistance and political movements. In this context, the term "politics" usually refers to political parties, parliamentary institutions, elections, and other aspects of formal political processes.

Gendered notions of politics result in myriad assumptions about women's involvement, one of which is that women's informal, less-organized, and often less-recognized participation in (male-led) political or revolutionary movements is by definition not political. For example, the "support" activities of Palestinian women during the 1936–1939 revolt—spying on British troop movements, hiding weapons, and carrying water—were not considered "political" in the same way that fighting as an armed *thā'ir* (revolutionary) was.

Second, women's historical activism in charitable, social, educational, and developmental associations is assumed to have little political content and is thus of little interest to historians, other than those who study women and gender. These philanthropic activities are viewed solely as precursors or even prerequisites to political involvement. Although this is true to an extent, this limited view divorces these activities from their own historical political contexts and does not take into account women's interactions with, and responses to, political situations other than national or externally generated crises. Because the social critique of the women's associations was implicit rather than explicit, focusing on "domestic" concerns, their work is relegated to the "social" sphere, which is conceptualized as distinct and separate from the political. In this view, the personal is *not* necessarily the political; social, economic, and cultural aspects of women's lives are often conceptually segregated from the political processes that have shaped them.[30] Instead, discussions of "women's concerns" are placed squarely in the domain of tradition, culture, and religion rather than in the realm of politics and power, which are not only conceptually constructed as "men's concerns" but defined as what *men do.*

Another reason for historical neglect lies in the fact that while other fields "have made great strides in the study of Middle Eastern women, the field of history has been less able or willing to bring gender in."[31] In recent years, this situation has begun to change, with a long overdue increase in the production of historical works on Middle Eastern women; however, women are not integrated into general works in the field of Middle East history, as a look at the index of most history books will indicate. Furthermore, unlike other writing in Middle East history, the research agenda of many women's historians has not, interestingly, focused on the history of women's political participation, but rather on other areas of interest such as women's position within the family, women and Islamic law, women in Islamic history, and women and Islam.[32]

In this context, it is worth noting that, despite the development of a strong anti-Orientalist critique provoked by the debate surrounding Edward Said's *Orientalism,* religion—specifically, Islam—still retains a tenacious hold within scholarship as an overarching explanatory paradigm,[33] particularly in analyses of women and gender. Marnia Lazreg notes: "The point is neither to dismiss the role that Islam plays in women's and men's lives, nor to inflate it. More importantly, it is to study the historical conditions under which religion becomes significant in the production and reproduction of gender difference and inequality."[34] The continued focus on religion and the essentializing category of "Muslim women" rendered religion the sole determinant of women's experiences, limiting intellectual exploration of other aspects of women's existence.

Third, the interest of scholars from other disciplines in contemporary women's political participation is often linked quite openly with feminist intellectuals' personal experiences and explicit political agendas, which are oriented toward achieving concrete, positive changes in women's political, legal, and economic situations in their societies. Women activist scholars are compelled by the urgency of current problems, conflicts, and situations, and often history may seem like a self-indulgent, meaningless intellectual exercise.

But history is not so easily swept aside. As often as not, it is invoked for models, warnings, or belated recognition.[35] One would hope that it is axiomatic in this day and age to point out that history that excludes women is a half-told tale. Women's developing their own movements was part of an overall historical process in which changes in women's position and the redefinition of gender relations in Middle Eastern societies were at the heart of searing questions revolving around the nature of culture, national and personal identity, and the meaning of modernity. Such transformations and the furious debates they provoked were rooted in political as well as social and cultural change, no matter how much tradition, religion, and culture have been highlighted. Politics is intricately implicated with the process of change, which affected women and notions of gender. The history of this process and all the constituent parts interwoven with it, and embedded within it, would be incomplete without the history of women's political involvement.

History of the Movements

In order to make sense of such a broad, rich, and diverse sweep of history, I make the risky proposition of arranging it into three roughly thematic stages of development, purely as a heuristic device. These stages do not necessarily follow a linear chronology because the progressive development of the individual women's movements varied, with stages overlapping, coinciding, preceding, and following one another, at times obscuring the demarcation lines among them.[36] In some cases, several of these stages occurred almost simultaneously, and in other cases, certain women's movements have yet to experience one or another of these stages. The first stage—the so-called awakening—was that phenomenon whereby women and men began to raise the issue of women's status and question previously unchallenged social practices, but not necessarily the social (or political) structures or institutions that governed them. It was during this stage that reformers and other intellectuals initiated debate on women's status in various forums, including the press. This stage also witnessed the development of myriad social, religious, literary, charitable, educational, and in some cases political women's organizations. A major characteristic of the second stage was women's adoption of nationalism as a liberating discourse, linking it and their own direct involvement in nationalist movements to female emancipation. The third stage is characterized by women's co-optation by, and collusion and/or collision with, the state-building project, resulting in the evolution of state feminism. Of the movements studied here, only Iran and Turkey experienced this stage of development before 1940.

It seems judicious before discussing the specific historical experiences of the women's movements to clarify the use of the terms "awakening" and "movement(s)" to characterize the heterogeneity of the various women's groups that were established. Discursive references to a "women's awakening"[37] began to appear as early as the late nineteenth century in the Middle East, particularly in the women's press; in the Arabic-speaking parts of the Middle East, the term seems to have been more commonly used in the earlier part of the twentieth century. Many women's organizations used the word in their names.[38] As Beth Baron points out, although the phrase originally referred to a literary movement, "it took on a broader cultural and social resonance."[39] I have chosen to use the word because women's utilization of it demonstrates its significance to them. The danger in using this term, however, is that the word "awakening" "presupposes sleep," an often reiterated but false assumption about women's passivity during the nineteenth century.[40] It also contained political connotations and implicit association with the Arab "awakening," a movement whose history continues to be contested and debated more than a century after its inception. Over time the ubiquity and frequency of the term's utilization approached something of a cliché, with all the generality and stereotyping that implies.[41] For that reason, I use the word advisedly and in quotation marks.

The word "movement"[42] began to be used around the 1920s to refer to a wide range of women's public activities that were taking place throughout the region. Increasingly, it began to replace the word "awakening" in this context. "Movement" at its most elemental level is defined as "a series of organized activities working toward an objective" or "an organized effort by supporters of a common goal."[43] My use of the term is deliberately broad. Although many of the different women's societies, organizations, federations, and unions that were established may not have been working toward commonly shared, explicitly delineated and agreed upon goals, it can be argued that women in each Middle Eastern society that experienced this phenomenon perceived their efforts as part of a broader whole, however ill-defined or assorted the myriad and sometimes discordant groups that formed its constituent parts. The emergence of women's movements in the Middle East during this period was not an isolated occurrence but was part of a broader global phenomenon in almost all parts of the world, including India, the United States, Europe, Latin America, and parts of Africa and Asia. Analogous to their counterparts throughout the world, most of the women's movements in the Middle East shared for the most part a basic "transformational character" that provoked reexaminations of gender roles, whether or not this was a specific goal.[44] Each of these movements, individually (on national or local bases) and collectively (on a regional basis), shared a "common concern with improving the position of women in society," despite often indirect ways of working toward achieving this goal and a lack of cohesive, unified strategies.[45]

The women's movements that arose in the early part of the twentieth century also shared a number of characteristics, demonstrating the links and connections between and among women of the region. Bonds of culture, religion, solidarity, and common political concerns were specifically articulated at a number of regional and international women's conferences attended by Middle Eastern women in the 1930s and 1940s. During crises in individual states, women from all over the region expressed solidarity and support for their "sisters" through demonstrations, telegrams, and various

protest actions. The press in the Middle East played a major role in facili-
tating communication and the spread of information through its coverage
of the activities of the different women's movements throughout the region,
as well as feminist movements elsewhere.[46] Women activists established
local and regional networks through correspondence and personal contacts. Prominent Egyptian women activists such as Huda Sha'rawi and
Amina Sa'id made speaking tours and were feted by their cohorts in the
Mashriq, for example, during the 1940s. By the end of World War II, a
solid network of women's organizations existed throughout the region that
had fairly extensive contacts and, in some cases, formal organizational ties
to each other.

The history of how this developed, however, is rich, variegated, and complex. Despite a certain amount of solidarity, there was no monolithic
"Middle Eastern women's movement," and the specific histories of the individual movements which formed a very loose collective reflect its constituent elements' heterogeneity and often, contradictions.

Stage One: The "Awakening"

Most of the commentaries on the women's movements locate their shared
intellectual foundations in the different reform movements, secular and
Islamist, that arose initially during the late nineteenth century. Male reformers have been highlighted for their role in voicing protests about, and
promoting improvements in, women's status. Ironically (and perhaps not
surprisingly), it was a man, Qasim Amin, the Egyptian judge and author of
the influential *The Liberation of Women* (1899), who was long considered
by many (mistakenly, according to Leila Ahmed) the "father of Arab feminism."[47] Historians have not focused much attention on the fact that, although the heated debates that ensued in the literate world during this early
period were ostensibly *about* women and frequently *among* men, women
themselves, far from being merely the objects of this debate, energetically
engaged in these contestations, challenging conservative male polemicists as
well as other women. In Egypt, for example, two women battled in the
press on opposing sides of the issue of women's suffrage as early as 1892.[48]
In Turkey, Fatma Aliye Hanim, provoked by a series of articles promoting
polygyny, set forth her views in a monograph entitled *The Women of Islam,*
which "predate[d]" (1891) and "foreshadow[ed]" many of Amin's arguments in *The Liberation of Women.*[49]

In the early twentieth century, intellectuals in Iran, Turkey, Egypt, and
Greater Syria all debated the issue of women within the context of modernity, which was understood to encompass "technological progress, secu-
larism, the rule of law, women's emancipation, and a monogamous family
system."[50] Women's status became a potent symbol and barometer of a so-

ciety's modernity. The porousness of political boundaries during this period facilitated contact, intellectual exchange, and the sharing of many of these concepts among intellectuals and reformers from all over the Middle East. Amin's writings reached beyond the Arab world, influencing, for example, Iranian intellectuals such as Seyyid Hosein Taqizadeh, a Majles (Parliament) representative and newspaper editor who defended women's right to establish their own associations during the convening of the first Majles in 1907.[51] Although Amin's feminist credentials have been recently subjected to critical reevaluation and his feminism may not stand up to contemporary scrutiny, the influence he had upon his peers cannot be discounted.[52] Reformers began to promote women's education and openly challenge and criticize social and cultural practices oppressive to women. Turkish author Ahmad Mithat Efendi attacked forced marriage, concubinage, and polygamy as "social ills," writing about such subjects in his novels.[53] The Iraqi poet Jamil Zahawi, who appealed to the Ottoman government in Istanbul to open a school for girls in Iraq, was fired from his position as professor of law after writing a newspaper article criticizing veiling and fathers' control over their daughters' marriage decisions.[54]

These intellectuals and reformers were attempting to come to terms with socioeconomic, cultural, and political transformations in the region, including the encroachment of Western institutions and structures of domination, which were beginning to penetrate their societies. Shifts in power between rural and urban elites, increased commercialization of agriculture, the Middle East's accelerating integration into the world market, and the effects of Western industrialization on local economies all affected social practices and political responses. The development and gradually increasing dissemination of education helped to foment an intellectual and cultural critique that looked both internally and externally for solutions to perceived social, cultural, and political ills. Criticism took place within both an Islamist framework and a secular one. Many male reformers "found the plight of women a powerful vehicle for the expression of their own restiveness with social conventions they found particularly stultifying and archaic. 'Modern' men often felt alienated from . . . patriarchal structures which curtailed their own freedom considerably, even though women were the more obvious victims of the system."[55] Others have pointed out how the "woman question" in many respects became "part of an ideological terrain" upon which other concerns—most prominently "questions of cultural and national integrity"—were "articulated and debated."[56]

The status of women and issues of feminism, as Thomas Philipp points out, "touched perhaps more directly than any other aspect of the modernist movement upon the personal life of people. . . . One could proclaim oneself in favor of . . . nationalism, constitutional rule, or the validity of modern sciences without necessarily having to change one's private life very

much. But new ideas about the role of woman in society had direct bearing on the private life of each individual."⁵⁷ Reformist, Western-oriented
men were seeking to modernize *themselves,* albeit through focusing their
attention on women. Educated, with experience abroad or in increased
dealings with foreigners, they began to perceive their own societies within
a broader, international context and reflexively turned their attention to
women, targeting them as the backward, atavistic embodiments of all that
was wrong with "tradition" and traditional culture and religion. "The
main enemy of early reformers was 'backwardness,' rather than 'foreign-
ness'";⁵⁸ "backward" women would retard society as a whole. As Amin
put it: "The status of women is inseparably tied to the status of a nation.
When the status of a nation is low, reflecting an uncivilized condition for
that nation, the status of women is also low, and when the status of a nation is elevated, reflecting the progress and civilization of that nation, the
status of women in that country is also elevated."⁵⁹ In some ways, this placing the burden of the nation's "civilization" upon women is a variant on
the honor paradigm, which places another of society's burdens on
women—that of male honor, defined by the preservation of *women's* sexual purity.

The primary focus of many of these concerns centered on improving
middle-class women's effectiveness in their roles as wives and mothers, particularly as educators of children, the men of the future. Suddenly, women
had to be "scientifically" trained and educated to learn how to be modern
wives and mothers. A woman could not "run her household well unless she
attain[ed] a certain amount of intellectual and cultural knowledge"; likewise, an "ignorant mother" could not "transform her child's personality to
include good qualities" if she were unaware of such qualities.⁶⁰ As Kumari
Jayawardena points out, increasingly, "the new bourgeois man . . . needed
as his partner, the 'new woman' who was presentable in . . . society yet
whose role was primarily in the home."⁶¹

Women fought back against some of the criticisms levied against their
sex by men, supposedly in the name of elevating the nation. Bibi Khanum,
an Iranian intellectual, responded to an essay entitled "The Chastisement
of Women" with her own heated and satirical defense of her sex, entitled
"The Vices of Men" (1896). "The creators of the misfortunes of society
were men," she admonished. "The least they could do . . . was to stop
going around advising women" and instead, seek "a remedy for their own
corruption."⁶²

Yet other women endorsed some of the ideas about "reforming" women.
They started to articulate their own views on the subject, particularly
through writing in the press. Beginning in the late nineteenth century,
women began to contribute articles to general-interest mainstream periodicals, often anonymously.⁶³ But it was the evolution of a separate women's

press, first in Egypt and Turkey and then in Iran and Syria, that marked a significant development.[64] For the first time, an explicitly female voice found its way into print, disseminated to an (admittedly limited) literate public. Egypt led the way, with the publication of the first women's periodical, *The Young Woman (al-Fatāh),* founded by Hind Nawfal in Alexandria in 1892. Turkey's earliest women's publication was *The Ladies Own Gazette (Hanimlara Mahsun Gazete),* which began publishing in 1895. Appearing twice weekly, it circulated widely throughout the Ottoman Empire and even in Muslim areas of the Russian Empire. In Iran, where the women's press confronted particularly harsh hostility and many obstacles, a woman "oculist," Dr. Kahhal, began publication of the country's first women's magazine, *Knowledge (Danish),* in 1910. Damascene Mary Ajami founded *The Bride (al-'Arūs)* in 1910; Lebanon's first women's journal was *Girl of Lebanon (Fatāt Lubnān),* introduced by Salima Abu Rashid in 1914.[65]

These early efforts heralded in an impressive wave of publications "by, for, and about women" with local journals often reaching wider audiences throughout the region.[66] In numerous cases, women's periodicals were founded in association with women's organizations. The quality of writing, range of topics, longevity, and circulation figures varied. Some of the earlier periodicals were constrained in their goals and in what types of subjects they covered; Iranian women were instructed by *Majles,* the journal of the newly established Iranian parliament during the first constitutional crisis (1906–1908), to "keep out of politics and affairs of the government." The Iranian women's paper *Knowledge* published a cautious disclaimer on its masthead stating that it "would only publish issues pertaining to domestic questions and 'under no circumstances discuss politics and the issues of the nation.'"[67] Although most of the women's journals during the early years restricted their coverage to "women's topics" such as the home, domestic work, child raising, education, fashion, and the like, this was by no means the case everywhere. The women's press during the second constitutional period in Turkey (1908–1919) severely criticized men for disregarding their promises to emancipate women once they took power. One woman, Ismet Hakki, wrote an article entitled "The Need to Fight" in which she argued that "rights can only be obtained by fighting and . . . rights obtained through struggle [are] easier to safeguard."[68]

A distinct women's press did not evolve everywhere, being notably absent in those parts of the Middle East that did not have large cities with a minimal number of literate women readers. In Palestine, for example, a women's press never really developed.[69] But women's experience in writing and publishing, be it in their own women's publications or in the general-interest mainstream press, ultimately resulted in their increasing recognition and use of the powerful propagandistic possibilities of the press to articulate their concerns and interests, which over time became more overtly political.

The Development of Women's Organizations

The "new" women themselves took advantage of these fermenting debates. Despite the ambivalent and contradictory roots, motivations, and concepts of female emancipation articulated in reformist discourse, such discourse did provide openings that empowered women to be innovative in their time and place: to organize themselves in associations for a common goal or good, often oriented toward "uplifting" their fellow women. This activity usually took the form of charitable or social welfare organizations, which were established in some parts of the Middle East as early as the mid-nineteenth century. The first women's associations generally focused on improving the status of women through working in such areas as health; the care of poor women, infants, and orphans; vocational training; and literacy. The Sisters of Love in Lebanon, for example, established in 1847, ran a school, a tuberculosis sanatorium, and a home for wayward girls.[70] Palestine's first women's association, the Orthodox Aid Society for the Poor, founded in Acre in 1903, provided clothes and trousseau items for poor young girls to "prevent them from remaining unmarried."[71] Many of the earliest philanthropic projects were founded by individual women motivated by specific crises,[72] but over time women's associations formed explicitly for the purpose of fulfilling social welfare functions.

One of the initial impulses to organize arose from a sentiment of noblesse oblige on the part of the wealthy toward the less fortunate, which was based upon a "tradition of public service" among both women and men in Islamic societies[73] and, in the case of Christians, upon notions of Christian charity. Indeed, most of the first efforts were primarily religiously based and segregated by confession, with Muslim and Christian women setting up separate organizations. This soon changed, however, and, as Margot Badran points out, it was women who led the way in "extricat[ing] social service from the exclusive hold of religious (or religiously affiliated) institutions."[74] One of the first such secular philanthropic societies was the Mabarrat Muhammad 'Ali, a dispensary for poor women and children, founded in Egypt in 1909.[75] By the 1920s, many, if not most, of the women's organizations then active—both charitable and otherwise—had members and leadership of mixed religious affiliation, and no longer identified themselves primarily as religious associations.

The historical chronology of these various efforts differed from place to place; in Iran and Turkey, for example, women's establishment of their own organizations followed a different trajectory than that of the Arab countries. In the latter, beginning in the late nineteenth century, religiously based charitable societies were generally founded first, followed in the post–World War I period by more overtly social and political groups. The first women's organizations in Iran, with few exceptions, catapulted themselves immediately into national politics, becoming involved in the first constitutional crisis in 1906. In Turkey, it was in the context of a "new atmosphere of freedom" during the second constitutional period (1908–1919), led by the CUP revolution, that women's societies first formed. "No less than a dozen" women's organizations were founded during this period; the Balkan Wars (1912–1913) also acted as a catalyst for some endeavors. The Red Crescent Women's Center, for example, was founded in 1912, as was another women's "club" that organized a hospital and helped war refugees.[76] This first wave of organizing included both religiously oriented charities and more feminist-oriented women's associations. In 1914 the Society for the Defense of the Rights of Women was founded; listed among its aims were several seemingly conflicting goals, including "to fortify woman in the home"; "to render mothers capable of bringing up their children according to the principles of modern pedagogy"; "to initiate Turkish women into life in society"; and "to encourage women to earn their own living by their own work."[77]

Although women's charitable activities have been dismissed by some as "bourgeois" and politically irrelevant, nonetheless their inauguration marked something new and distinct. Middle- and upper-class women had been benefactors and even supervisors of Islamic trusts (*awqāf*) for centuries,[78] but actively setting up and running charitable organizations required women to employ particular skills and engage themselves in public. These organizations also proved to be eminently suitable training grounds for political organizing. As Beth Baron suggests, elite women perceived the social welfare arena as "fertile ground for building a power base and pushing toward the center of politics."[79] Upper-class women found themselves working for the first time in direct contact with the lower classes,[80] an experience that opened the eyes of many, although not to the extent of including poorer women as peers and leaders among their ranks—something that was to ultimately limit the groups' organizational power, growth, and overall effectiveness.

Women also discovered strength in collective work, and they experienced "self-discovery"; "working towards collective goals tapped wellsprings of creativity that had been quiescent."[81] They learned that they could wield authority and influence from within a group, reducing the isolation and powerlessness they might feel as individuals and creating "new networks and bonds among themselves."[82] They had to develop and use organizational skills, exercise control over resources, and manage their own organizations.

Many women were publicly involved at multiple levels, belonging to a number of different groups and building upon and gaining from these

experiences. Although Huda Sha'rawi, as always, is renowned for her numerous involvements, many other, less well-known individuals, such as
Palestinian Nahid al-Sajjadi, actively participated in a wide range of activities; starting in the 1920s, al-Sajjadi was a member of the Arab Women's
Union, the Red Crescent Society, the Women's Solidarity Society, and (later,
during the 1948 war) the Society of the Wounded Fighter.[83] One of the re-
markable "pioneers" of Iranian feminism, Sedigheh Doulatabadi, was a
founding member of the first women's group in that country, the Women's
Freedom Society (1907); a member of the National Ladies' Society; a
founder of the Isfahan Ladies Company; the creator of the newspaper
Women's Voice; and a contributor to the journal *Patriotic Women,* among
other things.[84]

The women who were involved in these early efforts were almost all educated and from middle- and upper-class backgrounds, as was the case in
women's organizations in other parts of the world during this period. Their
educations acted as a catalyst, encouraging them to seek change and giving
them the confidence and ability to act.[85] They also had more leisure than
the poorer urban and peasant women who constituted the majority of
women in most Middle Eastern societies. Class played a major role in influencing their organizing styles, the issues they worked on, and their politics. Although eventually many women came to see themselves as part of
a women's movement, their concept of "movement" did not necessarily incorporate the mass of women in their societies. Instead, they tended to treat
lower-class women more as clients than as constituents.[86] They generally
did not address the "root causes," nor did they develop an explicit "critical awareness" of, their societies' "profound social inequities and economic
distress."[87] In this, they mirrored many of the attitudes of the male reformers, liberal politicians, and nationalists who were their allies during
this period.

On the other hand, women's very recognition of the need for the social
welfare services their organizations provided constituted a kind of *tacit* political act and implicit criticism of the deficiencies of prevailing political and
social institutions. By stepping in to fill perceived gaps, women were fulfilling functions that, over time, became recognized as the responsibility of
the local authorities or governments and, when they eventually came into
being, the nation-states. (Later, instead of trying to perform the duties of
government themselves, women increasingly turned to demanding that the
government fulfill its obligations to provide the services that the women's
organizations had initially supported.) Through their involvement with
charitable work, women began to interact with governmental and state institutions (where they existed), ultimately gaining political skills such as the
ability to negotiate with male officials and work the corridors of power. In
the process, some women became more analytic and politicized. However,

their focus on the positive role of the nation-state in enacting "reform" and legislating change, which intensified particularly after World War I, was to limit their critical analysis and effectiveness.

Elite women organized not only for the benefit of their poorer sisters but, on another level, for their own personal and intellectual development, forming social clubs, intellectual societies, and literary salons. These efforts provided forums for women to gather and discuss intellectual, social, and political concerns and, in many cases, provided training grounds for public speaking. At some of these gatherings, women delivered formal lectures. Such groups naturally tended to form in the larger cities such as Beirut, Damascus, and Cairo, where the concentration of literate women was higher than in the smaller towns and rural areas. Some of the earliest efforts included a salon established by Mariana Marrash in Aleppo in the late nineteenth century; several Cairo intellectual societies, including the Women's Refinement Union (1914), the Ladies Literary Improvement Society (1914), and the Society for the Women's Awakening (1916); the Arab Girls' Awakening Society, formed in Beirut in 1914; and Nazik 'Abid's Women's Literary Club, founded in Damascus in 1920.[88] In societies where public education was extremely limited, these groups played an educational role for the women—many individually tutored or instructed—who attended them.

Perhaps the most significant contribution, and a major priority, of many of the first women's organizations was the establishment of girls' schools. We have seen how the issues of national progress and women's emancipation were directly linked to education in reformist and intellectual discourses during the late nineteenth and early twentieth centuries. This link was one of the major vehicles for the development of a national consciousness among women. The idea of "lifting" the nation by "lifting" women pervaded the earliest stages of women's "discreet public activism"[89] in the first decade of the twentieth century, and it was in the arena of education where many of the women's groups focused their energies toward this end.[90]

The founder of one of Palestine's first women's associations, the Jaffa Orthodox Ladies Society, explicitly linked education, charity, and the nation in her description of how she and a group of Orthodox women "decided to found a national women's association to bring up and educate orphan girls and those in need." She made a point of stating in her memoir that this was "the first national women's association founded in Palestine" (in 1910). The society set up a girls' section of the previously all-male National Orthodox School.[91] When the Russian government, during the second constitutional crisis in Iran in 1911, asked Iranian women to compare their status to that of European women, their response was that European women's status was "preferable because they possess skills, but

not for any other reasons." The Iranian women directly related their comparative lack of skills to the lack of education for women in Iran.[92]

Government-sponsored public education did not become widely available for girls and women until after World War II in most of the Middle
East. In the countries that had been part of the Ottoman Empire, after
World War I, European Mandatory governments narrowly expanded female education beyond the Ottoman government's tentative beginnings,
which had been initiated on a limited basis in some of the Arab provinces
in the late nineteenth century; in Iraq, for example, the first girls' school
was established in 1899.[93] In Turkey itself, the first government girls'
schools were established in the 1850s as part of the Tanzimat (reforms) of
the nineteenth century; a secondary school for girls was founded in 1858,
and a vocational school in 1869.[94] In Iran, state-sponsored female education was established for the first time in 1918.[95] Egypt's first public educational establishment for females was the School for Midwives, instituted in
1832 during Muhammad 'Ali's reign; several girls' schools were subsequently founded in the late 1880s and 1890s.[96]

Because government-sponsored schools for girls were extremely limited
in number and accessibility, missionary and private schools tended to out-
number public schools in the period under study. Women themselves became early and enthusiastic participants in founding, administering, funding, and teaching in the first schools for girls. The Egyptian Nabawiyya
Musa, who experienced many struggles in her career as a teacher and administrator, devoted most of her energy and, indeed, almost her entire life
to women's education, founding several schools herself.[97] Many of the first
women's organizations focused their efforts on this one particular issue.

One stimulus to women's associations' founding of educational establishments was the desire for schools that were independent, and not directly
under the control of foreign and missionary institutions. In Lebanon, for
example, where women's associations took the lead in establishing schools
as early as 1847, two women's societies built and supported "national girls'
schools as an alternative to missionary schools."[98] The issue of "national"
schools came to the forefront as early as the 1880s in Lebanon, probably
because of that country's long history of missionary and foreign involvement in education. Criticism of these schools' deculturizing effects intensified during the Mandate periods in Palestine and Syria/Lebanon,[99] with the
result that the establishment of independent schools became imbued with
nationalist significance.

Syrian and Lebanese women's groups were prominent in founding many
schools, some of whose graduates became renowned in the women's movement in the early twentieth century.[100] Palestinian women, as noted above,
established girls' schools in 1910, starting a trend that continued throughout the almost thirty-year duration of the British Mandate; some of the

schools opened by women's associations in the 1920s operate to this day. In Iran, although it was individual women who took the initiative in founding girls' schools during the first constitutional period, "the new schools were in close organizational relationship with the women's anjumans." By 1913, there were sixty-three private girls' schools with a combined enrollment of 2,500 in Iran.[101] Women's associations in Egypt, interestingly, do not seem to have followed this trend; school founders tended to be individuals, such as Nabawiyya Musa. Beginning in the 1920s, women's associations started to focus their efforts on demanding that the state take on the responsibility for educating girls; this became a contentious issue between the associations and the European colonial governments, highlighting even more emphatically the articulation between education, women, and the nation.

Stage Two: Women and Nationalism

> *You who talk about rights of the nation, who talk about law, who speak of honor and zeal—we are also part of this nation, we ask for our share in these rights, too.*
>
> *—Anonymous Iranian woman, 1907*

The history of women's role in national struggles in the Middle East has increasingly begun to attract scholarly interest. Until recently, women's participation was selectively remembered and celebrated in tales of individual heroism and self-sacrifice, or in scattered references to isolated incidents in which women participated. What has not been methodically studied or recorded is the history of women's organized, sustained efforts on behalf of nationalism. The different women's movements in the Middle East experienced instructive contrasts and parallels in their activities, discourses, strategies, and politics. Nearly all of these movements struggled within the context of a male-defined nationalist agenda, which resulted in their developing complex and ambivalent relationships with the mainstream nationalist movements.

Nationalism was not an abstract issue for women; they were directly affected by the changes brought about by nationalist regimes that came to power—such as in Turkey—as well as by the changes taking place in states that experienced direct or indirect forms of colonial rule, which endured in one form or another in the Middle East throughout the 1930s. After the turn of the twentieth century, nationalism became a predominant political trend in the Middle East, as peoples under imperialist forms of control increasingly began to turn the liberalist ideologies of the imperialists against them in order to question the legitimacy of foreign rule. Also, importantly, nationalism constituted a potential unifying force in a world where mass mobilization was becoming a key component of modern political ideologies. In the Mashriq, Arab nationalists began to organize secretly for independence within the framework of the Ottoman Empire; the seeds of Turkish nationalism were sown in the Anatolian heartland during the second constitutional period, which followed the 1908 CUP revolution. The British occupation of Egypt after the 1882 'Urabi revolt contributed to the evolution of Egyptian nationalist sentiment. In Iran, Russia's and Britain's virtual dictatorship over the country's economy and politics, in addition to Russia's military occupation during the second constitutional crisis in 1909–1911, provoked a strong, organized nationalist response.

World War I was a watershed in transforming simmering nationalist sentiment into full-fledged nationalist movements in the Middle East. Postwar settlements, which reinforced European domination in the former territories of the dismembered Ottoman Empire, directly contributed to the development of nationalist movements in the Arab former provinces that were relegated to European Mandatory rule: Palestine, Iraq, Syria, and Lebanon. In the truncated remains of the former empire, Turkish nationalists waged a full-scale war of national liberation against European-imposed restrictions, resulting in the establishment of a new and independent Turkish republic under Mustafa Kemal Atatürk in 1923. Egypt remained under British rule, but not acquiescently; in 1919, the Wafdist revolution flared up, forcing Britain to make nominal concessions to Egyptian national sovereignty.

Women, along with men, became ardent nationalists and actively participated in all of these national movements, albeit in different ways than men. Their reasons for doing so varied. In some cases, women saw nationalism as a survival issue. This was obviously the case in Palestine, where the Arab population confronted a colonialist movement, Zionism, whose express purpose was to make the country its own, reducing the majority indigenous population to minority, second-class status. In other situations, women linked economic survival to the national struggle. This happened during the constitutional crisis in Iran, during which women were prompted to organize against government borrowing from, and subsequent economic dependence upon, foreign powers; women were very active in street protests against food shortages and hoarding, which occurred as a result of these policies.

In many instances, women perceived nationalism as an opportunity. It was indeed the "honorable door" through which women could enter in order to participate at new levels of public life. Nationalism became a legitimizing discourse for women, initially as a means to "justify stepping out of their narrowly prescribed role in the name of patriotism and self-sacrifice for the nation" and, ultimately, as a way to "earn" emancipation.[103] Yet nationalist women were careful to incorporate their feminist demands within the safe confines of nationalist ideology, since this was the only ideology permissible to them. "While it was possible for nationalists to be nonfeminists, it was not tolerated or possible for feminists to be nonnationalists."[104] Although nationalism did facilitate women's integration into society, it also "reaffirm[ed] the boundaries of culturally accepted feminine conduct and exert[ed] pressure on women to articulate their gender interests within the terms of reference set by nationalist discourse." Thus, feminism was effectively relegated a "maidservant to nationalism" through explicit or implicit acceptance of the strategy "national liberation now, and women's liberation later."[105] For Palestinian women, this "two-stage" theory became a kind of tacit pact between themselves and the mainstream nationalist movement. One sees vestiges of this approach in the cautious pronouncement of Zlikha Shihabi, president of the Palestinian Arab Women's Union, who, speaking to reporters after the 1944 Arab Women's Conference in Cairo, stated that Palestinian women would not demand more rights than those granted by Islamic law; that "demanding women's rights was before its time."[106]

Although nationalist women generally took care not to promote feminist demands at the "expense" of nationalist ones, there were public discussions of women's political equality—particularly in the press—and a few efforts to raise the issue of women's suffrage. In Iran, one brave delegate proposed that women be granted the right to vote during the second Majles (in 1911), but the proposal was rejected on the basis that (in the words of the clerical leader and deputy, Mudarris) "God has not endowed them with the ability to be electors. . . . Moreover, in our religion, Islam, they are under supervision: 'Men are in charge of women.' . . . They are in our charge. They will have absolutely no right to elect."[107] During the 1920s and 1930s, while Syria and Lebanon were under French Mandate, women attempted to claim their suffrage rights, which were debated in their respective parliaments, but without success.[108] (It should be noted that women in France had not yet obtained the vote either during this period.) The only Middle Eastern women to gain suffrage before 1940 were Turkish women, a development discussed below.

Feminism, or demands for female emancipation, were considered potentially divisive topics in struggles where concepts of the nation being fought for tended to be articulated in communal terms, in order to unify people and elide sources of potential difference.[109] "National feminists" developed a brand of feminism that did not challenge patriarchal social, cultural, and political norms so much as complement them by presenting women as working "alongside men" to "save the nation" and protect it from external threats. Women's ostensibly essential and innate qualities—such as motherhood and self-sacrifice—were channeled to the national cause, recasting women's traditionally gendered roles as new "'national' actors: mothers, educators, workers and even fighters."[110]

Despite the inherent limitations of nationalist discourse, women's actual experiences did have a "releasing effect." One cannot discount the excitement and the positive sense of empowerment, unity, and purpose that involvement in political movements engenders in individual participants. Women's participation in nationalist movements demonstrated their commitment, courage, strength, and ability, serving as a major source of personal and collective development. Their potential for providing a base of support and source of legitimacy to newly emerging national regimes was to influence the state-building projects that followed independence.

Women's involvement took various forms; by and large, they were mobilized by, or cooperated with, the mainstream (i.e., male-led) nationalist movements in mass activities, but they rarely participated within the actual male-led organizations themselves. The case of Turkey provides the exception. During the national liberation struggle after World War I, a handful of individual women, such as Nakiye Elgün and Halide Edib, were prominently involved within the mainstream nationalist movement. In most instances, however, women formed separate associations and engaged in their own segregated activities, occasionally coordinating with the male-led groups. In Egypt, for example, women formed their own branch of the Wafd Party, the Wafdist Women's Central Committee. In Iran, women founded numerous "patriotic" organizations, beginning with the Patriotic Women's League in 1906. Palestine's major women's organization, the Arab Women's Association (later renamed the Arab Women's Union), organized and led most of the women's nationalist campaigns during the 1930s and 1940s, establishing branches in the major towns and cities.

The leaders of these organizations, as was the case with the women's charitable and social welfare associations, tended to be from the educated, urban, upper and middle classes. They were frequently related to male nationalists or politicians, but this did not necessarily translate into their playing a role as "auxiliaries" to, or rubber stamps for, the male-led nationalist movements. In Palestine, for example, political differences often erupted between husbands and wives who were both active in the nationalist and women's movements. The Wafdist Women's Central Committee, an ardent supporter of the nationalist Wafd Party during the struggles against the British, eventually split from the Wafdist government when it came to power in Egypt over serious disagreements on both nationalist and feminist issues.[111]

One of the earliest, most visible, and most dramatic manifestations of women's nationalist activity was the large-scale demonstration, in which women, either alongside men or on their own, confronted colonial governments or their proxies. These were significant events in societies where urban women's public visibility and mobility were restricted. Sometimes women were killed or wounded in these demonstrations. During the first constitutional crisis in Iran in 1906, women demonstrated against the shah, stoning troops from rooftops, marching in huge crowds, and participating in a three-week-long occupation of the British legation. In one street protest, a woman shot and killed an anticonstitutionalist speaker, and was herself immediately killed by a mob.[112] In Syria, women organized their own nationalist demonstration during the visit of the King-Crane commission to Damascus in 1919.[113] Egyptian women were key participants in the turbulent upheavals that ensued after the British refused to allow Egyptian representation at the post–World War I Paris peace conference in 1919. Palestinian women, who had sporadically taken part in anti-Zionist disturbances in the 1920s, regularly joined men in major demonstrations in Nablus, Jaffa, and Jerusalem in the early 1930s. They also frequently held large, autonomous women's demonstrations, particularly during the 1936–1939 strike and revolt. Women's militancy often exceeded men's. In one incident, Palestinian women were demonstrating and getting arrested for curfew violations while the male leadership was praying at the mosque.[114]

Nationalists, both men and women, manipulated gender for political purposes during mass protests. Men in Iran encouraged their wives to attack foreign consulates and installations, since women were unrecognizable due to their being covered by veils.[115] Separate women's demonstrations drew extraordinary publicity for their novelty, making them effective as propaganda tools. The Arabic press in Palestine, for example, faithfully and closely covered women's demonstrations throughout the region, particularly in Syria, Egypt, Turkey, and Iraq. Palestinian women were aware of this propagandistic potential, using mnemonic devices in their statements to the press and manipulating "traditional" concepts of gender in order to draw attention to their demonstrations.[116]

A common pattern that emerged in this manipulation of gender norms was the manner in which nationalists employed women's presence in mixed-sex demonstrations to achieve a variety of tactical objectives. Women defused violent reactions from the police or troops deployed to put down demonstrations by force. The British in Palestine complained that the tactic of surrounding marching women with men created a buffer between the police and the "mob" during demonstrations in 1933. In Iran, the same objective was achieved in the opposite way; it was women who formed barricades around the men to protect them during the 1906 demonstrations. Sometimes women acted to incite men during demonstrations. During the 1922 nationalist demonstrations in Syria, women marched at the head of the crowd, ululating "at an unbearably high pitch, bringing the thousands of men behind them to an explosive roar" and causing the French to balk at using force.[117]

The women's movements played a particularly active role in the economic sector, which soon became an arena for nationalist struggles. Many of the nationalist leaders targeted unfair competition or advantages enjoyed by foreign goods in indigenous economies, issues that directly affected women in their everyday lives. As consumers, women played a pivotal role in supporting and upholding economic strikes and boycotting foreign goods. The women's organizations promoted "national" industries by sponsoring workshops that produced indigenous products and by contributing to national banks and funds. During the constitutional crisis in Iran, women donated funds and jewelry and offered to buy shares in the National Bank in order to alleviate dependence upon foreign loans; similarly, women contributed generously to the National Fund in Palestine during the 1930s. The women's movements saw such activities as within their particular purview, and they organized sustained campaigns focused on bolstering their national economies. They aggressively took the lead, acting as enforcers of boycotts through intimidation or outright coercion. During the 1891 tobacco boycott against British monopolies in Iran, women attacked shops that remained open during a national protest. A group of Palestinian women in Haifa was arrested by the British for smashing the shop windows of a strike-breaking merchant during Palestine's 1936 general strike.[118]

Upper- and middle-class women also played a seminal role in generating external support for nationalist causes, effectively utilizing new forms of communication to reach the wider world. They relied extensively on the press and on telegrams, drawing upon their contacts with other women's movements and even foreign governments to solicit international and regional sympathy and solidarity. Women in Iran sent telegrams of protest to foreign governments during the second constitutional crisis when the Russians delivered an ultimatum forcing the Majles to fire its American adviser or face occupation by force.[119] A veritable barrage of telegrams flew back and forth on the issue of Palestine in the 1930s: The Arab Women's Association exchanged telegrams with the Islamic Union in India; women's associations in Iran, India, Britain, and the Arab world; and the governments of Iraq, Egypt, Transjordan, Saudi Arabia, Britain, and Kuwait. They frequently highlighted their protests by publishing their telegrams to the British government in the press.[120]

Beginning in the early 1930s, Arab women began to develop a form of pan-Arab nationalism that extended their efforts beyond their own local national causes, directly supporting each other's nationalist struggles through fund-raising, demonstrating, and writing protest telegrams on each other's behalf. (One of the more interesting examples of the latter is a telegram that Syrian women wrote to the Daughters of the American Revolution on behalf of the Palestinian women's cause!) During 1931 demonstrations in Nablus, the Egyptian Sa'adist Ladies Committee (the successor of the disbanded Wafdist Women's Central Committee) sent greetings to the women of Nablus, congratulating them for their "sacrifice" in the face of oppression. Palestinian women sent telegrams of congratulation to the Syrian "women strugglers" *(mujāhidāt)* when they demonstrated in 1933 against the proposed treaty between France and Syria over the terms of Syria's entry into the League of Nations.[121]

The national struggle in Palestine was the focus of a kind of pan-Arab feminism that also included Muslim women of the "East" and that had the effect of uniting women in the region across national and even religious boundaries, specifically with regard to Christian Arab women. One of the major manifestations of this trend was the convening of the "Eastern" (or "Oriental") Women's Conference in Cairo in 1938, during the height of the 1936–1939 Palestine revolt.[122] At this conference, Arab women established a central, coordinating committee under the leadership of Huda Sha'rawi, formalizing their regional relationships. One of their principal aims was to aggressively combat negative portrayals of the conflict in the international press; they called for the establishment of their own propaganda and information bureau.[123] Separate Women's Committees to Defend Palestine were established in the Arab countries; the Syrian chapter was particularly active, sending money and organizing demonstrations in response to events in Palestine.[124]

Another domain in which women participated was armed conflict, often spontaneously, individually, and secretly, but also within their own organizational frameworks. They concealed and smuggled weapons; spied and conveyed intelligence on troop movements; hid men in their homes; provided medical and food aid to combatants; and, occasionally, took up arms alongside men. The women who directly fought tended to be peasant women; this was the case in Turkey during the war of liberation, in Syria during the 1925 rebellion against the French, and in Palestine during the 1936–1939 revolt. Battles often took place in the countryside, where women were more directly threatened by and involved in the violence. The upper- and middle-class women who worked in organizational structures supported the rebellions through covert support activity such as fundraising, nursing, and arms smuggling. In some instances, special military units for women were formed, usually noncombatant. Nazik 'Abid, who had been granted the honorary military rank of captain by King Faisal, participated in the resistance against the French occupation of Syria in the battle of Maysalun in 1920, wearing a military uniform and heading a woman's medical unit called the Red Star. During the 1948 war in Palestine, women in the Jaffa area formed a secret nursing troop called the Camomile Flowers *(zahrat al-uqhuwān)*, which also provided the fighters with arms.[125] Women paid a high price for their involvement in armed conflict, no matter what form it took. Palestinian women who smuggled arms and ammunition to the rebels during the 1936–1939 revolt were arrested and sentenced to long prison terms. Women were killed in battles in Iran during the civil war that followed the first constitutional crisis, and in Palestine during the revolt. For the most part, however, women's direct participation in armed conflict was relatively limited.

Although women took part in nationalist struggle as individual members of a national collective, it is important to recognize the autonomous organizational structures within which women also participated. The women's movements that emerged during nationalist eras gained valuable organizing experience, enabling them to consolidate their strength and extend their agendas. In many instances, the fact that these groups were *not* integrated into the mainstream nationalist organizations—particularly the leadership—was a source of vitality and autonomy for their own movements. It is striking that the proliferation of new and independent women's organizations occurred principally during periods when nationalist feelings were at their peak. Some of these groups became politically sophisticated and enduring (unless dissolved by the nationalist regimes that subsequently came to power, as discussed below). During the chaotic interregnum between the second constitutional crisis and the consolidation of Reza Khan's regime (1911–1921) in Iran, for example, the women's movement became more independent, structured, and organized; a veritable efflorescence of organizations and women's periodicals took place, among them left-wing, socialist groups.[126] In Palestine, the turbulent 1920s and 1930s saw the establishment of numerous locally active women's associations affiliated with the larger Arab Women's Association. Most of the new women's groups incorporated their more "traditional" social welfare work within a nationalist framework. Thus, for example, groups that focused on promoting women's employment could cast such employment as a patriotic duty, as was the case in Turkey, where women's organizations attempted to facilitate women's entry into the workplace in order to contribute to the war economy during World War I and the war of liberation.

"Women's work"—whether supporting the nationalist struggle or engaging in social welfare activities oriented toward "uplifting the nation"—has too often been considered auxiliary, conservative, and nonpolitical. Rethinking both feminism and nationalism requires eschewing gendered notions of politics and resistance. In the nationalist context, gendered notions of what was considered meaningful in the way of "active" or "passive" resistance have contributed to obscuring the nature of women's participation. The kind of work women engaged in was crucial to the nationalist struggles; for one thing, the fact that women were involved at all contributed to legitimizing nationalism as a communal, collective, unifying ideology. For another, no movement can endure without the sustenance of daily, mundane "support" activities. The provision of necessities such as food, medicine, and funds; and, on another level, the dissemination and use of information for intelligence and propaganda purposes, are not secondary. History's gendered focus on the "main" struggle—armed battles and rebellions, confrontations between nationalist leaders and colonial powers, diplomatic and political maneuverings—obscures the urgent necessity of the work that takes place in what is perceived as the margins. It is perhaps only because the "marginal" work is performed by women that it is considered the footnote to the nationalist narrative rather than constituting the "real" work in and of itself. A history that expands the central narrative to incorporate the margins and that recasts these limited concepts would allow us to more fully recognize the complete contours of the nationalist narrative in all its richness and complexity.

This complexity would include the mixed legacy that nationalism has left to women. Nationalism was, in many cases, the midwife for feminism in the Middle East, although, as Beth Baron wryly notes, "women have served nationalism, but nationalism, in some respects, has failed women."[127] Deniz Kandiyoti notes the "persistent tensions" between different trends within nationalism: a "modernist" trend, which favored an emancipatory role for women, extending the promise of "rights" and equality, and an "organicist" trend, which concerned itself with "the dilution and contamination of cultural values and identity in a post-colonial context."[128] The problem for nationalist women was that they attempted to harness conservative forms of nationalism—performing their nationalist activities within the culturally prescribed confines of the "organicist" trend—to serve the modernist brand of nationalism. Women were unable to resolve these tensions and ended up, in effect, serving two masters at once.

Women participated enthusiastically in nationalist movements, believing that the culmination of national goals—the achievement of the sovereign nation-state—would inextricably lead to their emancipation as citizens within this newly constituted political entity. A Palestinian activist gives a telling explanation for why the women's movement in Palestine was not as involved in pushing for reforms enhancing women's status as movements in Egypt and Turkey: "Such measures of reform [as women's rights] can only be introduced by National Government, or by persons deriving their authority from the people."[129] Thus, Palestinian women, along with their sisters in the region, explicitly linked their future achievement of rights to a national government that they, perhaps naively, equated with "the people." This concept of "rights" was embedded within and inextricably interwoven with a legalistic notion of citizenship that could only be conferred by a national government; it did not address internal structures and sources of inequities in society. What national feminists did not take into account was the fact that, historically, the mere establishment of a sovereign state did not automatically bestow "rights" on women, that disenfranchised groups had to fight for these rights. Egyptian women learned this almost immediately after the establishment of the Wafd government in 1924, when their efforts on its behalf did not translate into enfranchisement or representation within the new government. "No nationalism in the world has granted women and men the same privileged access to the resources of the nation-state."[130] The faith of women's movements in the benevolence of the nation-state as a "possible resource for more progressive gender politics" was to prove misplaced, as those women who experienced national sovereignty were to discover.[131]

Stage Three: State Feminism

Turkey and Iran, unlike the Mashriq and Egypt, became sovereign states after World War I. After Turkey's war of independence resulted in the establishment of a republic, Atatürk effected dramatic transformations in all domains of Turkish society: political, cultural, religious, economic, and social. One of the first of numerous laws enacted by the new republic was the abolition of the Islamic caliphate. In 1926 the family code was secularized, revised, and modified, using the Swiss civil code as its model. Women were enfranchised, after repeated demands from feminist groups, through a gradual process beginning at the municipal level in 1930 and ultimately resulting in equal enfranchisement with men on the national level in 1935. Polygamy was outlawed, Islamic dress and veiling were actively discouraged by the state, and women were encouraged to enter the workforce and public life.

The woman question, it has been suggested, was a "pawn" in Atatürk's struggle to establish a "republican notion of citizenship" through the modernization, secularization, and westernization of Turkish society.[132] Although Atatürk made the issue of women central to these efforts, his goal was not to transform and equalize gender relations so much as to make a complete break with the Ottoman past in order to "catapult Turkey to the 'level of contemporary civilizations' (i.e., Western economies and societies)."[133] Despite the fact that women gained important rights in the changes in family law enacted in the 1926 civil code—such as the rights to initiate divorce and inherit equally with men—they are not equal under the law. Wives remain under patriarchal control in marriage, since only men can have legal status as the head of the household. A woman must request permission from her husband to work outside the home; she must take her husband's name and follow her husband to a new domicile, since only the husband has the right to determine where the couple lives.[134]

In Iran, a military officer, Reza Khan, took control of the government in a military coup in 1921; events here followed a different yet, in some respects, parallel trajectory. Reza Khan was an admirer of Mustafa Kemal and watched his state-building venture closely.[135] Both politicians embraced the notion of establishing strong, centralized states with authority concentrated at the top; in Turkey, it was the ruling People's Party, controlled by Atatürk, that monopolized power. In Iran, Reza Khan directly consolidated power as the autocratic head of state. In 1925 he became shah, establishing the Pahlavi dynasty; he quickly moved to repress any left-wing political currents. The Bolshevik revolution in neighboring Russia in 1917, the proletarianization of urban society, and the rise of a labor movement had all contributed to creating a "radical political atmosphere . . . which resulted in an upsurge of feminism, socialism and communism."[136] Reza Shah banned political parties in 1931, stripped the Parliament of power, censored the press, and exiled, imprisoned, or executed leaders of the liberal opposition and leftist parties. The women's movement was not exempt. The offices of the Patriotic Women's League were destroyed by a mob while the police looked on; the leaders of a pro-communist women's organization, the Messenger of Women's Prosperity, were imprisoned and the organization banned.[137]

In both Turkey and Iran, during the process of consolidating the centralized state, the regimes reined in and controlled the women's movements. In Turkey, the new republican state both "circumscribed and defined [the] parameters" of the feminist movement, stifling and discouraging its independence, as the case of the Women's People Party demonstrates. Formed in 1923, this party aimed to modify "'the consciousness, the negligence, the grave situation' that had made womanhood the lowest class of society in all previous periods."[138] Its first major project, an educational congress, was quickly co-opted by the Ministry of Education, which instead held its own conference on the same topic, forcing the party to cancel its effort. Not long after the party's establishment, the government refused permission for it to incorporate on the grounds that women were not yet enfranchised, suggesting that it instead reconstitute itself as an association. The subsequent Turkish Women's League worked on social welfare and suffrage issues. In 1935, two weeks after Istanbul hosted the Twelfth Congress of the International Federation of Women, the government ordered the league to disband. The president of the organization rationalized its closure and the dispersal of its assets by stating that, since its goals (enfranchisement and "complete equality") had been fulfilled, it had served its purpose, and "there was no further justification for its continued existence."[139]

In Iran, the state had a similar program for modernization, secularization, and westernization, but, unlike in Turkey, where part of the state-building project entailed the development of representative institutions that held out the promise of democracy, power in Tehran was firmly controlled by the executive. Reza Shah moved more coercively to force social and economic change, and to control the women's movement. After closing down and banning the independent women's organizations, the shah established a state-sponsored women's association, the Ladies Center, in 1935, under the honorary presidency of one of his daughters. The center's goals were to prop up and reinforce domestic gender roles by educating women in child rearing and housekeeping on a "scientific basis." It held lectures on subjects such as unveiling, women's chastity and virtue, and health issues. One of the main objectives of the founding of the association was to lay the groundwork for women's unveiling, which became compulsory by decree in 1936.[140]

Although the independent women's movement in Iran was virtually obliterated, some of its leaders participated in the Ladies Center. Parvin Paidar's explanation for their co-optation (my word) is that the state-supported association provided them with both financial and personal security (they no longer had to deal with "fanatics"), and legitimacy. Afsaneh Najmabadi warns against considering these women (or Turkish women, for that matter) as "pawns in men's games," however; "these women had their own agendas as well."[141] Many of the shah's policies, such as integrating women into society through increased education and employment, were popular among certain limited segments of the population. His repressive measures against the opposition were also effective in limiting resistance.[142]

The 1931 Iranian civil code, however, left women's legal inequality virtually intact in almost every sphere. Women were not enfranchised, and the one hundred articles that were devoted to the family corresponded almost exactly to previous Islamic law as it had generally been practiced in Iran. Divorce remained the sole prerogative of men, women inherited unequally to men, and polygamy remained legal. Indeed, under the article on *sigheh* marriage, a Shi'i practice, men had the right to marry an unlimited number of women for periods of as short as one hour. "The project followed by Reza Shah . . . was to bring modernity to Iran through the establishment of Iranian 'culture' rather than Islam. Within this project, the familial position of women as advocated in the Iranian 'culture' and 'Islam' happened to be more or less the same."[143]

Women were at the heart of the building of the "modern" nation-state in both Turkey and Iran, particularly during the late 1920s and 1930s. Women's participation in nationalist movements had earned them the prerogative to articulate demands for the rights due them as citizens and members of a national collectivity. But one of the major problems in translating their participation into the achievement of rights was that "women's rights" were not conceived of as "part of the problematic of civil liberties and individual rights," but rather were "formulated within the framework of policies that aim[ed] to serve the 'social good.'"[144] Women themselves rejected notions of "individualistic interpretations of feminism,"[145] stressing the socially redeeming potential of their liberation in order to enable them to "serve the nation." Furthermore, "since the new social order was not based on the individual, defined as male, women seemed part of the collectivity rather than needing to enter it through the principle of individual rights."[146]

In Turkey, scholars postulate that the state's granting women rights without their having to fight for them during the state-building era weakened the women's movement, making it acquiescent and passive.[147] "Feminism" became synonymous with "Kemalism," resulting in dependence upon the state and the development of a "pattern of special interaction between the state and women."[148] The state made decisions from above and discouraged grassroots participation in the decisionmaking process. Women "internalized the patriarchal system to the extent that going beyond its laws was unthinkable." This is cogently summed up by Nakiye Elgün, who said in 1927, when women's enfranchisement was being discussed in the press: "Why don't we nominate women candidates? Because the law does not permit it. Therefore it is not our time yet. Our government has granted us every right our women deserve, in fact more than deserved."[149]

In both Turkey and Iran, the symbolic value of women's emancipation was more important than the substance, since suffrage and/or women's increased social participation and public visibility bolstered the external image of these states as "modern" nations.[150] Both Turkey's and Iran's membership in the "international society of states" was "fragile," and "full acceptance by the other members as a true equal . . . rated very high on the agenda of nationalists."[151] Thus, seemingly trivial issues such as women's dress, for example, became highly charged and imbued with meaning. Women in the "modern" nation-states of Iran and Turkey had to "look like the civilized women of the world," namely European women, in order for these states to be accepted in this international society of states.[152]

Mervat Hatem makes the point that state feminism was a "mixed blessing" in that although women benefited from the "state's support of women's rights . . . [the state] made gender a political tool used to satisfy state interests," thus undermining women's autonomy.[153] Although independent states were not established in the rest of the Middle East until the 1940s, some form of state feminism would appear in the Arab nationalist regimes that arose in the 1950s and 1960s. Nilüfer Çağatay and Yasemin Nuhoğlu-Soysal observe that women's movements could not develop autonomously because the ideologically heterogeneous nationalist regimes in the Middle East shared at least one "common trait": a "need to monopolize political power in their effort to mobilize the masses" and to suppress all "autonomous movements once a movement [had] acquired state power."[154]

State feminism undermined women's ability to develop a broad-based feminism that incorporated the interests of women from the lower classes, and particularly women in the rural areas, where the social engineering of the state did not take root. Sirin Tekeli notes that the few women who benefited from "rights"—educated, professional elites—"experienced the excitement of being pioneers ... so passionately that they could not realize that their own position did not reflect the real conditions of most Turkish women. And so they were led into a tragic 'schizophrenic' illusion: the new identity of these women was not one that they had selected themselves, but an ascribed one. And the ascriber was the state."[155] When the state decreed or forced supposedly emancipatory social change on the population, feminism was discredited because of its association with autocratic, westernizing regimes. And feminism was perceived as a culturally "unauthentic," imported, alienating Western ideology with little relevance to the women of the Middle East. Such associations severely limited feminist agendas and diluted their influence on, and effects in the lives of, the majority of women, making their task more difficult.

Conclusion

Although much of the focus above has been on highlighting the unity and analogousness of women's movements in the Middle East, it is important to recognize their heterogeneity and individual characters. Obviously, the specific historical contexts within which each movement operated are crucial. The Palestinian women's movement, for example, has the dubious distinction among those studied here of still being engaged in the struggle for national sovereignty (at the time of this writing). This fact, and the intractability of the Palestinian struggle, has left the troublesome relationship between feminism and nationalism intact and, often, not closely challenged, leaving a distinctive imprint on the Palestinian women's movement.[156]

Other factors that affected the individual character of each of these women's movements were the complex and variegated male responses to women's pushing the boundaries of proscribed female behavior. Paradoxically, the Iranian women's movement was among the most radical and militant at its inception during the constitutional crisis, yet Iranian women lived under some of the most oppressive restrictions in the region at the time, and male responses to their mobilization were often quite severe.[157] Nonetheless, Iranian women did not hesitate to become involved in violent confrontations. In other countries, such as Turkey and Palestine, men sometimes encouraged and even chastised women to get involved in politics.[158] Women often calibrated their organizing styles in response to men's reactions. But it is safe to generalize that male responses tended to be at least ambiguous and, in some circumstances, strongly opposed to women's increased public participation in political movements. As long as women remained segregated within women's organizations and focused their endeavors on social welfare and support activities oriented toward uplifting the nation, men gave cautious nods of approval to their involvement.

The organizing styles of the movements differed; in Iran, strong, autonomous regional women's associations developed in places like Tabriz and Isfahan as well as in Tehran, whereas in Egypt, the movement was more centralized, limited primarily to a few urban areas, Cairo in particular. This was also the case in Turkey and the Mashriq, where, although local women's organizations formed in the smaller towns and cities, a central association usually dominated the national matrix. This sometimes created a certain amount of tension within the individual movements.[159] The issue of unity within the national frameworks of the movements has not been closely examined in the Arab contexts;[160] in Turkey and Iran, on the other hand, writers have pointed to how competition and divisiveness within the women's movements led to a lack of centralization, coordination, and planning, ultimately weakening them.[161]

Despite the individual characters of the movements, however, one is struck by the common, identifiable patterns in their issues, organizing tactics, and ideological expressions, as well as their strong sense of cultural and regional identity and shared concerns. Women articulated this unity when they wrote for publications or assembled at women's conferences, as illustrated by the following statement delivered at the 1944 Cairo Arab Women's Conference by a Christian Arab woman, who began her speech by saying: "I'm the daughter of one nation, one language, one upbringing, one set of customs, one system of mores and one set of goals."[162]

This unity was not limited to Arab women. The first two Eastern Women's Conferences, held in Damascus and Baghdad in 1932, were attended by women from Iran and Afghanistan. The third Eastern Women's Conference, held in Tehran, reaffirmed support for the resolutions drawn up at the earlier meetings (mostly proposals for reforms in women's legal status), and added its own: (limited) female enfranchisement, the retention of "sound morals" by Eastern women, the avoidance of "evil Western customs and morals," and vocational training for repentant prostitutes.[163] The Tehran conference was "the last semi-independent activity" undertaken by Iranian women before the state hijacked the women's movement by establishing the Ladies Center.[164]

During the 1940s, the paths of the various women's movements in the Middle East diverged more distinctly, continuing a process that had already begun in the 1920s and 1930s, particularly in Turkey and Iran. Different political situations inevitably affected the movements. A pan-Arab trend developed among the Arab countries, as manifested in the women's conferences held in Cairo in 1938 and 1944.[165] Most of the Arab states became independent, subsequently turning toward their own state-building projects. State feminism ultimately became the predominant model in many of these newly independent states, and was solidified in Turkey and Iran.

One question that arises about the history of the women's movements concerns the legacy they left to subsequent generations. How important is this history? Can women learn from it? What is the role of history in relation to current politics? History is not simply something that happened to other people, something we can objectify and look at from a distance. It is something continuously unfolding—something to which we look for the origins of ourselves, our societies, our politics and culture. "The only past we can know is one we shape by the questions we ask; yet these very questions are also shaped by the context we come from, and our context includes the past."[166] It is a cliché that, without learning from history, we are condemned to repeat the mistakes of the past. A critical examination of the history of the women's movements should not be a condemnatory or congratulatory exercise, however, but rather part of a project to expand the contours of Middle East history by asking the unasked questions.

Notes

I would like to thank Afsaneh Najmabadi, Elizabeth Thompson, and Chris Toensing for their comments on earlier drafts of this essay; Lisa Pollard for support and advice; and Camron Amin and Afsaneh Najmabadi for helpful linguistic and other information. I take responsibility for conclusions drawn and any mistakes made.

1. Leila Ahmed, "Between Two Worlds: The Formation of a Turn-of-the-Century Egyptian Feminist," in *Life/Lines: Theorizing Women's Autobiography,* ed. Bella Brodzki and Celeste Schenck (Ithaca: Cornell University Press, 1988), 156.

2. In the interests of feasibility and scope, this essay will primarily be limited to literature in English and restricted to the Mashriq (the Arab East), Egypt, Turkey, and Iran; there is, unfortunately, very little literature on women's movements in North Africa during this period.

3. Marnia Lazreg, *The Eloquence of Silence: Algerian Women in Question* (New York and London: Routledge, 1994), 7.

4. See, e.g., Chandra Talpade Mohanty, "Cartographies of Struggle: Third World Women and the Politics of Feminism," in *Third World Women and the Politics of Feminism,* ed. Chandra Talpade Mohanty, Ann Russo, and Lourdes Torres (Bloomington: Indiana University Press, 1991); Chela Sandoval, "U.S. Third World Feminism: The Theory and Method of Oppositional Consciousness in the Postmodern World," *Genders* 10 (Spring 1991): 1–24; and Anne McClintock, "'No Longer in a Future Heaven': Women and Nationalism in South Africa," *Transition* 51 (1991): 104–123.

5. Mohanty, "Cartographies," 13.

6. Ibid., 6.

7. Janet Afary, *The Iranian Constitutional Revolution, 1906–1911: Grassroots Democracy, Social Democracy, and the Origins of Feminism* (New York: Columbia University Press, 1996), 10.

8. Marnia Lazreg, "Feminism and Difference: The Perils of Writing As a Woman on Women in Algeria," *Feminist Studies* 14 (Spring 1988): 101.

9. Sharon Sievers, "Six (or More) Feminists in Search of a Historian," in *Expanding the Boundaries of History: Essays on Women in the Third World,* ed. Cheryl Johnson-Odim and Margaret Strobel (Bloomington: Indiana University Press, 1992), 326.

10. Margot Badran, *Feminists, Islam, and Nation: Gender and the Making of Modern Egypt* (Princeton: Princeton University Press, 1995), 19–20.

11. Ibid., 19.

12. For this reason, I have deliberately used the phrase "women's movements" in the title of this essay. I have chosen to respect women's ambiguity, or historically different concepts about their own activism, despite the fact that *I* would consider their acts as feminist. Although it may seem both contradictory and a fine distinction, I believe there is a difference between women's own conception of their experiences and how we historians retrospectively categorize and name them. We should be explicit and self-conscious about this difference.

Furthermore, neither Arabic nor Persian have a specific word for "feminist" or "feminism," making the issues of language, meaning, and intent even more problematic.

13. Guida West and Rhoda Lois Blumberg, "Reconstructing Social Protest from a Feminist Perspective," in *Women and Social Protest,* ed. Guida West and Rhoda Lois Blumberg (Oxford: Oxford University Press, 1990), 15.

14. This theme has been continually reiterated by Palestinian women throughout history. See my "The Nation and Its 'New' Women: Feminism, Nationalism, Colonialism, and the Palestinian Women's Movement, 1920–1948," Ph.D. dissertation, Georgetown University, 1996.

15. Huda Sha'rawi, *Mudhakkirat ra'idat al-'Arabiyya al-haditha* [Memoirs of a modern Arab woman pioneer], introduced by Amina al-Sa'id (Cairo: Dar al-Hilal, 1981), 322, quoted in Badran, *Feminists,* 88.

16. Ruth Woodsmall, *Moslem Women Enter a New World* (New York: Round Table Press, 1936), 363.

17. This is not to say that all women in this historical period did not have or develop feminist "consciousness." Clearly such women existed, as has been amply documented by scholars such as Badran and Parvin Paidar, in *Women and the Political Process in Twentieth-Century Iran* (Cambridge: Cambridge University Press, 1995). On the other hand, the threat to national identity and even survival was so overwhelming an issue in some cases, such as the Palestinians', that feminist consciousness was much more muted and not as overtly articulated as in, say, the Egyptian women's movement.

18. Sandoval, "U.S. Third World Feminism," 15.

19. Mohanty, "Cartographies," 38.

20. For more on the contradictory, conflicting, and contentious interests *within* colonialist structures of power, see Ann Laura Stoler, "Rethinking Colonial

Categories: European Communities and the Boundaries of Rule," *Comparative Studies in Society and History* 31 (1989): 134–161.

21. It should be noted that some women's movements failed to creatively adapt, undermining their effectiveness. This was the case with the Palestinian women's movement during the 1940s, when it was unable to develop a broader base beyond its narrow middle- and upper-class constituency. See Fleischmann, "The Nation and Its 'New' Women," 348–349.

22. For example, Julie Peteet, *Gender in Crisis: Women and the Palestinian Resistance Movement* (New York: Columbia University Press, 1991); Sondra Hale, *Gender Politics in Sudan: Feminism, Socialism, and the State* (Boulder: Westview Press, 1996); Haideh Moghissi, *Populism and Feminism in Iran: Women's Struggle in a Male-Defined Revolutionary Movement* (London: St. Martin's Press, 1994); Guity Nashat, ed., *Women and Revolution in Iran* (Boulder: Westview Press, 1983); Nermin Abadan-Unat, ed., *Women in Turkish Society* (Leiden: E. J. Brill, 1981); and Sirin Tekeli, ed., *Women in Modern Turkish Society: A Reader* (London: Zed Press, 1995).

23. (I refer, of course, to Western-language researchers. But this is also true to a great extent of Arabic-language scholarship. Scholarship in Turkish and Persian may suffer less from a similar lacuna.) To date, there are few monographs devoted to the history of women's political and social activism. Some exceptions include Badran, *Feminists,* and Paidar, *Women and the Political Process.* Where such coverage does exist, it is usually in the form of a chapter or passing reference in a book, article, or anthology devoted to contemporary women's movements. See, for example, Leila Ahmed, "Feminism and Feminist Movements in the Middle East, a Preliminary Exploration: Turkey, Egypt, Algeria," *Feminist Studies International Forum* 5, no. 2 (1982): 153–168, and her "Early Feminist Movements in the Middle East: Turkey and Egypt," in *Muslim Women,* ed. Freda Hussain (New York: St. Martin's Press, 1984); Nashat, *Women and Revolution in Iran;* Abadan-Unat, *Women in Turkish Society;* and Deniz Kandiyoti, ed., *Women, Islam, and the State* (Philadelphia: Temple University Press, 1991). Kumari Jayawardena's valuable book *Feminism and Nationalism in the Third World* (London: Zed Press, 1986) has chapters devoted to the Turkish, Egyptian, and Iranian women's movements.

24. See, e.g., Margot Badran's: *Feminists;* "Dual Liberation: Feminism and Nationalism in Egypt, 1870s–1925," *Feminist Issues* 8, no. 1 (1988): 15–34; "Competing Agenda: Feminists, Islam, and the State in Nineteenth and Twentieth Century Egypt," in *Women, Islam, and the State,* ed. Deniz Kandiyoti (Philadelphia: Temple University Press, 1991); "Independent Women: More Than a Century of Feminism in Egypt," in *Arab Women: Old Boundaries, New Frontiers,* ed. Judith E. Tucker (Bloomington: Indiana University Press, 1993); and "From Consciousness to Activism: Feminist Politics in Early Twentieth Century Egypt," in *Problems of the Middle East in Historical Perspective,* ed. John Spagnolo (London: Ithaca Press, 1992). See also Mervat Hatem, "Egyptian Upper- and Middle-Class Women's Early Nationalist Discourses on National Liberation and Peace in Palestine (1922–1944)," *Women and Politics* 9, no. 3 (1989): 49–70; Selma Botman, "The Experience of Women in the Egyptian Communist Movement, 1939–1954," *Women's International Forum* 2, no. 5 (1988): 117–126; Thomas Philipp, "Feminism and Nationalist Politics in Egypt," and Afaf Lutfi al-Sayyid

Marsot, "The Revolutionary Gentlewomen in Egypt," both in *Women in the Muslim World,* ed. Lois Beck and Nikki Keddie (Cambridge: Harvard University Press, 1978); and Beth Baron, "Mothers, Morality, and Nationalism in Pre-1919 Egypt," in *The Origins of Arab Nationalism,* ed. Rashid Khalidi et al. (New York: Columbia University Press, 1991).

25. See, e.g., Paidar, *Women and the Political Process;* Afary, *Iranian Constitutional Revolution;* and Afsaneh Najmabadi, "*Zanhā-yi millat:* Women or Wives of the Nation?" *Iranian Studies* 26, nos. 1-2 (1993): 51–72. Some earlier writings include: Janet Afary, "On the Origins of Feminism in Early Twentieth-Century Iran," *Journal of Women's History* 1, no. 2 (Fall 1989): 65–87; Eliz Sanasarian, *The Women's Rights Movement in Iran: Mutiny, Appeasement, and Repression, from 1900 to Khomeini* (New York: Praeger, 1982); Simin Royanian, "A History of Iranian Women's Struggles," *RIPEH* 3, no. 1 (Spring 1979): 17–29; and Mangol Bayat-Philipp, "Women and Revolution in Iran, 1905–1911," in *Women in the Muslim World,* ed. Lois Beck and Nikki Keddie (Cambridge: Harvard University Press, 1978).

26. On Palestine there is a burgeoning body of literature on women's participation in the resistance movement of the 1960s–1970s and, later, the *intifada,* that sometimes includes glancing references to the past. A partial list includes: Peteet, *Gender in Crisis;* Orayb Najjar with Kitty Warnock, *Portraits of Palestinian Women* (Salt Lake City: University of Utah Press, 1992); Soraya Antonius, "Fighting on Two Fronts: Conversations with Palestinian Women," *Journal of Palestine Studies* 8 (1979): 26–45; Rita Giacaman and Muna Odeh, "Palestinian Women's Movement," in *Women of the Arab World,* ed. Nahid Toubia (London: Zed Press, 1988); Nuha Abu Daleb, "Palestinian Women and Their Role in the Revolution," *Peuples mediterranéens* 5 (1978): 35–47; Hamida Kazi, "Palestinian Women and the National Liberation Movement: A Social Perspective," in *Women in the Middle East,* ed. the Khamsin Collective (London: Zed Press, 1987); and Islah Jad, "From Salons to Popular Committees: Palestinian Women, 1919–1989," in *Intifada: Palestine at the Crossroads,* ed. Jamal R. Nassar and Roger Heacock (Birzeit and New York: Birzeit University Press and Praeger, 1991). To my knowledge, the only work that focuses on pre-1948 women's activity is my own writing, which includes "Jerusalem Women's Organizations During the British Mandate, 1920s–1930s," Jerusalem: Palestinian Academic Society for the Study of International Affairs, 1995; and "The Nation and Its 'New' Women."

The only work in English that deals with the Lebanese and Syrian women's movements is Elizabeth Thompson's "Engendering the Nation: Statebuilding, Imperialism, and Women in Syria and Lebanon, 1920–1945," Ph.D. dissertation, Columbia University, 1995. (Works in Arabic exist, but are also limited.)

There is hardly anything written in English or Arabic on the Iraqi women's movement. One of the few examples is Doreen Ingrams's *The Awakened: Women in Iraq* (London: Third World Center, 1985).

27. Berenice Carroll, introduction to *Liberating Women's History,* ed. Berenice Carroll (Urbana: University of Illinois Press, 1976), ix; and Joan Wallach Scott, *Gender and the Politics of History* (New York: Columbia University Press, 1988), 17.

28. Space does not permit me to discuss in depth the myriad problems facing researchers, both indigenous and foreign, in the Middle East. All who have engaged

in historical research in the region are familiar with the litany of difficulties: The inability to gain access to archival or other materials; travel restrictions to many places; and the dispersal, disappearance, or lack of documentation are just a few. These types of problems are compounded when one researches women, who often did not leave, or are not present in, written records.

29. This equation was illustrated for me when I was doing research on the Palestinian women's movement during the British Mandate period. During an interview with the president of the Arab Women's Association, I asked her: "Did this group do nationalist work as well as social work?" She responded: "National work—what do you mean? In politics, you mean." Samah Nusseibeh, interview by author, Jerusalem, November 23, 1993.

30. Thus, contemporary Palestinian women activists have tended to share these assumptions about the dichotomy between "social work" and "politics." These notions place "feminism" within the social rather than political realm. In 1994, for example, Maryam Zaqout, a Palestinian feminist in Gaza, commented that Palestinian women have "concentrated on the political struggle and not on women's issues" because they defined their main concern as the "occupation, not social problems. That was a mistake. . . . We've realized that social and political freedom are one—they go together." Joel Greenberg, "Women in Gaza See Gains," *New York Times,* July 17, 1994.

31. Fatma Muge Gocek and Shiva Balaghi, "Reconstructing Gender in the Middle East Through Voice and Experience," in *Reconstructing Gender in the Middle East: Tradition, Identity, and Power,* ed. Fatma Muge Gocek and Shiva Balaghi (New York: Columbia University Press, 1994), 12.

32. A limited list of such historical writing includes: Judith E. Tucker, *Women in Nineteenth-Century Egypt* (Cambridge: Cambridge University Press, 1985); Nikki Keddie and Beth Baron, eds., *Women in Middle Eastern History* (New Haven: Yale University Press, 1992); Leila Ahmed, *Women and Gender in Islam: Historical Roots of a Modern Debate* (New Haven and London: Yale University Press, 1992); Leslie Peirce, *The Imperial Harem: Women and Sovereignty in the Ottoman Empire* (New York: Oxford University Press, 1993); Beth Baron, *The Women's Awakening in Egypt: Culture, Society, and the Press* (New Haven: Yale University Press, 1994); Lazreg, *Eloquence of Silence;* Denise Spellberg, *Politics, Gender, and the Islamic Past: The Legacy of 'A'isha bint Abi Bakr* (New York: Columbia University Press, 1994); Amira E. Sonbol, ed., *Women, the Family, and Divorce Laws in Islamic History* (Syracuse, N.Y.: Syracuse University Press, 1996); and Judith E. Tucker, *In the House of the Law: Gender and Islamic Law in Ottoman Syria and Palestine* (Berkeley: University of California Press, 1998).

33. An interesting indication of this trend is the recent increase in academic job listings that are categorized as "Islamic Studies" rather than within a particular discipline.

34. Lazreg, *Eloquence of Silence,* 14 (emphasis in original).

35. Palestinian women, for example, often refer to Algerian women's experience—loss of the status gained during the war of liberation—as a warning to themselves. See Nahla Abdo, "Nationalism and Feminism: Palestinian Women and the Intifada—No Going Back?" in *Gender and National Identity: Women and Politics*

in Muslim Societies, ed. Valentine Moghadam (London: Zed Press; Karachi: Oxford University Press, 1994), 148.

36. For a slightly different "historical typology" of Arab (not Middle Eastern) feminism, see Margot Badran, "Feminism As a Force in the Arab World," in *Contemporary Arab Thought and Women* (Cairo: Arab Women's Solidarity Association, 1990), 56.

37. The phrase that was widely used in Arabic was *al-nahda al-nisā'iyya.* (*Nahda* can also be translated as "resurgence," "revival," or "renaissance," but "awakening" has been the most commonly rendered translation.) "Awakening" was also used in the Turkish and Iranian contexts. See, e.g., Badr ol-Moluk Bamdad, *From Darkness into Light: Women's Emancipation in Iran,* ed. and trans. F. R. C. Bagley (Hicksville, N.Y.: Exposition Press, 1977); and Sanasarian, *Women's Rights Movement,* 33. More research needs to be done to more accurately trace the historical etymology of use of the term.

38. E.g., the Ladies Awakening *(nahdat al-sayyidāt)* in Beirut (no date); the Women's Revival *(al-nahda al-nisā'iyya,* founded in 1924 by Ibtihaj Qaddura and Julia Dimashqiyya), also in Beirut; the Society for the Women's Awakening (jam'iyyat al-nahda al-nisā'iyya, f. 1916) in Cairo; the Women's Awakening Club in Iraq (f. 1923); and Women's Awakening *(nahzat nisvan)* in Iran (originally the Association of Revolutionary Women, changed to the Women's Awakening by order of the Shah c. 1927). The state feminism project initiated by the Pahlavi regime in Iran in the 1930s was also called the Women's Awakening. Baron, *Women's Awakening,* 20; Thompson, "Engendering the Nation," 91; Badran, *Feminists,* 55; Ingrams, *The Awakened,* 92; Sanasarian, *Women's Rights Movement,* 36–37; and Camron Amin, personal correspondence, May 26, 1997.

39. Baron, *Women's Awakening,* 2.

40. This is Lisa Pollard's cogent observation. Personal communication, March 1, 1997.

41. It is interesting to note, however, that the word continues to resonate today, as indicated by its recurrence in the contemporary Iranian women's press, for example. See Afsaneh Najmabadi, "Feminism in an Islamic Republic: 'Years of Hardship, Years of Growth,'" in *Islam, Gender, and Social Change,* ed. Yvonne Yazbeck Haddad and John L. Esposito (Oxford: Oxford University Press, 1998), 71–72.

42. During the Mandate period in Palestine, for example, the press frequently referred to women's organized activity as a "movement" *(haraka).* See, e.g., the Palestinian newspapers *Filastīn, Sirāt al-Mustaqīm, al-Difā'* in the years 1927–1948 for frequent use of the word "movement." As with "awakening," more research needs to be done on the historical uses of the word.

43. *Webster's Ninth New Collegiate Dictionary* (Springfield, Mass.: Merriam-Webster, 1988), 776; and *The American Heritage Dictionary of the English Language,* 3rd ed. (Boston: Houghton Mifflin, 1992), 1182.

44. Mary Fainsod Katzenstein and Carol McClurg Mueller, *The Women's Movements of the United States and Western Europe* (Philadelphia: Temple University Press, 1987), 5, quoted in Diana Rothbard Margolis, "Women's Movements Around the World," *Gender and Society* 7, no. 3 (September 1993): 379.

45. Myra Marx Ferree, "Equality and Autonomy: Feminist Politics in the United States and West Germany," in *The Women's Movements of the United States and Western Europe,* ed. Mary Fainsod Katzenstein and Carol McClurg Mueller (Philadelphia: Temple University Press, 1987), 173, quoted in Margolis, "Women's Movements," 379.

46. For example, starting in the 1920s, the Palestinian newspaper *Filastīn* began to publish articles on Turkish women and their "awakening," the women's "awakening" as articulated in the Egyptian and Lebanese women's press, and the women's "awakening" in Iran. *Filastīn,* "Ladies Magazine," December 17, 1921; "The Turkish Woman," August 1, 1924; "Turkish Ladies in the New Civil Law," November 9, 1926; "Woman's Rights and Her Duties," March 4, 1927; "Women's Awakening in Turkey," April 5, 1930; "The Women's Awakening and Unveiling [in Iran]," May 27, 1932; and "The Women's Awakening in Egypt," June 5, 1932. The Egyptian Feminist Union published articles on other women's movements in its house organ, *L'Égyptienne* (see, e.g., "Lettre de Palestine," November 1932; and "Le progrès de la femme palestinienne," August 1932). Sanasarian notes that "an interesting feature of feminist periodicals in Iran were translations and articles about the status of women in other countries" *(Women's Rights Movement,* 38). Coverage and support of women's rights was not limited to the women's press in Iran; proconstitutionalist periodicals also "wrote about the accomplishments of women in other nations of the East such as Japan, China, India, Turkey, and Egypt." Afary, *Iranian Constitutional Revolution,* 200.

47. Ahmed, *Women and Gender,* 162–163. As Margot Badran points out, due to history's reliance on "conventional questions, methods and sources," the history of feminism in Egypt (and one can safely extrapolate this to include the Middle East) has been "largely the history of men's feminism written within the framework of men's history." Margot Badran, "The Origins of Feminism in Egypt," in *Current Issues in Women's History,* ed. Arina Angerman, Geerte Binnema, Annemieke Keunen, Vefie Poels, and Jacqueline Zirkzee (London and New York: Routledge, 1989), 154.

48. Hanna' Kawrani, a Syrian Christian, took a position against, while Zaynab Fawwaz, a Muslim, published an article in support in the *Newspaper of the Nile.* Badran, *Feminists,* 15.

49. Deniz Kandiyoti, "End of Empire: Islam, Nationalism, and Women in Turkey," in *Women, Islam, and the State,* ed. Deniz Kandiyoti (Philadelphia: Temple University Press, 1991), 26–27; and Elizabeth Brown Frierson, "Unimagined Communities: State, Press, and Gender in the Hamidian Era," Ph.D. dissertation, Princeton University, 1996, 76.

50. Paidar, *Women and the Political Process,* 27.

51. Ibid., 98. Taqizadeh edited the pro–Revival Party newspaper, *Kaveh,* in which he "praised the efforts of the Islamic reformers such as Qasim Amin to change the 'pathetic position of Muslim women.'" Ibid. Iran, according to Paidar, did not experience Islamic reformism similar to that in Egypt, where attempts were made to "bring Islamic theory into line with modern social relations while maintaining its authority as a religious system"; instead, reformist movements typically involved either pre-Islamic or antiestablishment Islamic concepts, since Islam was conceived of

as an "imported" religion. But the influences from other Islamist movements affected Iran. Ibid., 45.

52. See Ahmed, *Women and Gender,* 155–165. Amin's influence and arguments continued to resonate in the Middle East long after the publication of his books. (He published a second book, *The New Woman,* in 1900.) Palestinian intellectuals, for example, were still citing him in debates on the "woman question" in the Palestinian press during the 1920s. See Fleischmann, "The Nation and Its 'New' Women," esp. chap. 3.

53. Kandiyoti, "End of Empire," 26.

54. Ingrams, *The Awakened,* 81.

55. Kandiyoti, "End of Empire," 26.

56. Deniz Kandiyoti, "Slave Girls, Temptresses, and Comrades: Images of Women in the Turkish Novel," *Feminist Issues* 8, no. 1 (1988): 35.

57. Thomas Philipp, "Women in the Historical Perspective of an Early Arab Modernist (Gurgi Zaidan)," *Die Welt des Islams* 18, nos. 1-2 (1977): 66.

58. Deniz Kandiyoti, "Identity and Its Discontents: Women and the Nation," *Millennium* 20, no. 3 (1991): 431, quoting Sami Zubaida, "Islam, Cultural Nationalism and the Left," *Review of Middle East Studies,* no. 4 (1988): 7.

59. Qasim Amin, *The Liberation of Women,* trans. Samiha Sidhom Peterson (Cairo: American University in Cairo Press, 1982), 6.

60. Ibid., 12, 26.

61. Jayawardena, *Feminism and Nationalism,* 12.

62. Paidar, *Women and the Political Process,* 48–49.

63. Nükhet Sirman, "Feminism in Turkey: A Short History," *New Perspectives on Turkey* 3, no. 1 (Fall 1989): 5; and Baron, *Women's Awakening,* 59–60.

64. The discussion of the women's press that follows is necessarily sketchy and general, since much more research on the evolution of the various women's publications remains to be done.

65. Frierson, "Unimagined Communities," 71; Afary, "On the Origins," 70; and Thompson, "Engendering the Nation," 285–286.

66. Beth Baron, "Readers and the Women's Press in Egypt," *Poetics Today* 15, no. 2 (Summer 1994): 218. Baron reports that an Egyptian woman editor translated and used selections from the Turkish women's press, and that there was even a bilingual Turkish-Arabic journal published by Sa'diya Sa'd al-Din in Alexandria in 1901. Baron, *Women's Awakening,* 61.

67. Afary, "On the Origins," 70.

68. Sirman, "Feminism in Turkey," 7 n. 10. (This interesting article provides rich quotations from some very feisty women writers in the press during this period.)

69. What did transpire during the British Mandate, however, was women's extensive use of the mainstream press to articulate their political concerns, which happened to dovetail neatly with the male-run press's own politics, particularly in the nationalist arena. The mainstream press devoted a considerable amount of coverage to women's political activities. A number of Palestinian women became prominent journalists, writing for the major newspapers, sometimes in special women's pages. They usually covered "women's topics" as columnists. Notable among them

are Mary Shihada, Sadhij Nassar (who coedited the paper *al-Karmil* with her husband), Fa'iza 'Abd al-Majid, and Asma Tubi. See my "The Nation and Its 'New' Women," chap. 3 and 272–277.

70. Thompson, "Engendering the Nation," 369.

71. Asma Tubi, *Abīr wa Majd* (Beirut: Matba'at al-Qalalat, 1966), 122–123.

72. For example, during the Italian invasion of Libya in 1911, Malak Hifni Nasif founded a relief society and a nurses' training center. Badran, *Feminists*, 50.

73. Marsot, "Revolutionary Gentlewomen," 264.

74. Badran, *Feminists*, 50.

75. Ibid.

76. Sirman, "Feminism in Turkey," 6; Kandiyoti, "End of Empire," 29; Yesim Arat, *Patriarchal Paradox: Women and Politicians in Turkey* (Cranbury, N.J.: Fairleigh Dickinson Press, 1989), 26; and Margaret Smith, "The Women's Movement in the Near and Middle East," *Asiatic Review* (April 1928), 189.

77. Smith, "Women's Movement," 190.

78. On women and *waqf*, see Mary Ann Fay, "Women and Waqf: Toward a Reconsideration of Women's Place in the Mamluk Household," *International Journal of Middle East Studies* 29, no. 1 (February 1997): 33–51; Carl Petry, "Class Solidarity Versus Gender Gain: Women As Custodians of Property in Later Medieval Egypt," in *Women in Middle Eastern History*, ed. Nikki Keddie and Beth Baron (New Haven: Yale University Press, 1992); and Gabriel Baer, "Women and Waqf: An Analysis of the Istanbul Tahrir of 1546," *Asian and African Studies* 17, nos. 1-3 (1983): 9–28.

79. Baron, *Women's Awakening*, 171.

80. Badran, *Feminists*, 51.

81. Ann Firor Scott, *Natural Allies: Women's Associations in American History* (Urbana: University of Illinois Press, 1991), 2.

82. Badran, *Feminists*, 51.

83. Fleischmann, "The Nation and Its 'New' Women," 176.

84. Paidar, *Women and the Political Process*, 68–69, 93, 96. Doulatabadi was an indomitable feminist. Paidar reports that after her organization and newspaper were banned and she was exiled from Isfahan, the Isfahan chief of police told her, "You have been born a hundred years too early," to which she replied, "I have been born a hundred years too late, otherwise I would not have let women . . . become so enchained by men today." Paidar, *Women and the Political Process*, 93, quoting Pari Sheykholeslami, *Zanan Ruznamehnegar Va Andishmand Iran* [Women journalists and free-thinkers of Iran] (Tehran: Chapkhaneh Mazgraphic, 1972), 97. It was Doulatabadi's wish that, after her death, no veiled woman participate in her burial ceremony or visit her grave, which was subsequently attacked "by a fanatic mob" shortly after the 1979 revolution. Sanasarian, *Women's Rights Movement*, 33.

85. Selma Botman makes this same point in describing Egyptian women involved in left-wing politics; Botman, "The Experience of Women," 125.

86. Indeed, one can discern uneasiness, fear, and a deep-seated conservatism among some of these pioneering feminists on the issue of class. Matiel Mogannam, a participant in the Palestinian women's movement, commented that Zionism imported "Bolshevik principles" into the country, producing an "effect on the popu-

lation, not by its propaganda only, but by the genuine uneasiness which it inspired amongst the Arabs, especially amongst the poorer classes." Matiel Mogannam, *The Arab Woman and the Palestine Problem* (London: Herbert Joseph, 1937), 217.

87. Baron, *Women's Awakening,* 175.

88. Badran, *Feminists,* 55; and Thompson, "Engendering the Nation," 370.

89. Badran, *Feminists,* 47.

90. Indeed, the idea still lives, as recently demonstrated by the following comments of the president of the World Bank, James Wolfensohn, delivered at a women's conference on May 22, 1997: "The single best investment is in a girl's education. If you educate a boy, you educate a boy. If you educate a girl, you educate a family or a nation." Nora Boustany, "Diplomatic Dispatches," *Washington Post,* May 23, 1997.

91. Adele 'Azar, unpublished personal memoir, 1965 (kindly provided to the author by Hana Nasir; emphasis mine). (The word "national" in this passage is used for the original Arabic *watanī.*) In Palestinian history, there is a tendency to retroactively attribute "nationalist" motivations to many activities, it should be noted. For an exploration of this subject, see Ted Swedenburg, *Memories of Revolt: The 1936–1939 Rebellion and the Palestinian National Past* (Minneapolis: University of Minnesota Press, 1995).

92. Paidar, *Women and the Political Process,* 60.

93. Ingrams, *The Awakened,* 81. Specific information about female education in the Arab countries under Ottoman rule is difficult to come by, because serious studies of the subject have yet to be published. I have been unable to ascertain the dates of establishment of the first girls' schools anywhere else.

94. Kandiyoti, "End of Empire," 28.

95. Paidar, *Women and the Political Process,* 92–93.

96. Badran, *Feminists,* 8–9.

97. Ibid., esp. 38–48, 56–60.

98. Thompson, "Engendering the Nation," 369.

99. A writer in the Palestinian press questioned the nature and goals of the education girls received in missionary establishments, since they did not learn about their own history, national heroes, or language. She called upon girls to demand their rights to an education that included learning about Arabic culture and language, and upon parents to support national schools. Su'ad Khuri, "Schools and Woman," *al-Difā',* July 22, 1935.

100. Thompson, "Engendering the Nation," 369–370.

101. Afary, *Iranian Constitutional Revolution,* 184.

102. Anonymous letter, *Tamaddun,* April 17, 1907, 3–4, quoted in Afsaneh Najmabadi, *"Zanhā-yi millat:* Women or Wives of the Nation?" *Iranian Studies* 26, nos. 1-2 (1993): 66.

103. Kandiyoti, "Identity and Its Discontents," 432.

104. Paidar, *Women and the Political Process,* 76.

105. Kandiyoti, "Identity and Its Discontents," 432; McClintock, "'No Longer in a Future Heaven,'" 122; and Rita Giacaman and Muna Odeh, "Palestinian Women's Movement in the Israeli-Occupied West Bank and Gaza Strip," in *Women of the Arab World,* ed. Nahid Toubia (London: Zed Press, 1988), 61.

106. *Filastīn,* December 13, 1944.

107. Quoted in Najmabadi, *"Zanhā-yi millat,"* 55.

108. See Thompson, "Engendering the Nation," 346–368, for a discussion of the battle for women's suffrage in Syria and Lebanon during the French Mandate period.

109. Nilüfer Çağatay and Yasemin Nuhoğlu-Soysal, "Comparative Observations on Feminism and the Nation-Building Process," in *Women in Modern Turkish Society: A Reader,* ed. Sirin Tekeli (London: Zed Press, 1995), 267.

110. Kandiyoti, "Identity and Its Discontents," 432–433.

111. See Fleischmann, "The Nation and Its 'New' Women," 243–248; and Badran, *Feminists,* 80–88.

112. Paidar, *Women and the Political Process,* 53–54, 58.

113. Thompson, "Engendering the Nation," 351.

114. Fleischmann, "The Nation and Its 'New' Women," 218–219. Women sometimes defied the male nationalist leadership by holding their own demonstrations against the latter's wishes. *Al-Karmil,* November 8, 1933.

115. Paidar, *Women and the Political Process,* 54.

116. See Fleischmann, "The Nation and Its 'New' Women," 272–287.

117. Fleischmann, "The Nation and Its 'New' Women," 271; Janet Afary, "The Debate on Women's Liberation in the Iranian Constitutional Revolution, 1906–1911," in *Expanding the Boundaries of History: Essays on Women in the Third World,* ed. Cheryl Johnson-Odim and Margaret Strobel (Bloomington: Indiana University Press, 1992), 104–105; and Philip Khoury, *Syria and the French Mandate: The Politics of Arab Nationalism, 1920–1945* (Princeton: Princeton University Press, 1987), 124. It should be noted that the presence of women in the Syrian demonstration did not deter the French from ultimately shooting three demonstrators dead and wounding others, including women.

118. Paidar, *Women and the Political Process,* 51; and Fleischmann, "The Nation and Its 'New' Women," 219. Among the Haifa women was the notorious activist Sadhij Nassar, secretary of the Haifa Women's Union, who was later imprisoned by the British without charges for seventeen months during the 1936–1939 revolt.

119. Paidar, *Women and the Political Process,* 59.

120. Many were published in the newspaper *Filastīn.*

121. Fleischmann, "The Nation and Its 'New' Women," 304–305.

122. A series of regional "Oriental" women's conferences were held in the 1930s in Beirut, Damascus, Baghdad, and Tehran.

123. *Al-mar'a al-'Arabiyya wa qadiyyat Filastīn* (Cairo 1938: Conference publication), 173. For more on the conferences and pan-Arabism, see Fleischmann, "The Nation and Its 'New' Women", 300–319, and Badran, *Feminists,* 223–250.

124. This can be partially explained by the fact that during the revolt, much of the Palestinian national leadership was in exile in Syria. Furthermore, the ties between Syrians and Palestinians were close on many levels; there were frequent intermarriages, for example, and some people owned property in both countries.

125. Nermin Abadan-Unat, "Social Change and Turkish Women," in *Women in Turkish Society,* ed. Nermin Abadan-Unat (Leiden: E. J. Brill, 1981), 9 n. 13; Thompson, "Engendering the Nation," 351–352; and Khadija Abu 'Ali, *Muqaddimāt hawla al-waqi'a al-mar'a wa tajribatiha fi al-thawra al-Filastiniyya* (Beirut: General Union of Palestinian Women, 1975), 47.

126. Paidar, *Women and the Political Process,* 91.

127. Baron, "Mothers, Morality, and Nationalism," 272.
128. Kandiyoti, "Identity and Its Discontents," 429.
129. Mogannam, *The Arab Woman,* 53.
130. McClintock, "'No Longer in a Future Heaven,'" 105.
131. Kandiyoti, "Identity and Its Discontents," 429.
132. Kandiyoti, "End of Empire," 33, 38, 42.
133. Çağatay and Nuhoğlu-Soysal, "Comparative Observations," 269 (quoting Atatürk's speeches).
134. Abadan-Unat, "Social Change and Turkish Women," 14.
135. He visited Turkey in 1934 and was particularly impressed by women's visible participation in work, education, and politics. Paidar, *Women and the Political Process,* 104. Houchang Chehabi describes how Reza Shah developed an attitude of "keeping up with the Joneses at an international level" in the relationship between the two countries. Atatürk was to return the visit, and Reza Shah did not want him to witness Iran's "comparative 'backwardness.'" Houchang E. Chehabi, "Staging the Emperor's New Clothes: Dress Codes and Nation-Building Under Reza Shah," *Iranian Studies* 26, nos. 3-4 (Summer-Fall 1993): 215.
136. Paidar, *Women and the Political Process,* 92–93.
137. Ibid., 101–102.
138. Kandiyoti, "End of Empire," 42; Ayşegül C. Baykan, "*The Turkish Woman:* An Adventure in History," *Gender and History* 6, no. 1 (April 1994): 108.
139. Kandiyoti, "End of Empire," 42. Feminists from other parts of the world, who often expressed admiration for Atatürk's positions on women, were clearly puzzled by this move and at a loss to explain it. See Woodsmall, *Moslem Women,* 359–360.
140. Paidar, *Women and the Political Process,* 104–105. For a detailed account of how coercive the unveiling and other dress code decrees were during Reza Shah's reign, see Chehabi, "Staging the Emperor's New Clothes."
141. Afsaneh Najmabadi, personal correspondence, January 19, 1998.
142. Paidar, *Women and the Political Process,* 105–106.
143. Ibid., 109–110, 113–114.
144. Çağatay and Nuhoğlu-Soysal, "Comparative Observations," 265.
145. Baykan, "*The Turkish Woman,*" 112; and Parvin Paidar, "Feminism and Islam in Iran," in *Gendering the Middle East: Emerging Perspectives,* ed. Deniz Kandiyoti (Syracuse, N.Y.: Syracuse University Press, 1996), 52.
146. Baykan, "*The Turkish Woman,*" 112.
147. Abadan-Unat, "Social Change and Turkish Women," 12.
148. Sirin Tekeli, "Emergence of the Feminist Movement in Turkey," in *The New Women's Movement: Feminism and Political Power in Europe and the USA,* ed. Drude Dahlerup (London: Sage Publications, 1986), 193.
149. Tezer Taşkiran, *Cumhuriyetin 50: Yilinda Türk Kadin Haklari* [Turkish women's rights in the fiftieth year of the republic] (Ankara: Başbakanlik Basimevi, 1973), 125, quoted in Arat, *Patriarchal Paradox,* 22.
150. Ibid., 112; Arat, *Patriarchal Paradox,* 30.
151. Chehabi, "Staging the Emperor's New Clothes," 222.
152. Ibid., quoting Hesam al-Din Ashna, ed. *Khoshānat va farhang: asnād-e mahramāneh-ye kashf-e hejāb* (1313–1322) (Tehran: National Archives, 1992), 249.

153. See Chapter 2.
154. Çağatay and Nuhoğlu-Soysal, "Comparative Observations," 267.
155. Tekeli, "Emergence," 185.
156. This has begun to change in recent years, however, as Palestinian feminists have started to problematize the relationship. See, e.g., Giacaman and Odeh, "Palestinian Women's Movement"; and Penny Johnson and Rita Giacaman, "The Palestinian Women's Movement in the New Era," *Middle East Report,* no. 186 (1994): 22–25.
157. The journal *Zaban-i Zanan,* for example, faced such dire threats that its editor, Sedigheh Doulatabadi, was forced to close it down and move from Isfahan to Tehran, where the political and religious climate was less conservative. Afsaneh Najmabadi, personal correspondence, January 19, 1998.
158. Fleischmann, "The Nation and Its 'New' Women," 147; and Kandiyoti, "End of Empire," 39.
159. This was the case in Palestine, for example. See Fleischmann, "The Nation and Its 'New' Women," 249–261.
160. Arab women who have written about their experiences in the movements during this period tend to stress in glowing terms their unity, whereas my own research, at least, has revealed contradictions in some of these portrayals. See, e.g., 'Anbara Sallam al-Khalidi, *Jawla fī al-dhikrayyāt bayna Lubnān wa Filastin* (Beirut: Dar al-nahar lil-nashr, 1978).
161. See, e.g., Baykan, *"The Turkish Woman,"* 108; and Sanasarian, *Women's Rights Movement,* 40.
162. Mrs. Munir Khuri, *Filastin,* December 15, 1944.
163. Fleischmann, "The Nation and Its 'New' Women," 301–303.
164. Paidar, *Women and the Political Process,* 102.
165. Related to this trend was the development of a minor conflict over the naming of the 1938 Eastern Women's Conference in Cairo. Akram Zu'aytir, a Palestinian nationalist who helped organize the 1938 conference, argued with Huda Sha'rawi to change its name to the Arab Women's Conference, but Sha'rawi refused. (Only two non-Arab women attended this conference, which focused on the Palestine problem.) See Fleischmann, "The Nation and Its 'New' Women," 309 n. 42.
166. Carolyn Bynum, "Why All the Fuss About the Body? A Medievalist's Perspective," *Critical Inquiry* 22 (Autumn 1995): 30.

References

Abadan-Unat, Nermin. *Women in Turkish Society.* Leiden: E. J. Brill, 1981.
Abdo, Nahla. "Nationalism and Feminism: Palestinian Women and the *Intifada*—No Going Back?" In *Gender and National Identity: Women and Politics in Muslim Societies,* ed. Valentine Moghadam. London: Zed Press; Karachi: Oxford University Press, 1994.
Abu 'Ali, Khadija. *Muqaddimat hawla al-waqi'a al-mar'a wa tajribatiha fi al-thawra al-Filastiniyya.* Beirut: General Union of Palestinian Women, 1975.

Abu Daleb, Nuha. "Palestinian Women and Their Role in the Revolution." *Peuples méditerranéens* 5 (1978): 35–47.

Afary, Janet. "On the Origins of Feminism in Early Twentieth-Century Iran." *Journal of Women's History* 1, no. 2 (Fall 1989): 65–87.

_____. *The Iranian Constitutional Revolution, 1906–1911: Grassroots Democracy, Social Democracy, and the Origins of Feminism.* New York: Columbia University Press, 1996.

Ahmed, Leila. "Feminism and Feminist Movements in the Middle East, a Preliminary Exploration: Turkey, Egypt, Algeria." *Feminist Studies International Forum* 5, no. 2 (1982): 153–168.

_____. "Early Feminist Movements in the Middle East: Turkey and Egypt." In *Muslim Women,* ed. Freda Hussain. New York: St. Martin's Press, 1984.

_____. "Between Two Worlds: The Formation of a Turn-of-the-Century Egyptian Feminist." In *Life/Lines: Theorizing Women's Autobiography,* ed. Bella Brodzki and Celeste Schenck. Ithaca: Cornell University Press, 1988.

_____. *Women and Gender in Islam: Historical Roots of a Modern Debate.* New Haven and London: Yale University Press, 1992.

Amin, Qasim. *The Liberation of Women,* trans. Samiha Sidhom Peterson. Cairo: American University in Cairo Press, 1982.

Antonius, Soraya. "Fighting on Two Fronts: Conversations with Palestinian Women." *Journal of Palestine Studies* 8 (1979): 26–45.

Badran, Margot. "Dual Liberation: Feminism and Nationalism in Egypt, 1870s–1925." *Feminist Issues* 8, no. 1 (1988): 15–34.

_____. "The Origins of Feminism in Egypt." In *Current Issues in Women's History,* ed. Arina Angerman, Geerte Binnema, Annemieke Keunen, Vefie Poels, and Jacqueline Zirkzee. London and New York: Routledge, 1989.

_____. "Feminism As a Force in the Arab World." In *Contemporary Arab Thought and Women.* Cairo: Arab Women's Solidarity Association, 1990.

_____. "Competing Agenda: Feminists, Islam, and the State in Nineteenth and Twentieth Century Egypt." In *Women, Islam, and the State,* ed. Deniz Kandiyoti. Philadelphia: Temple University Press, 1991.

_____. "From Consciousness to Activism: Feminist Politics in Early Twentieth Century Egypt." In *Problems of the Middle East in Historical Perspective,* ed. John Spagnolo. London: Ithaca Press, 1992.

_____. "Independent Women: More Than a Century of Feminism in Egypt." In *Arab Women: Old Boundaries, New Frontiers,* ed. Judith E. Tucker. Bloomington: Indiana University Press, 1993.

_____. *Feminists, Islam, and Nation: Gender and the Making of Modern Egypt.* Princeton: Princeton University Press, 1995.

Baer, Gabriel. "Women and Waqf: An Analysis of the Istanbul Tahrir of 1546." *Asian and African Studies* 17, nos. 1-3 (1983): 9–28.

Bamdad, Badr ol-Moluk. *From Darkness into Light: Women's Emancipation in Iran,* ed. and trans. F. R. C. Bagley. Hicksville, N.Y.: Exposition Press, 1977.

Baron, Beth. "Mothers, Morality, and Nationalism in Pre-1919 Egypt." In *The Origins of Arab Nationalism,* ed. Rashid Khalidi et al. New York: Columbia University Press, 1991.

_____. The Women's Awakening in Egypt: Culture, Society, and the Press. New Haven: Yale University Press, 1994.

Bayat-Philipp, Mangol. "Women and Revolution in Iran, 1905–1911." In Women in the Muslim World, ed. Lois Beck and Nikki Keddie. Cambridge: Harvard University Press, 1978.

Baykan, Ayşegül C. "The Turkish Woman: An Adventure in History." Gender and History 6, no. 1 (April 1994): 101–116.

Botman, Selma. "The Experience of Women in the Egyptian Communist Movement, 1939–1954." Women's International Forum 2, no. 5 (1988): 117–126.

Boustany, Nora. "Diplomatic Dispatches," Washington Post, May 23, 1997.

Bynum, Carolyn. "Why All the Fuss About the Body? A Medievalist's Perspective." Critical Inquiry 22 (Autumn 1995): 1–33.

Çağatay, Nilüfer, and Yasemin Nuhoğlu-Soysal. "Comparative Observations on Feminism and the Nation-Building Process." In Women in Modern Turkish Society: A Reader, ed. Sirin Tekeli. London: Zed Press, 1995.

Carroll, Berenice. Introduction to Liberating Women's History, ed. Berenice Carroll Urbana: University of Illinois Press, 1976.

Chehabi, Houchang E. "Staging the Emperor's New Clothes: Dress Codes and Nation-Building Under Reza Shah." Iranian Studies 26, nos. 3-4 (Summer-Fall 1993): 209–233.

al-Difā'. Jaffa, Palestine, 1920s–1940s.

L'Égyptienne. Cairo: Egyptian Feminist Union, 1930s.

Fay, Mary Ann. "Women and Waqf: Toward a Reconsideration of Women's Place in the Mamluk Household." International Journal of Middle East Studies 29, no. 1 (February 1997): 33–51.

Filastīn. Jaffa, Palestine. 1920s–1940s.

Fleischmann, Ellen. "Jerusalem Women's Organizations During the British Mandate, 1920s–1930s." Jerusalem: Palestinian Academic Society for the Study of International Affairs, 1995.

_____. "The Nation and Its 'New' Women: Feminism, Nationalism, Colonialism, and the Palestinian Women's Movement, 1920–1948." Ph.D. dissertation, Georgetown University, 1996.

Frierson, Elizabeth Brown. "Unimagined Communities: State, Press, and Gender in the Hamidian Era." Ph.D. dissertation, Princeton University, 1996.

Giacaman, Rita, and Muna Odeh. "Palestinian Women's Movement in the Israeli-Occupied West Bank and Gaza Strip." In Women of the Arab World, ed. Nahid Toubia. London: Zed Press, 1988.

Gocek, Fatma Muge, and Shiva Balaghi. "Reconstructing Gender in the Middle East Through Voice and Experience." In Reconstructing Gender in the Middle East: Tradition, Identity, and Power, ed. Fatma Muge Gocek and Shiva Balaghi. New York: Columbia University Press, 1994.

Greenberg, Joel. "Women in Gaza See Gains." New York Times, July 17, 1994.

Hale, Sondra. Gender Politics in Sudan: Feminism, Socialism, and the State. Boulder: Westview Press, 1996.

Hatem, Mervat. "Egyptian Upper- and Middle-Class Women's Early Nationalist Discourses on National Liberation and Peace in Palestine (1922–1944)." Women and Politics 9, no. 3 (1989): 49–70.

Ingrams, Doreen. *The Awakened: Women in Iraq.* London: Third World Center, 1985.

Jad, Islah. "From Salons to Popular Committees: Palestinian Women, 1919–1989." In *Intifada: Palestine at the Crossroads,* ed. Jamal R. Nassar and Roger Heacock. Birzeit and New York: Birzeit University and Praeger, 1991.

Jayawardena, Kumari. *Feminism and Nationalism in the Third World.* London: Zed Press, 1986.

Johnson, Penny, and Rita Giacaman. "The Palestinian Women's Movement in the New Era." *Middle East Report,* no. 186 (1994): 22–25.

Johnson-Odim, Cheryl, and Margaret Strobel, eds. *Expanding the Boundaries of History: Essays on Women in the Third World.* Bloomington: Indiana University Press, 1992.

Kandiyoti, Deniz. "Slave Girls, Temptresses, and Comrades: Images of Women in the Turkish Novel." *Feminist Issues* 8, no. 1 (1988): 35–50.

_____. *Women, Islam, and the State.* Philadelphia: Temple University Press, 1991.

_____. "Identity and Its Discontents: Women and the Nation." *Millennium* 20, no. 3 (1991): 429–443.

al-Karmil. Haifa, Palestine. 1920s–1940s.

Kazi, Hamida. "Palestinian Women and the National Liberation Movement: A Social Perspective." In *Women in the Middle East,* ed. the Khamsin Collective. London: Zed Press, 1987.

Keddie, Nikki, and Beth Baron, eds. *Women in Middle Eastern History.* New Haven: Yale University Press, 1992.

Al-Khalidi, 'Anbara Sallam. *Jawla fi al-dhikrayyat bayna Lubnan wa Filastin.* Beirut: Dar al-nahar lil-nashr, 1978.

Khoury, Philip. *Syria and the French Mandate: The Politics of Arab Nationalism, 1920–1945.* Princeton: Princeton University Press, 1987.

Lazreg, Marnia. "Feminism and Difference: The Perils of Writing As a Woman on Women in Algeria." *Feminist Studies* 14 (Spring 1988): 89–107.

_____. *The Eloquence of Silence: Algerian Women in Question.* New York and London: Routledge, 1994.

Al-mar'a al-'Arabiyya wa qadiyyat Filastīn. Cairo, 1938: conference publication.

Margolis, Diana Rothbard. "Women's Movements Around the World." *Gender and Society* 7, no. 3 (September 1993): 379–399.

Marsot, Afaf Lutfi al-Sayyid. "The Revolutionary Gentlewomen in Egypt." In *Women in the Muslim World,* ed. Lois Beck and Nikki Keddie. Cambridge: Harvard University Press, 1978.

McClintock, Anne. "'No Longer in a Future Heaven': Women and Nationalism in South Africa." *Transition* 51 (1991): 104–123.

Mogannam, Matiel. *The Arab Woman and the Palestine Problem.* London: Herbert Joseph, 1937.

Moghissi, Haideh. *Populism and Feminism in Iran: Women's Struggle in a Male-Defined Revolutionary Movement.* London: St. Martin's Press, 1994.

Mohanty, Chandra Talpade. "Cartographies of Struggle: Third World Women and the Politics of Feminism." In *Third World Women and the Politics of Feminism,* ed. Chandra Talpade Mohanty, Ann Russo, and Lourdes Torres. Bloomington: Indiana University Press, 1991.

Najjar, Orayb, with Kitty Warnock. *Portraits of Palestinian Women.* Salt Lake City: University of Utah Press, 1992.

Najmabadi, Afsaneh. "*Zanhā-yi millat:* Women or Wives of the Nation?" *Iranian Studies* 26, nos. 1-2 (1993): 51–72.

_____. "Feminism in an Islamic Republic: 'Years of Hardship, Years of Growth.'" In *Islam, Gender, and Social Change,* ed. Yvonne Yazbeck Haddad and John L. Esposito. Oxford: Oxford University Press, 1998.

Nashat, Guity, ed. *Women and Revolution in Iran.* Boulder: Westview Press, 1983.

Paidar, Parvin. *Women and the Political Process in Twentieth-Century Iran.* Cambridge: Cambridge University Press, 1995.

_____. "Feminism and Islam in Iran." In *Gendering the Middle East: Emerging Perspectives,* ed. Deniz Kandiyoti. Syracuse, N.Y.: Syracuse University Press, 1996.

Peirce, Leslie. *The Imperial Harem: Women and Sovereignty in the Ottoman Empire.* New York: Oxford University Press, 1993.

Peteet, Julie. *Gender in Crisis: Women and the Palestinian Resistance Movement.* New York: Columbia University Press, 1991.

Petry, Carl. "Class Solidarity Versus Gender Gain: Women As Custodians of Property in Later Medieval Egypt." In *Women in Middle Eastern History,* ed. Nikki Keddie and Beth Baron. New Haven: Yale University Press, 1992.

Philipp, Thomas. "Women in the Historical Perspective of an Early Arab Modernist (Gurgi Zaidan)." *Die Welt des Islams* 18, nos. 1-2 (1977): 65–83.

_____. "Feminism and Nationalist Politics in Egypt." In *Women in the Muslim World,* ed. Lois Beck and Nikki Keddie. Cambridge: Harvard University Press, 1978.

Royanian, Simin. "A History of Iranian Women's Struggles." *RIPEH* 3, no. 1 (Spring 1979): 17–29.

Sanasarian, Eliz. *The Women's Rights Movement in Iran: Mutiny, Appeasement, and Repression, from 1900 to Khomeini.* New York: Praeger, 1982.

Sandoval, Chela. "U.S. Third World Feminism: The Theory and Method of Oppositional Consciousness in the Postmodern World." *Genders* 10 (Spring 1991): 1–24.

Scott, Ann Firor. *Natural Allies: Women's Associations in American History* Urbana: University of Illinois Press, 1991.

Scott, Joan Wallach. *Gender and the Politics of History.* New York: Columbia University Press, 1988.

Sievers, Sharon. "Six (or More) Feminists in Search of a Historian." In *Expanding the Boundaries of History: Essays on Women in the Third World,* ed. Cheryl Johnson-Odim and Margaret Strobel. Bloomington: Indiana University Press, 1992.

Sirāt al-Mustaqīm. Jaffa, Palestine: 1920s–1940s.

Sirman, Nükhet. "Feminism in Turkey: A Short History." *New Perspectives on Turkey* 3, no. 1 (Fall 1989): 1–34.

Smith, Margaret. "The Women's Movement in the Near and Middle East." *Asiatic Review* (April 1928): 188–203.

Sonbol, Amira E., ed. *Women, the Family, and Divorce Laws in Islamic History.* Syracuse, N.Y.: Syracuse University Press, 1996.

Spellberg, Denise. *Politics, Gender, and the Islamic Past: The Legacy of 'A'isha bint Abi Bakr.* New York: Columbia University Press, 1994.

Stoler, Ann Laura. "Rethinking Colonial Categories: European Communities and the Boundaries of Rule." *Comparative Studies in Society and History* 31 (1989): 134–161.

Swedenburg, Ted. *Memories of Revolt: The 1936–1939 Rebellion and the Palestinian National Past.* Minneapolis: University of Minnesota Press, 1995.

Tekeli, Sirin. "Emergence of the Feminist Movement in Turkey." In *The New Women's Movement: Feminism and Political Power in Europe and the USA,* ed. Drude Dahlerup. London: Sage Publications, 1986.

Tekeli, Sirin, ed. *Women in Modern Turkish Society: A Reader.* London: Zed Press, 1995.

Thompson, Elizabeth. "Engendering the Nation: Statebuilding, Imperialism, and Women in Syria and Lebanon, 1920–1945." Ph.D. dissertation, Columbia University, 1995.

Tubi, Asma. *Abīr wa Majd.* Beirut: Matba'at al-Qalalat, 1966.

Tucker, Judith E. *Women in Nineteenth-Century Egypt.* Cambridge: Cambridge University Press, 1985.

_____. *In the House of the Law: Gender and Islamic Law in Ottoman Syria and Palestine.* Berkeley: University of California Press, 1998.

West, Guida, and Rhoda Lois Blumberg. "Reconstructing Social Protest from a Feminist Perspective." In *Women and Social Protest,* ed. Guida West and Rhoda Lois Blumberg. Oxford: Oxford University Press, 1990.

Woodsmall, Ruth. *Moslem Women Enter a New World.* New York: Round Table Press, 1936.

❀ 4 ❀

Debating Islamic Family Law: Legal Texts and Social Practices

Annelies Moors

"The Eclipse of the Patriarchal Family in Contemporary Islamic Law" is the telling title of an article published in 1968 by J. N. D. Anderson, one of the most prominent scholars in the field of Islamic law.[1] In this article he provides a concise and succinct summary of major twentieth-century reforms in Islamic family law. In doing so, he also presents a perspective on women and the family in Islamic law that has come under increasing criticism since the late 1970s.

Self-consciously employing the term "patriarchal," Anderson first describes the features characteristic of "the type of family set-up which has been typical of Islamic law throughout almost all the centuries of its development" (1968, 221). On the basis of classical legal texts, he argues that this patriarchal family was polygamous ("at least potentially, and often actually"), with women always under the threat of repudiation as men could divorce their wives at will. Women did not have similar rights and were obliged to obey their husbands in certain matters. The guardianship of children always belonged to the father, with mothers only having the right of custody over very young children. Fathers could arrange for compulsory marriages of minors, both male and female, and, in some schools of law, also of women in their legal majority who had not previously been married. Women themselves were, in most schools of law, only able to contract marriages with the cooperation of their marriage guardians. In respect to inheritance rights, agnates (patrilineal kin) held a privileged position.

141

Turning to codified twentieth-century family law, Anderson summarizes the major reforms that have taken place in almost all the Muslim countries. Both polygamy and the male right of repudiation have, to various extents, become restricted, and women may, under specific conditions, turn to the court to ask for annulment of marriage. The wifely duty of obedience is no longer enforced by returning a wife against her will to the marital home, and women's custody rights over their children have been extended. Both marriages of minors and compulsory marriages have largely been done away with. The special position of agnates in inheritance law has been restricted, and measures have been taken to favor the basic family unit at the expense of patrilineal heirs. These legal reforms signal, according to Anderson, the eclipse of the patriarchal family.

Shifting Positions and Perspectives

Until the early 1970s, the academic study of Islamic family law was largely the privileged terrain of Orientalists. Employing a textual approach, they considered family relations as the outcome of the provisions of Islamic law. Concentrating heavily on the classical texts of the leaders of the major law schools on the one hand, and on the texts of the newly codified twentieth-century laws on the other, they constructed an Islamic family that remained monolithic, static, and rigidly patriarchal until the promulgation of the twentieth-century legal reforms.

Since the late 1970s, the grounds of debate have fundamentally changed. An increasing number of historians and anthropologists have become involved in research on Islamic family law employing a greater variety of sources and methodologies and bringing different questions and new perspectives to the fore. Making use of, for instance, court documents and oral narratives, they do not assume the determining effect of law texts but rather question the ways in which these are related to other genres of legal discourse and to various forms of social practice.

This disciplinary shift intersects with the entry of a rapidly growing number of women in the field of Islamic family law, many of them either from the region itself or having close ties of family or residence, and with the development of women's studies as an academic field. This has led to more theoretically informed work on gender relations. Firmly held assumptions have come up for debate, and major shifts have occurred in conceptualizing women and gender relations. Rather than taking the meaning of gender for granted, the ways in which gender is constructed and how this relates to gendered social practices have become central issues. The exclusive focus on women's subordination has been modified by taking into account women's agency and by recognizing women as knowledgeable actors who make strategic use of the means and resources available, however limited these may, at times, be. With differences among women foregrounded, they are no longer seen as a homogeneous category, and the complex relations between gender and other axes of distinction, such as class, are elaborated on. Recent work, then, has focused on such topics as the construction of gender in various genres of Muslim legal discourse; the ways in which women's voices are represented in court cases and other court documents; and how oral narratives draw attention to the ways in which women from different backgrounds deal with the courts, devise strategies, and express their points of view about marriage, divorce, and inheritance.

Such inquiries subvert the Orientalist construct of the monolithic patriarchal family of classical Islamic law and question the assumption that family law reforms have greatly enhanced women's position and capacity to act. In this article I highlight the results of some of these studies.[2] First, I discuss how historians using court materials and other genres of legal texts bring to the fore women's agency and the strategies they employ. In the next section, I point to how twentieth-century law reforms are inscribed in highly charged debates on gender relations, and I contextualize these reforms within the framework of the development of the nation-state and its attempts to institutionalize new family models. In the last section, I address the relationship between legal texts and social practices, ending with a note on forms of modernity and feminism that do not take the West as its model, but position themselves within an Islamic tradition.

"Classical Islamic Law": New Sources, New Perspectives

In her historical study on women and gender in Islam, Leila Ahmed (1992) contrasts two major strands in Islam: "ethical Islam," with such central values as justice, piety, and the equality of all before God, and "legalistic Islam," the Islam of the dominant groups and the legal establishment, in which male dominance is a constitutive principle. Her emphasis on the existence of such divergent perspectives on gender relations in Islam is a forceful and convincing critique of the Orientalist trope of women's subordination. Still, her negative evaluation of "legalistic Islam" runs the danger of following conventional lines of thought that define Islamic family law as a quintessential patriarchal institution. Recent studies on the history of Islamic law that employ a greater variety of sources have criticized the one-sided evaluation of Islamic family law as a rigid and patriarchal institution and have also drawn attention to legal mechanisms women may use to their advantage.

Arguing for the Flexibility of Islamic Law

In their analyses of the history of Islamic law, Orientalists have often adopted the point of view of Muslim scholars. Whereas the first centuries

of Islamic history are seen as a golden age of lively debate and great intellectual activity, from the end of the third/ninth century on there was no
longer room left for independent interpretation *(ijtihad)*. By then Islamic
legal doctrine had fully developed, and four Sunni schools of law (Hanafi,
Hanbali, Maliki, and Shafi'i) had crystallized, all recognizing each other's
orthodoxy. Muslim jurists had only to apply and hand down the legal doctrine as formulated by the founders of these schools of law. A closure of
Islamic law had been effected.[3]

Recent scholarship has criticized the notion that there ever was a consensus that the law was no longer open to interpretation. Flexibility and
fluidity rather than rigidity were the hallmarks of Islamic law before codification (Messick 1992, 16; Mir-Hosseini 1993, 11). Basing itself on a plurality of authoritative texts, Islamic law was capable of accommodating individual needs and allowed for change. To underlined the openness of
Islamic law, Brinkley Messick (1992, 33) uses the metaphor of the branch-
ing tree. With the Qur'an (divine revelation) as the central authoritative
text, the Sunna (deeds and sayings of the Prophet Muhammad) may be seen
as an "expansive elaboration" of the Qur'an; the Qur'an and the Sunna,
taken together, are further elaborated upon by Islamic jurisprudence. After
the four standard Sunni schools of law were established, the authoritative
works of their founders were, in turn, subjected to commentaries and summaries. Individual scholars could diverge in their interpretations. Whereas
a concise manual may pertain to one point of view, commentators did not
cover up different points of view and inevitably brought to the fore points
of difference and debate. The concentration of Orientalists on the texts
composed by the founders of the legal schools and the summaries of their
doctrines has probably contributed to the notion of Islamic law as a closed
and static system.[4]

The flexibility of Islamic law is also underscored when turning to the debate on the origins of legal doctrine and practice. Focusing on the law's origins in terms of strictly separate and distinct traditions (Islamic law, local
customary law, and laws of European origin) neglects the heterogeneity of
legal practices (Dwyer 1990, 3). As long as they were not contrary to
Islamic principles, existing provisions were incorporated into the Islamic
legal system, providing space for considerable variability in legal practice;
in fact, local practices that are not forbidden in Islam are often seen as
Islamic (Rosen 1989). The acceptance of other additional principles of
Islamic law, such as consideration of the public interest *(istislah)* and the
principle of seeking the most equitable solution *(istihsan)*, also allow for
flexibility and the modification of legal doctrine.

Insights from New Sources: Fatawa *and Court Cases.* Investigating the
potential flexibility of Islamic family law, Judith Tucker (1997) does not re-

strict herself to the texts of the leaders of the major law schools, but makes use of *fatawa* collections and court documents and proceedings to gain insight into the gendered doctrine and practice of Islamic law in seventeenth- and eighteenth-century Syria and Palestine. *Fatawa* are authoritative, but not enforceable, opinions provided by muftis, in this case usually local men, who were part of an urban intellectual class and who functioned as legal advisers to the local community. In order to understand how this legal discourse on gender relates to social practice, the proceedings of the Islamic court are used. Because court documents focus on the arguments brought by the litigants, they are an important source of information about the strategies women employed.

Tucker's analysis of *fatawa* and court materials leads to conclusions that differ significantly from more conventional Orientalist studies about women and Islamic family law. It is true that both the muftis and *qadi*s assumed that gender difference was the natural state of affairs, a difference that also entailed elements of male dominance and women's subordination. But they also enforced men's obligations, upheld those elements of Hanafi law (the dominant legal school in the Ottoman Empire) that worked to women's benefit, and attempted to modify provisions that were harmful to women.

The muftis and *qadi*s emphasized that men's legal rights over women were not absolute. In respect to arranging marriages, they upheld the Hanafi position that a woman, upon reaching legal majority (that is, puberty), has both the right to refuse a marriage arranged for her by her marriage guardian and the right to arrange for her own marriage.[5] Men's rights were, furthermore, to some extent balanced by men's obligations to women. According to Islamic law, marriage is a contract that does not result in community of goods. With the signing of the contract, a husband is obliged to present his wife with a proper dower, which is to be her exclusive property. Neither her husband nor her kin hold any rights to it, and she is under no obligation to buy part of her trousseau *(jihaz)* with it. A husband is also obliged to provide maintenance for his wife, even if she has means of her own, and to do so at the level she is accustomed to. If he leaves her without support she may turn to the court, have a maintenance order drafted, and then borrow money with her husband owning the debt. In case of divorce, she is entitled to the balance of the dower and to maintenance during the waiting period. Legal scholars time and again enforced these obligations.

Attempts to modify elements working to women's detriment are evident in the ways in which the muftis and *qadi*s dealt with the very limited grounds (incurable male impotence) available to women under Hanafi law to seek annulment of their marriage. Hanafi muftis accepted Shafi'i and Hanbali rulings, according to which nonsupport, especially if due to disappearance, was also considered a ground for annulment. Whereas Hanafi judges could not grant such annulment themselves, they arranged for Shafi'i and Hanbali assistant judges to preside over such cases. Women themselves also used provisions that at first instance may seem harmful, such as the "oath of divorce," to their benefit. If this oath of divorce was tied to conditions regulating the husband's behavior, it could provide a wife with the right to claim divorce if her husband did not fulfill his promises. The effects then were similar to inscribing conditions in the marital contract.

The muftis provided some protection for women by taking a highly flexible position in respect to illicit sexual intercourse. They were very liberal in their applications of the doctrine of *shubha* (the notion that a couple had acted in good faith, assuming they had contracted a valid marriage) and were willing to recognize a child as legitimate if the couple married up to one month before birth. They also defended women against some social customs that were detrimental to them, strongly rejecting, for instance, the return of a bride to her family if she failed the virginity test on her wedding night. They argued that virginity had nothing to do with the constitution of a marriage, considered the woman herself as the only one able to testify about her virginity, and denied husbands or brothers the right to judge whether a woman had previously committed unlawful sexual intercourse.

Women and Property: Arguing Against Patriarchy

Women's rights with regard to property are a particularly apt topic to undermine one-sided notions of patriarchy and women's subordination. The main mechanisms through which women may gain access to property are the dower and inheritance, both of which are regulated through Islamic family law.[6] Also, as men are always obliged to maintain their wives, women may acquire property through their savings from paid labor. According to Islamic law, women have the same rights as men in dealing with property, be it in buying or selling it, donating it or receiving it as a gift, and so on. Historical studies based on *shari'a* court records provide insight into women's dealings with property; these studies emphasize that women were well aware of their legal rights and made ample use of them in practice. Topics discussed are the extent to which women had access to various types of property, the ways in which female property ownership ties in with the nature of the political system, and how political and economical transformations have affected women's access to property.

Studies of seventeenth- and eighteenth-century Ottoman cities have emphasized that independent property ownership was widespread among women (Jennings 1975; Gerber 1980; Marcus 1983). Women engaged in dealing in real estate and commercial property with both kin and nonkin, at times not hesitating to even sue their kin or husbands. It is true that women more often tended to sell property than to buy it and that they were more prominent in the trade in residential housing than in either commercial or agricultural property. Still, their involvement in property deals was considerable. In Aleppo, for instance, women constituted one-third of the dealers in commercial real estate, and one-third of these women were buyers; also, more than one-third of the founders of religious endowments were women. Within the family, the majority of women were buyers, whereas most men were sellers, resulting in family shares in houses moving from men to women. More generally, the fact that women were involved in from 40 percent (in Kayseri) to 63 percent (in Aleppo) of all property sales points to their widespread access to property.

Female property ownership has been linked to the nature of political organization in, for instance, studies about the Mamluk political systems of later medieval (Petry 1991) and eighteenth-century Egypt (Marsot 1996; Fay 1997), and about the Ottoman Empire of the sixteenth and seventeenth centuries (Peirce 1993). The ways in which households were central to political organization in these systems enabled women to participate actively in economic life. The (neo-)Mamluk regimes of slave-soldiers were characterized by strong rivalries and factionalism, and male competition for political power was often highly violent. In such unstable systems, women, who regularly outlived their husbands and male relatives, were crucial in providing continuity and stability. Because women were seen as the ideal custodians of estates, considerable property was turned over to them, and they were regularly appointed as caretakers of estates and as supervisors of endowments. Women's repeated marriages also gave them also increased access to property through the dower and inheritance.

Nineteenth-century transformations of the economy affected the access that women from different classes had to property in divergent ways. In early nineteenth-century Aleppo, as Margaret Meriwether (1993) states, the rush to buy property had similar effects for elite men and women. Elite women continued to own and manage property, held real estate in their own right, and were active as managers of religious endowments. Lower-class women, on the other hand, were negatively affected by the decline of textile production, which deprived them of productive activities. In nineteenth-century Egypt, upper-class women were still holders of large tax farms and managers of considerable property in religious endowments, but major trading opportunities were lost to Europeans (Tucker 1985; Marsot 1996).

Political and economic changes in early-nineteenth-century Nablus (Palestine) also affected dower arrangements. Tucker (1988) points to the different meanings of the dower to women from different classes and to changes in the contents of the dower. Whereas for the upper classes marriage was less a transfer of wealth than a means for forming economic and political alliances, to the lower classes the dower was an important means to acquire considerable property. If in the eighteenth century the dower also contained personal and household goods, in the nineteenth century the practice of including goods in the dower seems to have died out. Ceasing the display of such items may have been due to the increased monetarization of the region and to the stabilization of the upper class, with the dower less crucial as a status marker.

Whereas the focus on female property ownership has been an important contribution in countering a perspective that conceptualizes Islamic family law exclusively in terms of "patriarchy," there is a caveat here. By virtue of their sources, historians often have more information about the nature of the property than about the women concerned and their motives. Combined with a desire to "argue against" male dominance, women's property ownership may be seen as the automatic embodiment of women's power. As will be elaborated on below, contemporary studies show that the relation between gender, property, and power may well be more complex.

If some inquiries have a strongly quantitative bend in order to ground statements about women's ownership of specific types of property, with cases of individual women mainly used to illustrate an argument, other studies have combined a focus on women's property ownership with a detailed study of the life histories of individual women. Using the *waqfiyyat* (religious endowment deeds) of eighteenth-century Cairene Mamluk women as her main source, Mary Ann Fay (1997) has been able to amass considerable information about individual, named women of Mamluk households, which made it possible to link their personal and property histories with those of the households they were part of. Dealing with family relations in late eighteenth- and nineteenth-century Ottoman Aleppo, Meriwether (1999) has chosen to concentrate on families with family names (in casu the elite) in order to trace the activities of individuals and of families across generations.

Revisiting the Monolithic Islamic Family

Reconsidering the texts of the leaders of the major law schools by reading them from a woman's point of view further undermines the notion of a monolithic Islamic family. There are major differences between the provisions of Sunni and Shi'i law that may affect women's options substantially. In respect to inheritance, Sunni law is strongly partible and privileges male agnates if the deceased has no sons. If an only daughter and a distant male agnate are the sole heirs, the daughter will receive only half the estate, with the remainder going to the agnate. Shi'i law does not give such preference to agnates; parents and lineal descendants exclude all other heirs, allowing for limited partition of the estate. An only daughter may then inherit the whole estate, even excluding the grandfather (Coulson and Hinchcliffe

1978; Mundy 1988, 40–41). In respect to the affiliation of children, the differences between the Sunni Maliki school and Shi'i law are particularly striking. The Malikites allow for a maximum period of pregnancy of five years during which paternity can be claimed and give custody rights to the mother, revolving to the women in her line if she is not available or is deemed unsuitable. Shi'i law, in contrast, only recognizes a brief pregnancy period (with a maximum of ten months) and gives custody rights to the mother for only a limited period of time (for sons until they reach the age of two and daughters until they reach the age of seven), after which these revolve to the father's line (Mir-Hosseini 1993, 133ff.).

There are also differences among the various Sunni law schools in the ways in which they structure family relations (Ahmed 1992, 88ff.). For instance, there are great discrepancies between Hanafi and Maliki provisions about the marriage guardianship of women and about their options to ask for annulment of a marriage by the court. According to Hanafi law women in their legal majority may arrange for marriages themselves, but Maliki law demands the consent of the marriage guardian in the case of women entering their first marriage. Whereas Hanafites leave very few options for annulment, Malikites give women considerably more leeway in this respect, allowing for dissolution in case of nonmaintenance, desertion, or harm.

Studies focusing on social practice rather than on legal provisions further subvert the notion that there ever was a monolithic and unchanging Islamic family. The previous section on women and property shows how in this respect gender relations vary among the classes, depend upon the nature of the political system, and are strongly influenced by processes of economic change. One example here suffices to indicate that, also in respects other than property, family and gender relations could vary considerably. Through an analysis of marriage contracts and documents on divorce, maintenance, and the partition of estates, Tucker (1988) points out that whereas child marriage and polygyny were largely limited to the upper classes, divorce and remarriage were much more common among lower-class women.

In short, studies published since the late 1970s have pointed to the flexibility of classical Islamic law, have unearthed a wealth of sources that provide insight into the strategies that women from different backgrounds employed, and have modified the notion that there ever was one monolithic, rigid, and unchanging patriarchal family, either in doctrine or in practice.

Family Law Reform: The State, the Law, and Gendered Citizenship

Even if classical Islamic family law cannot be simply labeled as patriarchal, women's options were, generally, more limited than men's. This leaves open the question whether family law reform has greatly improved women's legal position. Changes in the substance of the law cannot be dealt with in isolation from transformations in the relations between states and their citizens (Sonbol 1996). Family law reform was part and parcel of the process of nation building, and changes in the substance of the law often aimed at institutionalizing new family structures. Taking these contexts into account complicates evaluations of the effects of family law reform on women. This is all the more important as family law has increasingly turned into a highly charged political symbol.

The Political Symbolism of Family Law Reform

From the mid-nineteenth century on, legal codes based on European models have rapidly replaced Islamic law in commercial, criminal, and administrative law in the Middle East. Personal status or family law, however, has largely retained the linkages between the legal and the sacred (with the notable exception of Turkey). One reason to single out family law from such wholesale replacement was that rulers did not perceive a pressing need to amend these laws. Western powers exerted considerable pressure on the Ottoman Empire to introduce, for instance, Western commercial law in order to facilitate trade with the region, and Ottoman reformists themselves supported efforts to modernize the empire. Family law, on the other hand, was of more limited interest. Distinguishing between the public and the private sphere, and relegating family relations to the latter, neither Western colonial administrators nor Muslim rulers felt an immediate need to intervene in Islamic family law. The main exceptions to this concurrence of interests was in respect to provisions about religious and family endowments *(waqf)*, which the Western powers strove to abolish, and with regard to the inheritance of state *(miri)* land.[7]

Another important consideration inhibiting the abolishment of Islamic family law was that this was perceived as a highly sensitive issue.[8] With gender relations at its core, Islamic family law has become "the preferential symbol" of Islamic identity (Hélie-Lucas 1994, 391). Because Orientalists and colonial administrators have often employed the "subordination of Muslim women" as legitimization for Western presence and interference, debates about women and gender relations have acquired a particularly strong symbolic edge (Ahmed 1992, 129ff.), with Islamic family law as a keystone of the state's commitment to Islam. This political symbolism of Islamic family law has become more pronounced with the growth of the Islamist movements from the 1970s on, which put pressure on the states to adapt family law to fundamentalist definitions of Muslim identity. As Marie-Aimée Hélie-Lucas (1994, 396) argues, governments fighting the Islamists on other fronts have been willing to give in on the issue of family law, using women as exchange money in order to pacify their fundamentalist opponents.

Now that Islamic family law has become such a powerful political symbol, replacing or even only reforming it may be perceived as betrayal of one's "own culture." Extending women's legal options then brings up the complex issue of engendering cultural change. Still, if Islamic family law has become such a crucial symbol, this does not preclude multiple interpretations and a range of alternative visions. A study of young Cairene university women (conducted by Zeinab Radwan; see Ahmed 1992, 222–228) underscores the divergent meanings that people can attach to symbols. A considerable number of these women support both women's equality in marriage and the imposition of Islamic law. Although they opt for Islamizing family law because they believe in the inherent justice and egalitarianism of Islam, which they assume must be reflected in its laws, neither the religious establishment nor the male leadership of Islamist movements would condone an emphasis on gender equality.

Building the Nation: Codifying the Law and Supervising the Courts

Whereas Middle Eastern rulers have avoided replacing Islamic family law with foreign legal systems, in most countries reforms of Islamic family law have been implemented. Such reforms have been part of the process of nation-state formation in the region and have been instrumental in transforming relations between states and their citizens. As Messick (1992) has argued, in the course of the twentieth century personal ties based on kinship have increasingly given way to the notion of a national and homogeneous citizenry. The state's control over the legal system has been greatly enhanced by the codification of law texts and by increased state supervision of the courts. This, together with increased bureaucratization and standardization, has also brought about changes in legal procedures. The earlier emphasis on oral witnessing has given way to the primacy of written evidence, in particular official documents such as birth certificates, marriage contracts, and divorce registrations.

If, in all countries where major reforms of Islamic family law were introduced this was part of the process of nation building, the outcome is by no means uniform. Deniz Kandiyoti (1991a) identifies some factors that influenced the ability of states to implement family law reforms: the ways in which national identity tied in with Islam and the particular meanings of Islam this entailed, the question of whether colonialism had encouraged the development of a defensive identity, and the extent to which the state was dependent upon kin and tribally based communities.

The first codification of Islamic family law was the Ottoman Law of Family Rights of 1917, which was also applied in the Arab provinces of the Ottoman Empire. Perceiving a strong need to modernize and strengthen the empire, Ottoman rulers in the course of the nineteenth century had instigated numerous reforms that involved "a progressive distancing between cultural nationalism and Islam" (Kandiyoti 1991b). Rather than encouraging a (pan-)Islamic identification, this led to the emergence of a Turkish nationalist ideology, the protagonists of which argued for a primordial (pre-Islamic) Turkish identity. After the establishment of the Turkish republic in 1923, Mustafa Kemal Atatürk took a series of measures to control the religious establishment, including the abolition of the Ottoman Law of Family Rights and its replacement in 1926 by a secular civil code based on that of Switzerland.[9]

In Iran, where codification started between 1928 and 1935, Reza Shah's attempts at nation building were similar to, and in fact inspired by, those of Mustafa Kemal. Religion, however, remained an important source of legitimacy. In contrast to Turkey, the Shi'i clergy had much greater autonomy vis-à-vis the state and was more supportive of the ruler's attempts of modernization. Iranian nationalism succeeded in drawing upon the specificities of Shi'i Islam and in integrating these with pre-Islamic notions. In Iran, Shi'i family law was reformed rather than replaced by a secular legal system (Najmabadi 1991).

In North Africa and in the Arab East, further codification of the law took place after independence, starting in the 1950s. Tunisia is a strong example of innovative legal reforms in a former colony. Although during the struggle against the French colonizers Habib Bourguiba had been against changing women's legal status, he became strongly in favor of implementing major changes in Islamic family law once independence had been won (1956). He adopted this position to show that Tunisia was a modern and civilized nation and to prove that a rational interpretation of Islam was indeed possible. Bourguiba was able to implement his legal reforms because, in contrast to Morocco and other countries, kin-based groups in Tunisia had only limited political autonomy (Hijab 1988, 22–24; Charrad 1990).

Whereas codification on the Arabian peninsula has been a slow process and reforms have remained limited, the former state of South Yemen is an outstanding example of an interventionist state aiming to radically alter its relations to its subjects through family law reform, enacted in 1974. Coming to power after a long period of British rule, the Marxist regime was committed to radical social and economic transformation, intent on mobilizing women in building up a socialist state and ideologically committed to the equality of men and women. At the same time, a major aim of state policy was to create a national entity by setting up a centralized and unified legal system throughout the national territory, dissolving old tribal and regional ties and identities (Molyneux 1991).

Reforming the Substance of the Law: Women, the Family, and Citizenship

Rulers made use of various mechanisms in order to reform Islamic family law. In the late nineteenth century the modernists had argued for a return to the sources (the Qur'an and the Sunna) to develop new interpretations and legal provisions better suited to modern times. By means of such reinterpretations, polygyny was outlawed in Tunisia. More commonly, legal reform was implemented through procedural devices, with rulers issuing administrative regulations and restricting the jurisdiction of the courts rather than changing the substance of the law. Procedural requirements, for instance, were used to discourage marriages of minors and out-of-court repudiations. Another device used to reform family law was to select the most suitable provisions *(takhayyur)* from among different schools of law, including minority opinions. This was one means employed to broaden the grounds on which women could, for example, turn to the court to request a divorce in areas in which classical Hanafi law had previously been applied (such as the territories of the former Ottoman Empire). The implementation of such reforms could be legitimized in Islamic terms by reference to "the public interest."[10]

Adapting Islamic family law to changed circumstances meant reworking family and gender relations. Family law reform has generally strengthened conjugal ties at the expense of kin relations. This should, however, not be interpreted as a sharp break with classical Islamic law. Classical law already acknowledged the importance of conjugal ties through, for instance, the obligation of a man to provide his wife with adequate housing *(maskan shar'i)*, which ensured privacy from the husband's natal family (see Antoun 1990). Still, twentieth-century reforms have put a greater emphasis on conjugal ties and the nuclear household, with such reforms also often affecting gender relations. In most countries the prerogatives of male agnates in inheritance law have been limited, to the benefit of the direct family, and kin control over marriage has been greatly diminished by setting minimum ages for marriage, by ensuring the woman's consent, and, in some cases, by allowing her to enter into marriage without recourse to a marriage guardian.[11] At the same time, reforms not only strengthened a woman's position vis-à-vis her male kin but also affected relations between husbands and wives. Women could now turn to the court for a divorce under specific conditions, usually nonmaintenance, cruelty, desertion, or the husband being afflicted with a dangerous disease. Also, women's custody rights over children were extended, and, under certain conditions, women's options to claim financial support after divorce were strengthened.

Not only have women's rights been strengthened but, at the same time, men's rights of polygyny and unilateral repudiation have, in some countries, been curtailed. Such restrictions were often imposed through procedural devices, such as requiring the consent of the court, giving women the option of divorce in the case of polygyny, and no longer allowing specific types of repudiation, such as triple repudiation in one session. The legal reforms implemented in Tunisia (1956), Iran (1967 and 1975), and South Yemen (1974) provide strong examples of this trend. In Tunisia polygyny was outlawed, whereas both in Iran and South Yemen polygyny required the permission of the court, which would only be given in specific circumstances such as barrenness and incurable illness. In respect to the dissolution of marriage, Iran and South Yemen enacted laws requiring all divorces to be arranged through the courts, with roughly equal grounds available for men and women; Tunisia worked toward equal rights for men and women in this area by expanding the grounds available to women.

Although reforms in the substance of the law have often worked to the benefit of women, this was not always the case. Ziba Mir-Hosseini (1993), for instance, argues that family law reform in Morocco, enacted in 1957, has reinforced certain patriarchal elements of the *shari'a* while doing away with classical leeways. With respect to paternal affiliation, the maximum duration of pregnancy during which paternity may be claimed, was reduced from five years to one year. In the case of the legal validity of unregistered *(fatiha)* marriages, women have become totally dependent on the goodwill of men; if men do not acknowledge the marriage, the only proof the court will admit is a marriage certificate. More generally, the strong sense of formality and the lengthy procedures of Moroccan courts, with their great emphasis on documentation, work against women, especially those who are poor. In other cases, family law reform may have divergent effects for different categories of women. In South Yemen, for instance, codified family law set an upper limit on the dower. Whereas this may be of benefit to educated and employed women, it may turn out to be disadvantageous to those women who do not have other sources of economic security.

If the reforms mentioned above were instigated in order to bring legal provisions closer to the demands of "modern times," more recent attempts at reform argue for Islamizing family law. After the 1979 Islamic revolution in Iran, the new government canceled the 1975 reforms (the Family Protection Act) as un-Islamic. The legal changes implemented to Islamize family law did away with the limitations the previous reforms had imposed on male unilateral divorce and polygyny, and severely curtailed women's custody rights (Kar and Hoodfar 1996). The unification of North and South Yemen in 1991 brought about a new family law in 1992 that abolished or modified many of the family law reforms implemented in South Yemen eighteen years earlier. Men no longer required the permission of the court for unilateral divorce; the only redress women had was their ability to claim extended maintenance in cases of "arbitrary divorce." And the permission of the court was also no longer needed for polygyny (Molyneux 1995).

Gender and Family Law Reform in Palestine: A Brief Historical Comparison. As several studies have recently been written about women and family law in Palestine, covering different historical periods (Welchman 1992; Moors 1995; Tucker 1997), a more detailed historical comparison of the impact of legal reform in Palestine is now possible. During the Ottoman period, Hanafi law was the official school followed by jurists. The Hanafi system was codified as the Ottoman Law of Family Rights in 1917 and applied during the British Mandate. In 1951, when the West Bank fell under Jordanian control, Jordanian legislators enacted the Jordanian Law of Family Rights, which was replaced in 1976 by the Jordanian Law of Personal Status. Finally, after the Israeli occupation of the West Bank, the Jordanian personal status law was applied to the Palestinian Muslim population, and jurisdiction was held by the *shari'a* courts.[12]

Legal reforms have been enacted in these laws, lessening the control of kin and husbands over women. Minimum ages for marriage have been introduced (fifteen for girls and sixteen for boys); as Hanafi law only allowed for forced marriages of minors, this new legislation has ended all marriage under duress. The duty of wifely obedience has eroded, as wives are no longer forcibly returned to the marital home. The very limited grounds for divorce allowed to the wife by Hanafi law have been widened to include nonmaintenance, "discord-and-strife," and abandonment. With respect to male unilateral divorce, conditional divorce has been abolished, all divorce is considered single revocable, and, in the case of "arbitrary divorce," husbands are obliged to pay maintenance for up to one year. Mothers' custody rights over their children have been extended from seven for boys and nine for girls to the onset of puberty.

Compared to the more radical reforms mentioned previously, these reforms may appear rather limited. Male unilateral divorce has hardly been restricted, for women injury by itself is still not a valid reason to request a divorce, and polygyny has not been subject to restraints.[13] Furthermore, some of these reforms are not as substantial an improvement as one might at first assume. The muftis and *qadi*s in seventeenth- and eighteenth-century Syria and Palestine already referred women to *qadi*s from other legal schools to enable them to request the dissolution of marriage, and in those days the "best interests of the child" were also taken into consideration (Tucker 1997). Other reforms, such as abolishing conditional and triple divorce, do not always work to women's benefit; in the past, women have made selective and strategic use of these in order to bring about a desired divorce. In respect to a woman's ability to give herself in marriage without the consent of her marriage guardian, legal reforms are not clear; in the case of women marrying for the first time, the formulations in codified law may well have undermined the strong position classical Hanafi law gave women in their legal majority (Welchman 1992). Also, the tendency to strive for equality between spouses has led to the enactment of some provisions benefiting the husband rather than the wife, such as those allowing the husband to include conditions into the marriage contract (previously a privilege of women only) and providing additional grounds for men to ask for a separation through the court, which severely limits men's financial obligations toward their former wives (Welchman 1988, 872). More recently, in 1984, pressures to Islamize legal codes have resulted in the application of Qur'anic rules of inheritance to *miri* land, restricting (at least on paper) women's access to agricultural land.

Women Activists and Legal Reform

Women themselves have actively participated in debates on family law reform. Women activists who were divided on other issues often agreed about the need for such reform. In early-twentieth-century Egypt, for instance, prominent women such as Huda Sha'rawi and Malik Hifni Nassef, who took different positions in respect to veiling, both advocated reforming marriage laws in respect to polygyny, unilateral repudiation, and early marriage (Ahmed 1992, 176ff). In Iran in the 1980s, family law reform was an issue around which women from various ideological persuasions (both Islamist and secular) united (*Middle East Report* 1996). At other times, however, women activists found themselves divided along political lines. When in Egypt in 1979 amendments were made with respect to family law (called "Jihan's law," after President Anwar al-Sadat's wife), some were caught between their opposition to Sadat's pro-Western policies and the fact that these reforms were in some ways beneficial for women (Hijab 1988, 30).[14]

In Palestine, local women's organizations have been active in matters of legal reform. In 1988 leaders from three of the four women's committees called for the replacement of communal laws with civil legislation (Giacaman and Johnson 1989, 168).[15] The Declaration of Independence and other steps taken toward Palestinian statehood raised the interest of the women's committees in family law. In 1990, at a conference on the *intifada* and women's social issues, one of the recommendations of the women committees' workshop was to "initiate a review of the laws and regulations dealing with personal status and family laws and draft changes" (Women's Studies Committee and Bisan Center 1991, 26). Personal law has, however, turned out to be a highly sensitive issue. In a publication of the Women's Centre for Legal Aid and Counselling (WCLAC) on women and the law, a section on personal status laws underscores that participants in a workshop organized by the centre in 1994 held divergent points of view about the possibility of reform through reinterpreting Islamic family law (WCLAC 1995, 71). As a result, the WCLAC initiated a research project to examine and compare family law and legal practice in the *shari'a* courts in the West Bank and Gaza Strip with specific reference to the protection of women's rights. In the meantime, starting in 1991, the WCLAC has published a number of brochures (on topics such as maintenance rights, custody rights, divorce, and registering special conditions in marriage contracts) in order to increase women's awareness of their legal rights.[16]

A major step toward internationalizing these local women's initiatives was taken in 1984 when the network Women Living Under Muslim Laws was set up to provide a space for discussion and action for women of Muslim background worldwide. A major aim of the network was to bring to the fore how governments and political movements made political use of religion by advancing local traditions that work to the detriment of women as Islamic. In 1988 an exchange program for women from different Muslim countries was organized to enable them to experience the great variety of social practices that are labeled "Islamic." Such interactions between women from various Muslim backgrounds in itself draws attention to the ways in which Muslim laws are grounded in history and culture (Hélie-Lucas 1994).[17]

Legal Reform and Social Change

If legal reforms strengthened women's legal position vis-à-vis their male kin and husbands, one set of questions centers on whether women have in practice benefited from these reforms. Have women indeed been able to turn to the courts to claim their rights and have judges been prepared to implement the new reformed legal codes? And what does it mean when women claim their rights? Another major issue for debate is the relation between legal reform and social change. Women's strategies are not only directed toward reforming the law. And individual women engendering or accommodating social change through contractual provisions may well be at least as important.

From Law Texts to Legal Practice:
The Judiciary and Women Litigants

In some cases the implementation of family law reform was stalled because of the attitude of the judiciary. This was the case, for instance, with the abolition of polygyny in Tunisia, with the new inheritance laws in Iraq, and with extending women's options to initiate divorce in Egypt.[18] In other cases judges are reported to have attempted to modify legal provisions working to women's disadvantage. In postrevolutionary Iran, for example, judges expressed their reluctance to allow for unilateral divorce through their repeated attempts to reconcile couples.[19]

In her work on legal practices in the West Bank, Lynn Welchman (1992, 1994) elaborates on how the attitude of the judiciary is linked to the nature of the issues at stake. In some respects the judges follow a conservative line. Their approach to the inclusion of stipulations in marriage contracts has been very literalistic; especially with respect to the delegation of divorce, exact and correct wording is of paramount importance.[20] In some issues left to its discretion, the court is not very supportive of women. For instance, the amounts awarded as maintenance, as "caretaker wages," and as suckling fees are very low. But in other respects the attitude of the judges can be far more lenient. They generally give a working woman the benefit of the doubt if her husband objects to her employment. Whereas according to the law no maintenance is due to a wife who works outside the home without her husband's consent, judges often assume that such consent has implicitly been given. Also, in the case of "arbitrary repudiation," the judiciary places the burden of proof on the husband. Every unilateral repudiation is assumed to be arbitrary (giving women the option to claim extended maintenance), unless the husband can provide good reason (Welchman 1992).[21]

Although it is clear that large numbers of women litigants have turned to the courts to claim their rights, women's active participation in legal matters is not simply an effect of legal reforms. Studies of Ottoman cities indicate that also in Ottoman times women did not hesitate to turn to the courts to argue their cases.[22] People from all walks of life appear in the Palestinian *shari'a* court archives (Doumani 1985). Still, the participation of rural women, in particular, has increased considerably in the course of the twentieth century.[23] Whereas the rural populations' greater access to urban institutions has had an effect here, women have also eagerly made use of the new options provided by the law. For instance, in Jabal Nablus, Palestine, after the 1976 reform, a large number of unilaterally divorced women claimed extended maintenance rights on the basis of "arbitrary divorce" (Moors 1995, 140), and in South Yemen after the 1974 reform, women turned in large numbers to the courts to seek divorces (Molyneux 1991, 259). The willingness of women to address the judiciary may be highly class-specific. Enid Hill (1979, 91) argues that when in the 1970s it had become easier for women in Egypt to obtain a "divorce by court action," it was mainly the poorer women who turned to the court, hoping to gain the support of the state authorities to force their husbands to pay them what they were entitled to. The elite and the middle classes, on the other hand, stuck to more traditional forms of separation.[24] The observation that, in this case especially, poorer women are more likely to turn to the court raises the question of what it signifies when women either turn to the court or refrain from doing so.

The Complex Meanings of Claiming One's Rights. Women regularly refrain from claiming rights they are entitled to under the law. Whereas historians in their studies on women's access to property tend to assume that claiming property rights is an indication of power, anthropologists, who have more opportunities to investigate women's points of view, have argued that "giving up" one's rights may be a strategy to gain other, more important, benefits.

Women from the Nablus region, for instance, only rarely turned to the courts to claim the remainder of their prompt dower if this had not been paid in full (Moors 1995, 102). A woman usually only did so if her husband also did not fulfill his obligations of providing adequate housing and maintenance. Rather than forcing their husbands into debt, these women preferred to "give up" some of their material rights, convinced that this would morally strengthen their position within the family. In a similar vein, a rural woman did not tend to turn against her father when he pocketed a considerable part of the dower himself (a practice both illegal and widespread in rural areas until the 1960s). She would only do so if it was not her father but another relative who had been her marriage guardian. Because a woman would return to her father's house in case of marital problems, turning against him would weaken rather than strengthen her position vis-à-vis her husband and his kin. Women were more often willing to raise a case against their uncles and other male kin in court, as they were convinced that these more distant relatives would feel less obliged toward them (Moors 1995, 97).

Women from Jabal Nablus also often refrained from claiming their inheritance rights. This was, however, not necessarily an expression of their subordination, nor was claiming their rights in an estate an indication of power (Moors 1995, 48ff; 1996). Some women received at least part of their share automatically because they were from a wealthy urban family background, where men would raise their own status by "giving" to their sisters. Their inheriting was first and foremost an expression of their class position rather than of gendered power. Others inherited because their husbands put great pressure on them to claim their share. Rather than indicating power, under such circumstances inheriting property may well undermine a woman's position. These women were not only likely to lose kin support but, as a result, would also often find themselves in a weaker position in regard to their husband and his kin. Other women, in particular daughters without brothers, claimed their share because they were in a highly vulnerable situation. On the other hand, when daughters renounced their rights to an estate, they often did so to underscore their kin's obligations toward them. And when a widow left her share to her sons, her position was generally strengthened rather than weakened.

To complicate matters further, women's legal claims may not coincide with what they expect to gain when they turn to court. In a comparative study of Islamic family law in Iran and Morocco, Mir-Hosseini (1993) shows that if a woman is intent on getting a divorce, it is not the divorce laws that are central but custody rules, dower practices, family structure, and employment opportunities. In Morocco, poor women turn to the court to claim maintenance to arrange for a divorce; in Iran, middle-class women use their dower claims to bring about a separation. Poor Moroccan women may want divorces because their husbands have failed as providers (among the poor, women may actually find it easier to gain employment), and they do not lose access to their children because of the matrilineal custody rights of Maliki law. They use maintenance claims to facilitate divorces, as the procedures for claiming maintenance are relatively straightforward. In Iran, on the other hand, where women have to hand over their children at a young age to the children's father, women use their dower claims (that is, they give these up) to convince their husbands to agree to a divorce of mutual consent and to negotiate special custody arrangements.[25]

Changing Gender Relations Through Contractual Provisions: The Marriage Contract

A focus on legal reforms may obscure how contractual provisions, in particular the marriage contract, may affect women's position. Also, when contractual provisions are discussed, the focus has often been on those areas in which legal reform has taken place, namely the inclusion of stipulations in the marriage contract. Changes in dower registrations may, however, be at least as important for realigning gender relations.

Stipulations: Tools for Change?   Whereas the various classical schools of law differed in their opinions about the effects of including stipulations in the marriage contract, legal reform has generally allowed for a wide range of such stipulations to be registered concerning such issues as the place of residence, the nature of the accommodation, the right to work, and the right to divorce, often under specific circumstances, such as if the husband takes another wife. By including such stipulations in her marriage contract, a woman can improve her legal position considerably. Registering marriage stipulations is, however, not a widespread practice. According to Welchman (1994), only 0.9 percent of the marriage contracts in the West Bank included conditions, mostly filed by urban women.[26] Among particular categories of women, however, recording conditions in the marital contract is becoming a more common practice. In Nablus, for instance, whereas only 2 percent of all marriage contracts included stipulations, the contracts of professionally employed women indicate a different pattern. In the 1970s and 1980s, about 13 percent of women teachers included stipulations in their marriage contracts, usually pertaining to their right to work as a teacher if they wished to do so or their right to use their wages as they saw fit (Moors 1995, 246–247).[27] Urban middle-class Saudi women are increasingly registering conditions in their marriage contracts, most often about their right to study and work after marriage (Wynn 1996, 116).

Revising marriage contract forms has been a tool used by the state to implement changes in legal gender relations without changing the law. Stipulations have played a crucial role in this regard. In Egypt in 1995, for instance, the Ministry of Justice prepared a draft proposal for a new marriage contract, including a number of conditions that the marriage parties had the option of agreeing or disagreeing with. Such a contract was considered a means of informing people of the rights available to them through the law. Supporters of the new contract saw it as a way of achieving reforms from within the *shari'a* (*Al-Ahram,* May 25–31, 1995).

In Iran, both under the Pahlavi regime and after the Islamic revolution, the revision of marriage contract forms has been a means of modifying the rules of Islamic law. When the Family Protection Law was drawn up (1967 and 1975), resulting in similar divorce rights for men and women, an attempt was made to claim some adherence to Islamic law by including the grounds available to women in the marriage contract as conditions. These, however, were obligatory, which goes against Islamic law (Mir-Hosseini 1993, 55). In the new postrevolutionary marriage contracts, which were first issued in 1982, several standard stipulations are included. The first requires the husband to pay his wife, if he wants a divorce and she is, in the eyes of the judiciary, not to blame, up to half of the wealth he has acquired during that marriage. The second gives the wife the delegated right to file for divorce under certain conditions, such as nonmaintenance, maltreatment, desertion, and polygyny, which are specifically mentioned in the contract (Mir-Hosseini 1993, 57–58). Although the husband must sign each of these conditions to make them legally binding (thus having the option of not doing so), the very fact that they are printed in the standard contract makes it easier for the woman to include them. In this way, legal rights can be modified through the marriage contract rather than through legal reform.[28]

The Dower: Major Changes Without Reform. Whereas legal reform has barely addressed the issue of the dower, the ways in which the parties concerned register the dower have been subject to great variations. As the dower often is an important means for women to gain some measure of financial security, new trends in dower registrations are closely related to transformations in gender relations.

In twentieth-century Jabal Nablus, for instance, a major shift has taken place in the proportion of the amount the groom has to pay at the conclusion of the marriage contract (the prompt dower) and the amount due in case of repudiation or widowhood (the deferred dower). In the 1920s and 1930s a deferred dower was registered in only a minority of marriage contracts, but by the 1970s virtually all contracts included a deferred dower, the amount of which often was considerably higher than that of the prompt dower. This greater centrality of the deferred dower ties in with the increased importance of the husband as provider. Rather than at the time of marriage, a woman is now perceived to need financial guarantees when she loses her husband, whether through widowhood or repudiation. Another major development in dower registrations also ties in with a greater emphasis on conjugal relations. Beginning in the early 1960s, a new trend developed to register only a token amount as the prompt dower, for instance one dinar, five dinars, or one gold coin. Although such a token dower was an "invention" of the modernizing urban elite, it did not take long for it to become a part of some contracts of the less well-off in the city as well as of women in rural areas. Registering a token dower entailed a change from the groom providing a dower payment as a legal obligation to his voluntarily providing gifts.

Although women may attempt to influence gender relations through dower registrations, women's dower strategies cannot be understood simply from the information these written marriage contracts provide. Oral sources, in particular women's narratives, point to the ways in which social practices coincide with or diverge from written contractual obligations. For instance, rural women often did not receive the full prompt dower, as their fathers kept part of it for themselves; the deferred dower stands out more on paper than in practice, as those entitled to it often have to face considerable obstacles to secure their entitlements; and registering only a token dower usually does not affect the nature of the gifts the groom is expected to provide to his wife.

Still, both dower registrations and women's narratives indicate that women have lost some of their access to and control over property. In addition to the growing trend of registering a token dower and the greater emphasis on the deferred dower, women themselves have become less interested in using their dower to buy productive property (such as livestock), investing it instead in their husband and his house. Their narratives provide insight into why they often acquiesce to or even actively support these developments. Losing property rights often coincides with gaining other advantages, such as a greater say in marriage arrangements and a rise in social status. This does not, however, affect all women in the same way. The prompt dower is generally more important for women from poor households than for those from wealthy families, as dower differentials between richer and poorer women were and are considerably less pronounced than the great differences in wealth among households.[29]

In general, registering a substantial dower is seen as strengthening a woman's position of negotiation with respect to divorce. Both Cairene women from low-income communities (Hoodfar 1996) and urban middle-class Saudi women (Wynn 1996) argue that a high dower paid at the conclusion of the marriage contract inhibits men from resorting to unilateral divorce, because they would not only lose everything they had paid but in order to remarry they would have to pay another large sum as dower. In Iran, women use the dower to modify their legal rights in negotiations over their marital relations or its breakdown (Mir-Hosseini 1993, 72ff.). The dower in urban Iran is usually high; the groom is not expected to pay in full, but the wife may demand payment whenever she likes (that is, it is a "prompt" dower, not "deferred"). Although a woman demanding payment of the dower cannot prevent her husband from divorcing her, her rights in this regard work as a strong disincentive. Dower claims can also facilitate a desired divorce to which a husband objects; all court cases in which women wanted a divorce involved dower claims, but a large number resulted in divorce by mutual consent, with the wife giving up her dower. Women, particularly those from better-off backgrounds or with their own sources of income, can use a demand for payment of the dower as means of negotiation, giving up their claims in order to effect a desired divorce or to change its terms (for instance, to gain full custody over children). Dower registrations in Iran also illustrate how changes in family law can effect contractual rights. The significant rise in the value of the dower after the Iranian revolution is, in part, due to men regaining the right to unilateral divorce and polygyny (Mir-Hosseini 1993, 75).

Temporary Marriage: Divergent Interpretations.   One particularly flexible contractual arrangement is that of temporary marriage, an institution about which various parties hold divergent points of view. Temporary marriage is a specific Twelver Shi'i institution, not acknowledged by Sunni Islam. It entails a marriage contract between a man and an unmarried woman who agree, often privately, to marry each other for a specific period of time. The man is obliged to pay a dower but has no maintenance obligations toward his wife, and the partners do not inherit from each other. Any children produced by the union are, however, fully legitimate and have rights to maintenance and inheritance. At the end of the contract, no divorce procedures are needed, but, as in permanent marriages, the woman must observe a waiting period (of two months or two menstrual periods) to certify paternity in case of pregnancy. Temporary marriages may be extended for an unlimited number of periods.

The ambiguities inherent in temporary marriage enable a variety of interpretations, as Shahla Haeri (1989) has elaborated. The points of view of men who engage in temporary marriage generally concur with the dominant Shi'i view, which sees such marriages as aiming at sexual pleasure (for men), as good for society's health, and as providing religious reward. The perspectives of women who have been involved in temporary marriage not only diverge to varying extents from those of men but diverge considerably among women as well. Whereas some women would agree with the dominant Shi'i perspective, others challenge the popular notion that women engage in temporary marriage for financial reasons and men for sexual pleasure. Some women underscore their active role in arranging for a temporary marriage and link this to female sexual desire, whereas others find fault with the fact that women are seen as the objects of pleasure in a temporary marriage.

Islamic Modernity, Islamic Feminism

Although modernization and feminism are often equated with secularization, some recent work deals with new trends in Islamic family law in terms of the development of "Islamic" modernity and feminism. Haeri (1994) analyses the statements made by Iranian president Hashemi Rafsanjani in 1990 about female sexuality and temporary marriage. During the reigns of the Pahlavi shahs, the institution of temporary marriage had become marginalized. Aiming at modernization along Western lines, the Pahlavi regimes had worked toward the desegregation of public life and the unveiling of women. These efforts were accompanied by an avoidance of any public discussion on sexuality, with unveiled urban middle-class women proving their respectability by resorting to chastity and modesty. Many of these women perceived temporary marriage as a relic of the past, as an institution resembling prostitution, as a threat to the stability of the family, or as yet another institution employed by men to exploit women.

After the Islamic revolution, the new regime set out to actively propagate temporary marriage as an indigenous Islamic institution well suited to contemporary life and as a valuable Islamic alternative to the decadent Western practice of "living together." Rafsanjani's comments on sexuality and the role of temporary marriage reflect long-standing Shi'i discourse, which sees sexuality as a positive force and defines sexual enjoyment, rather than procreation, as the main objective of temporary marriage. His statement did not, however, simply signify a return to Shi'i traditions. In contrast to established Shi'i discourse, Rafsanjani explicitly acknowledged female sexuality, argued that there was nothing wrong with women themselves taking the initiative to propose temporary marriage, and suggested that it was an institution suitable for young adults. Temporary marriage was presented as a quintessentially "modern Islamic" institution.

There is, however, a need for caution, as Haeri (1994) emphasizes. Engaging in a temporary marriage is risky for women. Culturally, there is considerable disapproval of the institution and of the women (but not the men) who engage in it. Also, because of the widespread notion that a woman entering her first permanent marriage ought to be a virgin, engaging in a temporary marriage may well jeopardize her chances on a respectable permanent marriage. Another problem is the ambiguity about male responsibilities and commitments; paternity in temporary marriages, for instance, can be denied much more easily than in permanent marriages. In the conventional Shi'i idiom, temporary marriage is basically a contract that a man concludes for sexual pleasure, suitable to his natural need for multiple sexual partners. Many women seem unaware of these assumptions inherent in temporary marriage and engage in it in hopes of companionship and of achieving a meaningful and affectionate relationship. Almost all women involved in temporary marriages expressed a desire to be married permanently. Many of them are divorced women from the lower classes, trying through temporary marriage to escape the marginality of their status as divorcees.

Mir-Hosseini (1996, 286) refers to "the emergence of a feminist re-reading of the shari'a texts" in discussing how, with the establishment of the Islamic Republic in Iran, debates on "women and Islam" have fundamentally changed. Contending that implementation of the *shari'a* would strengthen the family and raise women's status, the leaders of the Islamic Republic have to deliver on their assurances, and they are held accountable for injustices experienced by women. As a result, "feminist" reinterpretations are gaining prominence both in official and in oppositional Shi'i discourse.

The effects of the abolition of the Family Protection Law, especially the reinstatement of men's rights to unilateral divorce and custody of children, resulted in strongly felt social injustice, women's protest actions, and, eventually, shifts in the official discourse. In 1985 Ayatollah Khomeini modified Shi'i rules, allowing a widow to keep her children even if she remarried and granting her (rather than her late husband's father) the right to receive his pension (Mir-Hosseini 1993, 159). Another important new development, part of the 1992 divorce amendments and the result of women's activism, has been in respect to divorce procedures. In cases of divorce requested by the husband where the wife is, in the eyes of the judiciary, not to blame, the court may rule that the wife is entitled to payment for her labor during the years of the marriage ("wages for housework").[30]

The oppositional discourse, which Mir-Hosseini calls "post-fundamentalist," has come to the fore in a series of legal articles published in *Zanan,* an Islamic women's magazine. Tackling issues pertaining not only to family law but also, for instance, to criminal law and women's employment as judges and *mujtahids,* this discourse on gender is very different from the official one. In contrast to official discourse, which sees gender inequality as grounded in the *shari'a* and in harmony with the laws of nature, these new voices argue for gender equality on all fronts, seeing women's sexuality as a social construct rather than as defined by nature and divine will. By using Shi'i scholarship to argue for the need to reinterpret the old texts in changed conditions, Islam rather than the West is taken as source of inspiration and legitimization.

Conclusion

Twentieth-century reforms of Islamic family law have ushered in the eclipse of the patriarchal family, Anderson argued in 1968. He based his statement, in many ways exemplary for oriental studies, on a comparison between the substance of these reformed and codified laws and that of the texts of the leaders of the main schools of classical Islamic law. Studies published since the late 1970s have seriously questioned such an approach. Taking differences among individual women into account, these newer studies have taken issue with the underlying concept of a monolithic, static, and patriarchal family, employing more nuanced and finely tuned notions than male oppression versus female subordination to deal with gender relations. With a focus on women's strategies, they do not limit themselves to analyzing legal provisions but also pay attention to social practices. In doing so, such studies employ a much greater variety of sources, including court documents and oral history.

To start with, a comparison of legal provisions "from a woman's point of view" already brings out substantial differences among the classical schools of law as well as among the various codified and reformed national family laws. Even on paper, gender relations were neither monolithic nor exclusively patriarchal. According to Hanafi law, women in their legal majority were able to arrange for their own marriages; according to Maliki law, they could ask for a divorce under specific circumstances; and according to Hanbali law, they were able to include certain conditions in the marriage contract. According to all classical schools, women were able to manage their property in whatever way they wished. Legal reforms, on the other hand, did not always increase women's options. In doing away with some of the flexibility that classical law provided, as with respect to paternity claims, these reforms actually may work against women's interests.

Recent studies have employed written sources other than the texts of the leaders of classical law schools and the new codified laws. In doing so, they have further undermined notions of the patriarchal Islamic family and its eclipse. Scholars have used *fatawa* and court cases to discuss how gender is constructed in specific legal discourses and practices. They have pointed to the ways in which muftis and *qadis* enforced women's rights and, at times, attempted to modify provisions that would affect them negatively. Scholars working with court documents referring to property registrations, such as *waqfiyyat*, have provided ample evidence that women were, indeed, property owners. Summaries of court cases have been employed to prove that women did not hesitate to make use of the court system in order to claim their rights. And those researching contractual provisions such as the dower have elaborated on their flexibility and the great variety of arrangements made.

Still, the use of such written sources raises its own problems. The relation between the information provided by written sources and the reality of social practice always must be questioned. Authors working with women's narratives, whether they are historical (oral history and life stories) or contemporary (interviews, informal talks, and observations), have drawn attention to the at times substantial differences between the amounts registered as dower and the amounts received by women in practice. With respect to court actions, authors have pointed out that women may turn to the court to ask one thing (for instance, maintenance or the balance of the dower) in order to get something else (such as a divorce on their own conditions). In fact, women's turning to the court in itself may have divergent meanings. While such an activity indicates their ability to act in a legal capacity, it may also point to the lack of any other viable options available to them. In a similar vein, women's access to property does not necessarily imply gendered power; women may claim their share of an inheritance because they find themselves in a highly problematic situation rather than as an expression of strength. A major challenge is then to understand how specific genres of legal writing interact with social relations.

When the legal reforms of codified law are compared to classical Islamic provisions, there is more at stake than the issue of substance. As family law reform not only concerned the substance of the law but also entailed its codification, a greater emphasis on written and official documents, and a much greater control by the state over the court, it may well be argued that reforms have increased Islamic family law's rigidity. Exercising *ijtihad* has become the task of the legislature, with the limited room for maneuver left to individual *qadis* further circumscribed by the control of the court of appeal within the terms set by the law.[31] In setting clear standards for all, it has been pointed out, codification guarantees equal treatment of all citizens. There is, however, a contradiction between such proclaimed equality of men and women as cit-

izens and the gender differences that are inscribed in Islamic family law. If
the classical Islamic system was strongly gendered, the codification of Islamic
family law has further entrenched such gender differences.

Analyses of legal reforms have pointed to the need to place such reforms
within the context of the processes of state formation and nation building,
and have made evident that "the state" (whether in terms of its structure
or its policies) is far from gender neutral. In the classical period, Mamluk
political systems, for instance, encouraged particular household structures
and relations, which made women pivotal to the reproduction of households. In the process of twentieth-century nation building, Islamic family
law became a powerful political symbol; in Turkey, Iran, and Tunisia the
codification and reform of Islamic family law was seen as a strong sign of
the state's commitment to modernity. In Iran after the Islamic revolution,
the reforms instigated by the Pahlavi regime were immediately abrogated
in order to express the state's commitment to Islamize society. Codification
has also been employed to unify the nation-state, and legal reforms often
entailed attempts to create a new type of family. Although legal reforms
limiting the control of male kin and husbands may indeed strengthen
women's bargaining position, they may simultaneously lead to increased
state control over women's lives.

Women have dealt with these issues at two levels. On the one hand, they
have, sometimes collectively, argued for reforms of Islamic family law that
would extend women's options and support their interests. On the other
hand, women have also made the most of the options available to them
within the existing systems of Islamic family law, for instance by including
stipulations in the marriage contract or by registering particular forms of
dower. Women have also deliberately refrained from claiming certain legal
rights in other to gain other benefits. Yet such rights need to be acknowledged widely in order for women to be able to benefit from "giving these
up." This is a strong argument for a style of analysis that pays attention
both to various genres of legal texts and juridical practices and to women's
actions, narratives, and strategies.

Notes

I wish to thank the editors of this volume for their comments, their encouragement,
and their patience; and I am grateful to Lynn Welchman for her comments as well
as for providing me with a copy of her unpublished Ph.D. dissertation.

1. Anderson's academic affiliations, listed on the article's title page—Professor of
Oriental Laws, Director of the Institute of Advanced Legal Studies, and Dean of the
Faculty of Laws at the University of London—indicate the position of authority he
writes from.

2. This essay does not attempt to present an overview of books and articles on gender and Islamic family law. My aim is to present a selection of English-language publications in order to point to major shifts that have taken place since the late 1970s. I do not intend to argue here that history, anthropology, and women's studies are necessarily less implicated in the Orientalist discourse (in the Saidian sense; see Said 1978) than oriental studies. The point is that studies employing a critical approach and opening up new debates are mainly located in those fields.

3. In addition, two law schools (Ithna 'Ashari and Zaydi) have come to dominate Shi'i Islam. Although Shi'i Islam has preserved the right of *ijtihad,* it has, at the same time, restricted this to a hierarchy of religious scholars.

4. Throughout the history of Islam, but in particular from the late nineteenth century on, there have been appeals for a return to the sources, that is the Qur'an and the Sunna. Modernist reformers argue for doing so to substantiate their claim that Islam is essentially compatible with modernity. Distinguishing between provisions about religious observances (*ibadat,* the relation of person to God) and on social transactions (*mu'amilat,* the relation of person to person), they argue that whereas the former were eternally valid, the latter were open to individual interpretation (*ijtihad),* ought to be seen in their historical context, and may be adapted according to the needs of the age. Islamists also argue for a return to the sources in order to reclaim the pure Islamic message. They contend that modern life ought to follow the prescriptions found in the Qur'an and the Sunna, which were given for all times and places. Insisting on a literal interpretation of the scriptures but disregarding the work of the jurists and community consensus, they themselves engage in a good deal of individual interpretation.

5. That is, as long as the dower is fair and the husband is her "equal" in various respects such as religion, freedom, lineage, profession, piety, and wealth; otherwise, her marriage guardian may request annulment.

6. However, in the case of *miri* land (land to which individuals could acquire rights of usufruct and possession, with ultimate ownership vested in the state), a secular law of succession is applied, the Ottoman *intiqal* system. With respect to Islamic inheritance law, Powers (1990) argues that in early Islam, reforms of Islamic inheritance law turned an inheritance system into a collection of inheritance rules. If in early Islam Qur'anic rules were only applied in the absence of a valid will, in the course of the first/seventh century the possibility of designating an heir was largely eliminated. Yet Muslim jurists found ways to provide flexibility by means of the law of the gift (the alienation of property during one's lifetime). Often this was done to designate property as family endowments (*waqf ahli).*

7. As the European powers saw the inalienability and impartibility of *waqf* land as an obstacle to productivity and progress, they aimed at dissolving the *waqf* system (Mundy 1988, 10–11; Powers 1990). In addition to reforming *waqf* property, the European powers also instigated reforms with respect to *miri* land—land with ultimate ownership vested in the state, often with middlemen (such as tax farmers) between the direct producers and state authorities. In the case of *miri* land, a secular law of succession prevailed (the Ottoman *intiqal* system). Again, in order to promote small land-ownership, legal reforms attempted to arrange for secure tenure and partible inheritance. Whereas early forms of *intiqal* severely restricted the number of heirs, only recognizing the rights of sons, later legal reforms extended the

number of heirs; by 1868, daughters were also able to inherit (Schölch 1982, 21). Codified in 1913 as the Ottoman Law of Succession, this legislation's main principles had by then become gender neutrality and the distribution of the estate on the basis of generations (Schölch 1982, 21; Mundy 1988, 12). As a result, from then on daughters had the same rights as sons to inherit *miri* land, but not plantations, orchards, or vineyards.

8. Even the rulers of the former Marxist state of South Yemen refrained from totally detaching family law from Islamic law in order not to give ammunition to their adversaries. For the very same reasons, Israeli authorities have not interfered in the substance of family law on the West Bank.

9. The 1926 secular family code did, however, incorporate its own gender inequalities. For instance, the head of the marriage union was the husband, who was defined as the provider for his wife and children; the father had more legal rights over his children than the mother; the wife was assigned the family name of the husband; and women could not work outside the home without their husbands' permission (see Arin 1996).

10. According to Islamic law, the ruler-legislator has the right to make administrative regulations as long as they are not contrary to the *shari'a* and to specify which rules of Islamic law shall govern for particular purposes.

11. With respect to inheritance, an interesting case is the Iraqi family law reform of 1959, which extended the gender-neutral rules for state *(miri)* land to all forms of property. In 1963, however, the law was amended to apply the order of succession of Shi'i inheritance law to both the Sunni and the Shi'i communities (Coulson and Hinchcliffe 1978, 47).

12. The *shari'a* court system and the personal status law have been the major exceptions to Israeli interference in the legal system of the West Bank, as they have remained under Jordanian control. For the legal situation of the West Bank population under Israeli occupation, see Bisharat 1989 and Welchman 1990.

13. According to the 1917 Ottoman Law of Family Rights, a woman could include a condition in the marriage contract to the effect that she had the right to request divorce if her husband married another wife.

14. In various countries, women lawyers have actively participated in debates about family law reform. In Kuwait, for instance, the woman lawyer Badriya al-Awadhi published a comparative study of Islamic family laws in the early 1980s, when the first personal status law was drafted, and argued for restricting men's unconditional right to divorce (Hijab 1988, 25–26).

15. In the late 1970s grassroots women's committees were founded in the occupied territories. By the early 1980s four strands had developed in line with divisions in the Palestinian nationalist movement.

16. The need to increase women's awareness of their options under the law was widely felt. Many women (and men) were and are unaware of the correct ways to register conditions in the marriage contract, of the possibility of claiming compensation for arbitrary repudiation, of the option of "discord and strife" separation, of the fact that women cannot be pressured into giving up custody rights over children in order to obtain a divorce, and of the fact that women can no longer be forcibly returned to the marital home (Welchman 1992). In Iran, the publishing

house Roshangaran and Women's Studies Publishing, founded by Shahla Lahiji, has published brochures on similar subjects.

17. The network publishes a newsletter, containing both background articles and calls for action in particularly disturbing cases. Correspondence may be addressed to: Women Living Under Muslim Laws, Boîte Postale 23, 34790 Grabels, France.

18. The Tunisian and Iraqi cases are discussed in Coulson and Hinchcliffe 1978 (48–49). According to a study by Amina Shmeis on the Zananiri Personal Status Court (Egypt), a large proportion of the judges were against reforms extending women's rights in case of divorce, and some admitted having failed to apply the 1979 laws (*Al-Ahram*, May 25–31, 1995). An example of an early study comparing legal reforms with judicial practices is Layish 1975. Here, however, the case is complicated, as a "non-Muslim state" (Israel) becomes involved in Islamic family law issues.

19. Whereas in postrevolutionary Iran a number of reforms have been abrogated (especially regarding women's custody and divorce rights), Iranian judges are not tied to fixed procedures and have great discretionary powers in interpreting *shari'a* rules (Mir-Hosseini 1993, 189). This in contrast to, for instance, Moroccan judges, who have very little discretionary power and can only apply the code according to civil rules of procedure.

20. The judiciary has argued that delegating the divorce by the husband to the wife does not mean delegating the procedure. The main problem is that if the wording is not exact, it is not clear when the wife may use her power to divorce herself (Welchman 1994).

21. Establishing a good reason in such cases is difficult. The courts insist on a *shar'i* reason, such as blasphemy or adultery; they do not accept, for instance, barrenness (Welchman 1992).

22. According to Gerber (1980), the common people made use of the courts in Bursa; Marcus (1983) and Tucker (1985) argue the same for Aleppo and Cairo. Tucker (1997) states that women often came to the Damascus, Jerusalem, and Nablus courts in person to raise a claim or engage in business. The courts were expected to make arrangements for women who wished to seclude themselves (allowing them to use an agent to bring a claim to court or to defend themselves) but not to discourage nonsecluded women from appearing before the court.

23. Since the 1970s, rural women have also increasingly turned to the court to raise cases of nonpayment of a prompt or deferred dower. In the 1970s and 1980s, 37 percent of the women who were finally repudiated litigated in court to claim their deferred dowers. The proportion of women from the city, from the rural areas, and from the refugee camps roughly coincided with the occurrence of final repudiation (Moors 1995, 139).

24. Social change also had to be taken into account. Anna Würth argues that in Sana'a, Yemen, among lower-class families, kinship relations have become less important in marriage arrangements, and the role of communities in settling marriage disputes has decreased. As a result, these families increasingly take their marital disputes to court (Würth 1995).

25. The procedures for claiming maintenance in Morocco are relatively easy, because the husband has to prove his wife's nonsubmission. In Iran, on the other

hand, the burden is on the wife, who must prove her submission. Iranian women use dower claims to effect a separation because in urban Iran dowers usually are very high, with payment only demanded if serious marital problems occur; in Morocco, the dower is considerably lower and is paid at, or soon after, marriage (Mir-Hosseini 1993).

26. Welchman's work is based on a sample of marriage contracts concluded in 1965, 1975, and 1985 in the Hebron, Bethlehem, and Ramallah *shari'a* courts. Most of the stipulations concerned the place of residence and the nature of the accommodations. By registering such conditions, a woman may gain the option of dissolving her marriage if her husband breaks a condition, or he may have to pay a large cash fine (if this is specified). A husband's breaking a marriage condition may also provide his wife with a good defense against any claim of disobedience he may later raise (which, if successful, would allow him to refrain from paying marital maintenance) (Welchman 1992).

27. Although the latter is only a confirmation of an existing right, the fact that women deemed it necessary to include such a stipulation points to possible divergences between the law and social practice.

28. In Iran, the grounds for divorce available to women were extended in 1982, even for those women whose contracts included no stipulations. Following the *shari'a* principle that the sanction of a rule may be lifted when adherence creates hardship, the court can compel the husband to allow a divorce or act in his stead if marital life has become intolerable. Stipulations in marriage contracts are seen as identifying such circumstances (Mir-Hosseini 1993, 65).

29. Also in eighteenth- and early-nineteenth-century Nablus, the dower was a more significant sum in lower-class marriages (Tucker 1988, 177).

30. Although Kar and Hoodfar (1996, 31–34) point to the problems involved in the implementation of this law, they also argue for the symbolic significance of recognizing the economic importance of women's unpaid housework. Moreover, they consider this law as having set a precedent for unconventional interpretations of the *shari'a*.

31. For instance, Jordanian law clearly states that any matters not explicitly covered by its provisions should be decided by the majority opinion of the Hanafi school.

References

Ahmed, Leila. 1992. *Women and Gender in Islam: Historical Roots of a Modern Debate.* New Haven: Yale University Press.

Anderson, J. N. D. 1968. "The Eclipse of the Patriarchal Family in Contemporary Islamic Law." In *Family Law in Asia and Africa,* ed. J. N. D. Anderson, 221–234. London: Allen and Unwin.

Antoun, Richard. 1990. "Litigant Strategies in an Islamic Court in Jordan." In *Law and Islam in the Middle East: An Introduction,* ed. Daisy Dwyer. New York: Bergin and Garvey.

Arin, Canan. 1996. "Women's Legal Status in Turkey." In *Shifting Boundaries in Marriage and Divorce in Muslim Communities,* ed. Homa Hoodfar, 37–52. Montpellier, France: Women Living Under Muslim Laws.

Bisharat, George. 1989. *Palestinian Lawyers and Israeli Rule: Law and Disorder in the West Bank.* Austin: University of Texas Press.

Charrad, Mounira. 1990. "State and Gender in the Maghrib." *Middle East Report* 20: 19–25.

Coulson, Noel, and Doreen Hinchcliffe. 1978. "Women and Law Reform in Contemporary Islam." In *Women in the Muslim World,* ed. Lois Beck and Nikki Keddie, 37–52. Cambridge: Harvard University Press.

Doumani, Beshara. 1985. "The Islamic Court Records of Palestine." *Birzeit Research Review* 2: 3–30.

Dwyer, Daisy, ed. 1990. *Law and Islam in the Middle East: An Introduction.* New York: Bergin and Garvey.

Fay, Mary Ann. 1997. "Women and Waqf: Toward a Reconsideration of Women's Place in the Mamluk Household." *International Journal of Middle East Studies* 29: 33–52.

Gerber, Haim. 1980. "Social and Economic Position of Women in an Ottoman City, Bursa." *International Journal of Middle East Studies* 12: 231–244.

Giacaman, Rita, and Penny Johnson. 1989. "Palestinian Women: Building Barricades and Breaking Barriers." In *Intifada: The Palestinian Uprising Against Israeli Occupation,* ed. Zachary Lockman and Joel Beinin, 155–169. Boston: South End Press.

Haeri, Shahla. 1989. *Law of Desire: Temporary Marriage in Iran.* London: I. B. Taurus.

_____. 1994. "Temporary Marriage: An Islamic Discourse on Female Sexuality in Iran." In *In the Eye of the Storm: Women in Post-Revolutionary Iran,* ed. Mahnaz Afkhami and Erika Friedl, 98–115. London: I. B. Taurus.

Hélie-Lucas, Marie-Aimée. 1994. "The Preferential Symbol for Islamic Identity: Women in Muslim Personal Laws." In *Identity Politics and Women: Cultural Reassertions and Feminisms in International Perspective,* ed. Valentine Moghadam, 391–407. Boulder: Westview Press.

Hijab, Nadia. 1988. *Womanpower.* Cambridge: Cambridge University Press.

Hill, Enid. 1979. *Mahkama! Studies in the Egyptian Legal System.* London: Ithaca Press.

Hoodfar, Homa. 1996. "Circumventing Legal Limitation: Mahr and Marriage Negotiation in Egyptian Low-Income Communities." In *Shifting Boundaries in Marriage and Divorce in Muslim Communities,* ed. Homa Hoodfar, 121–142. Montpellier, France: Women Living Under Muslim Laws.

Jennings, Ronald 1975. "Women in Early Seventeenth-Century Ottoman Judicial Records: The Sharia Court of Anatolian Kayseri." *Journal of the Economic and Social History of the Orient* 18: 53–114.

Kandiyoti, Deniz. 1991a. Introduction to *Women, Islam, and the State,* ed. Deniz Kandiyoti. London: Macmillan.

_____. 1991b. "End of Empire: Islam, Nationalism, and Women in Turkey." In *Women, Islam, and the State,* ed. Deniz Kandiyoti, 22–48. London: Macmillan.

Kar, Mehranguiz, and Homa Hoodfar. 1996. "Personal Status Law As Defined by the Islamic Republic of Iran: An Appraisal." In *Shifting Boundaries in Marriage and Divorce in Muslim Communities,* ed. Homa Hoodfar, 7–37. Montpellier, France: Women Living Under Muslim Laws.

Layish, Aharon 1975. *Women and Islamic Law in a Non-Muslim State*. New York: Wiley.

Marcus, Abraham. 1983. "Men, Women, and Property: Dealers in Real Estate in Eighteenth Century Aleppo." *Journal of the Economic and Social History of the Orient* 26: 137–163.

Marsot, Afaf Lutfi al-Sayyid. 1996. "Entrepreneurial Women in Egypt." In *Feminism and Islam: Legal and Literary Perspectives*, ed. May Yamani, 33–49. Berkshire, England: Ithaca Press.

Meriwether, Margaret. 1993. "Women and Economic Change in Nineteenth-Century Syria: The Case of Aleppo." In *Arab Women: Old Boundaries, New Frontiers*, ed. Judith Tucker, 65–84. Bloomington: Indiana University Press.

_____. 1999. *The Kin Who Count: Family and Society in Ottoman Aleppo*. Austin: University of Texas Press.

Messick, Brinkley. 1992. *The Calligraphic State: Textual Domination and History in a Muslim Society*. Berkeley, Los Angeles, and Oxford: University of California Press.

Middle East Report. 1996. "Women and Personal Status Law in Iran." *Middle East Report* 26: 36–40.

Mir-Hosseini, Ziba. 1993. *Marriage on Trial: A Study of Islamic Family Law, Iran and Morocco Compared*. London: I. B. Taurus.

_____. 1996. "Stretching the Limits: A Feminist Reading of the Shari'a in Post-Khomeini Iran." In *Feminism and Islam: Legal and Literary Perspectives*, ed. May Yamani, 285–332. Berkshire, England: Ithaca Press.

Molyneux, Maxine. 1991. "The Law, the State, and Socialist Policies with Regard to Women: The Case of the People's Democratic Republic of Yemen, 1967–1990." In *Women, Islam, and the State*, ed. Deniz Kandiyoti, 237–272. London: Macmillan.

_____. 1995. "Women's Rights and Political Contingency: The Case of Yemen, 1990–1994." *Middle East Journal* 49: 418–431.

Moors, Annelies. 1994. "Women and Dower Property in Twentieth-Century Palestine: The Case of Jabal Nablus." *Islamic Law and Society* 1: 301–331.

_____. 1995. *Women, Property, and Islam: Palestinian Experiences, 1920–1990*. Cambridge: Cambridge University Press.

_____. 1996. "Gender Relations and Inheritance: Person, Power, and Property in Palestine." In *Gendering the Middle East: Emerging Perspectives*, ed. Deniz Kandiyoti, 69–84. London: I. B. Taurus.

Mundy, Martha. 1988. "The Family, Inheritance, and Islam: A Re-examination of the Sociology of Faraa'id Law." In *Islamic Law: Social and Historical Contexts*, ed. Aziz al-Azmeh. London and New York: Routledge.

Najmabadi, Afsaneh. 1991. "Hazards of Modernity and Morality: Women, State, and Ideology in Contemporary Iran." In *Women, Islam, and the State*, ed. Deniz Kandiyoti, 48–77. London: Macmillan.

Peirce, Leslie. 1993. *The Imperial Harem: Women and Sovereignty in the Ottoman Empire*. New York: Oxford University Press.

Petry, Carl. 1991. "Class Solidarity Versus Gender Gain: Women As Custodians of Property in Later Medieval Egypt." In *Women in Middle Eastern History:*

Shifting Boundaries in Sex and Gender, ed. Nikki Keddie and Beth Baron, 122–143. New Haven: Yale University Press.

Powers, David. 1990. "The Islamic Inheritance System: A Socioeconomic Approach." In *Islamic Family Law,* ed. Chibli Mallat and Jane Connors, 11–31. London: Graham and Trotman.

Rosen, Lawrence. 1989. *The Anthropology of Justice: Law As Culture in Islamic Society.* Cambridge: Cambridge University Press.

Said, Edward. 1978. *Orientalism.* New York: Vintage Books.

Schölch, Alexander. 1982. "European Penetration and the Economic Development of Palestine, 1856–1882." In *Studies in the Economic and Social History of Palestine in the Nineteenth and Twentieth Centuries,* ed. Roger Owen, 10–87. London: Macmillan.

Sonbol, Amira E., ed. 1996. *Women, the Family, and Divorce Laws in Islamic History.* Syracuse, N.Y.: Syracuse University Press.

Tucker, Judith E. 1985. *Women in Nineteenth-Century Egypt.* Cambridge: Cambridge University Press.

_____. 1988. "Marriage and Family in Nablus, 1720–1856: Towards a History of Arab Marriage." *Journal of Family History* 13: 165–179.

_____. 1997. *In the House of the Law: Gender and Islamic Law in Syria and Palestine, Seventeenth–Eighteenth Centuries.* Berkeley: University of California Press.

Welchman, Lynn. 1988. "The Development of Islamic Family Law in the Legal System of Jordan." *International and Comparative Law Quarterly* 37: 868–886.

_____. 1990. "Family Law Under Occupation: Islamic Law and the Shari'a Courts in the West Bank." In *Islamic Family Law,* ed. Chibli Mallat and Jane Connors, 93–119. London: Graham and Trotman.

_____. 1992. *The Islamic Law of Marriage and Divorce in the Occupied West Bank.* Ph.D. dissertation, School of Oriental and African Studies, University of London.

_____. 1994. "Special Stipulations in the Contract of Marriage: Law and Practice in the Occupied West Bank." *Recht van de islam* 11: 55–77.

Women's Studies Committee and Bisan Center. 1991. *The Intifada and Some Women's Social Issues.* Ramallah: Bisan.

Women's Centre for Legal Aid and Counselling (WCLAC). 1995. *Towards Equality: An Examination of the Status of Palestinian Women in Existing Law.* Jerusalem: Women's Centre for Legal Aid and Counselling.

Würth, Anna. 1995. "A Sana'a Court: The Family and the Ability to Negotiate." *Islamic Law and Society* 2: 320–340.

Wynn, Lisa. 1996. "Marriage Contracts and Women's Rights in Saudi Arabia." In *Shifting Boundaries in Marriage and Divorce in Muslim Communities,* ed. Homa Hoodfar, 106–121. Montpellier, France: Women Living Under Muslim Laws.

❀ **5** ❀

Gender and Religion in the Middle East and South Asia: Women's Voices Rising

Mary Elaine Hegland

*I*n years past, orthodox Muslims generally believed that women's voices, considered dangerously tempting and arousing, should not be heard by men who were not their kin. Now, however, Muslim women's religious voices have been rising, sometimes from mosque loudspeakers or the radio, sometimes even in mixed religious gatherings. Muslim women are finding moderating, alternative, and dissenting voices, and their voices and views are reaching men and revising Islamic beliefs and gender constructions.

Not long ago, Islamic women's religious activities were generally segregated, were often different from those of men, and received little outside attention. Now, women's religious presence and practices are becoming more visible and gaining community, media, government, opposition, and feminist attention. With the resurgence of political Islam, fundamentalism, and Islamism and given the core position of Islamic femininities with regard to these movements, women's roles and behavior vis-à-vis Islam have become central identity symbols. The connections between gender and Islam have been opened for discussion, debate, and conflict.

As they and their religiosity are the subject of so much discourse and direction, women have been provoked to think about their situation regarding Islam and themselves as religious, cultural, and national symbols. Middle Eastern women scholars are now studying and writing about Middle Eastern women, including women's religious activities and Islamic views of gender.[1] Women are not just the subjects of others' Islamic discourses but have themselves become active participants in discourse.[2]

Middle Eastern women are now all the more provoked into developing stances and philosophies of their own about Islam. A minority of Middle Eastern women have turned their backs on religion, arguing that Islam is inherently patriarchal and misogynist. In their views, Middle Eastern women's advancement can best (or can only) take place in a secular framework. Some are agnostics, atheists, or Marxists of one type or another. Some women from Muslim backgrounds have joined an international network, Women Living Under Muslim Laws, to publicize Muslim women's situations and pressure for solutions (Shaheed 1994). Another minority of women are openly problematizing Islamic sources, questioning male-dominated history, the Hadith, and Qur'anic exegesis. They are attempting to develop more accurate interpretations of Islam that better support women's rights and equality. Or women may accept Islam, while rejecting some or all aspects of the organized religion and the authority of Islamic clerics in favor of a personal belief system. Many women just do not give much attention to religious beliefs and practices. The great majority of Middle Eastern Muslim women, though, live in a social environment, which makes it difficult to overtly resist religious pronouncements on gender and the dependent status of women. Judging it difficult or even dangerous to turn their backs on their social communities, these women must work to find ways to address their spiritual and social needs without obviously straying outside of state, community, family, and self-imposed boundaries.

As they are the predominant group, in this article I will focus on the latter: women living within Islamic[3] frameworks and feeling able to question and modify Islamic gender rules only in subtle, private, or limited ways. These women largely accept their communities' Islamic frameworks[4] for their beliefs and their modes of living. Often they practice an accommodating resistance, accepting regulations to the level they feel necessary while attempting to use Islamic practices and precepts for their own interests or making inconspicuous modifications for their own benefit. My own work with gender and Islam has been with Shi'i[5] women in Iran and Pakistan.[6] I will concentrate on these Shi'i women as case studies to examine how Muslim women are speaking—explicitly and implicitly—for themselves about gender and religion. I emphasize anthropological approaches (my own academic field)[7] while also relying upon researchers in other fields for context.[8]

Gender and Islam Before 1979

Although urban women's rituals and contributions to religion were actually very significant,[9] before the recent Islamist movements, women's public religious participation, and feminist scholarship, neither Muslim males nor outsiders recognized their importance. In Middle Eastern urban Muslim tradition, women should not be seen or heard by nonrelated males. Women's religious voices and views did not much enter public discourse. Muslim clerics and community males have interpreted Islam for women and informed them of their makeup and responsibilities as Muslim women. Until recently, even women's religious activities were minimized and segregated. They were home based and thus largely invisible to males and outsiders. If present at religious gatherings, women should be hidden behind curtains or up on balconies. They usually did not go to mosques.[10] Female practitioners generally did not write or communicate to outsiders about women's religious views or practices. In earlier decades and up through the 1960s and 1970s, most researchers on-site to record Islamic practices were men, with no access to women or their beliefs and practices.[11]

Although women, as intermediaries, sometimes seek help by visiting shrines or donating meals to saints on behalf of male family members, such practices are trivialized by males and more educated females as superstition, as an excuse for socializing and gossiping, or even as near idolatry (Betteridge 1989; Tapper [Lindisfarne] 1990; Torab 1996).[12] Women developed modified religious beliefs and practices meaningful to themselves, but then were criticized for those religious activities. Yet, denied public rituals, if women also had little access to female rituals, their religious lives could be sparse indeed.

In contrast to urban women, rural women—peasants and nomads who composed the great majority of Muslim women until recent decades—most often had little formal religious outlet (Brink 1997; Friedl 1989; Hegland 1983, 1986). They did not enjoy the active informal ritual lives of many urban Muslim women. Rural women and less-advantaged urban women did not have the literacy, leisure, social networks, clothing, roomy homes, or financial resources to attend or host religious gatherings. Most rural women could not even fulfill the five pillars of Islam. They did not have the resources to go on hajj to Mecca or give alms. The schedules and work demands of rural Muslims generally prevented fasting during Ramadan. The great majority of rural women did not even have the time or knowledge to perform the required five sets of prayer each day. Illiterate, they could not read the Qur'an or other religious texts. Rural women and poorer urban women were fortunate if they could visit a local shrine, listen to a traveling religious storyteller, mumble a few words of prayer, or pay a bit to a specialist for an amulet or verbal formula to address physical or social problems.

Shi'i women and religious ritual in "Aliabad," Iran. The exclusion of women from male-dominated, formal religious activities and rituals cannot but send a negative message about females' religious competence and value. In Moharram[13] of 1978 and 1979, I noted Iranian women's exclusion from Aliabad village's[14] mourning rituals and processions. These rituals conveyed the male-centered nature of village Moharram commemorations.

Only men participated in the mourning processions circling through the narrow village alleyways. If present during the procession of flagellants, women were on the sidelines, peering out from behind their doorways, pressed against the walls of the alleyways, or sitting back from the edges of roofs, always carefully covering themselves with their veils. Women did not really belong at the commemorations, it seemed. The most pious and modest women did not leave their own courtyards during these days any more than they did otherwise.

On the third day after 'Ashura, villagers acted out the leading of the captive women, also played by men, to Damascus. In Aliabad, the part of Shemr, who killed Imam Husein, was played by a politically powerful person: the headman, the son of the headman, or another relative. Expected to have a loud and frightening voice, this person rode his horse around the procession, beating the "women" survivors of Imam Husein's band, who were played by politically weaker male villagers. The village mullah, a poor, soft-spoken relative of the village elite, played the part of Fatima Zahra, Imam Husein's mother and the Prophet Muhammad's daughter. When "Shemr" beat "Fatima Zahra," and the latter yelped in pain, people laughed.

In the 'Ashura myth, the women are not fighters but rather sit passively by and then are taken as battle spoils. The female gender is thus connected with powerlessness, insignificance, invisibility, and passivity. Women are to be loyal to their male relatives and make the concerns of these men their own primary concerns, the Karbala myth teaches them. Certainly, as women told me, when Zaynab left her husband to go to Karbala she was demonstrating independence from her husband. But it was to support the cause of her brother Husein, another male relative. Only when men are not available to take the predominant roles should women temporarily emerge from their suffering and retiring roles to follow the example of Zaynab, who, according to tradition, lived to broadcast the story of her brother's Karbala martyrdom.

Just as Emrys Peters (1956, 1972) found in his analysis of southern Lebanese Shi'i passion plays, Aliabad Moharram commemorations reflected local perceptions of social organization. Women's absence on these holy days correlates with the expectation that, in general, women have no proper place in public life and public ritual. Of course, women are indeed active in public life, and the suggestion that they are not is a myth (Hegland 1991). Women do the organizing, administering, and cooking for Moharram commemorative meals as well as preparing food to be distributed for vows.

In spite of men's dramatic public performances and women's public invisibility, in actuality, women too played significant roles in keeping the memory of Husein alive. Women were the ones who sponsored and funded weekly *rozeh* (martyrdom recitation) meetings throughout the year. A number of village women arranged for the local *rozehkhun,* the reciter of stories connected with Imam Husein's martyrdom, to come to their homes regularly each week. Women paid the several *toman*s weekly and provided cigarettes to the reciter as well as tea for all who came to join the sessions. The stories, weeping, and conversation provided a regular suffusion of spirituality and remembrance of Husein for neighborhood women and any family males who happened to be present. Whereas the women managed these quiet, unassuming, year-long, home-based congregations in honor of Husein and his family of martyrs, men monopolized the ringing and dramatic villagewide commemorations during the month of Moharram. Men received the greatest community gratitude and *savab* (religious credit) for keeping the memory of Husein alive. Women could not expect their own religious contributions, feelings, and voices to be much acknowledged or valued.

Shi'i women and religious ritual in Peshawar, Pakistan. Women related to rural elite menfolk and urban women generally had richer religious lives than poorer or less well-placed women. Although males' improved financial situation might well allow them to keep their women more strictly veiled and secluded at home—signaling the men's economic station and religious piety (Keddie 1991), these women could engage in many more segregated and household rituals. Some of these, such as gatherings to welcome home pilgrims to Mecca, attendance at weddings and funerals, and Shi'i commemorations of Imam Husein's martyrdom, may be similar to men's gatherings although held separately. Women predominate in holding and attending some types of rituals, such as life-cycle commemorations, Qur'an-reading gatherings of gratitude or entreaty, birthday celebrations for the Prophet, and—for Shi'i women—*majale*s (mourning rituals) for Imam Husein, *rozeh*s (martyrdom recitals), household miracle narrations (Schubel 1993), *sofreh*s (meals donated in honor of the Karbala martyrs), and visits to the local shrine.

Even when women have ample opportunity to engage in ritual practices, though, they are faced with symbols and teachings about women's religious inferiority and dependence. Well-off Mohajir and Qizilbash Shi'i women in Peshawar enjoyed highly active ritual lives, particularly during the two-and-a-half-month commemoration of Imam Husein's martyrdom.[15] In conjunction with strengthening Pakistani Shi'i political/religious identity and flourishing ritual life,[16] Peshawar Shi'i women enjoyed escalating religious opportunities. But these very opportunities further exposed them to belittling Islamic femininities. They mourned in segregated women's rituals. When attending men's rituals, they sat behind curtains or up on hidden balconies, and were not to speak, chant, or even strike their chests loudly enough to be heard by the men. Preachers—both female and male—

exhorted women to cover themselves, obey their husbands, stay away from nonrelated men, and follow Islamic gender laws. Male dominance permeated ritual sermons and ritual process. Males channeled their female relatives' ritual performances and participation. Women managers ensured female ritual compliance.

Further, the core ritual symbolic complexes were phallocentric. At the *majale*s dedicated to Hazrat-e Abbas (Imam Husein's younger half-brother, martyred with him at Karbala), one or more *alam*s, or battle standards, were brought out from the household shrine room into the women's assembly. The *alam*s, representing the battle flag held by Hazrat-e Abbas when he was martyred at Karbala, signaled women's frenzied weeping and self-flagellation. Near the front of Peshawar male mourning processions, prominent Shi'i men attended a white horse representing Imam Husein's wounded steed, who had returned riderless to the waiting women after the Karbala massacre, thereby announcing Imam Husein's martyrdom. After these processions, the horse's handler would lead him to the women's assembly waiting back at the Huseiniyyah (the building designated for mourning Husein). The women, replicating the Karbala womenfolk's reaction, would then beat their heads frantically and cry out their horrified sorrow in thundering, fast-paced chants.

Although women spent far more time mourning, men's mourning practices were more dramatic and meritorious. During processions and at the climax of some male *majale*s, several men, bared to the waist, beat flails across their backs, testifying their readiness to follow in Imam Husein's footsteps and become martyrs. Women, considered physically weak and already losing blood through menstruation, could not afford to give more blood. Their method of flagellation could only be striking their chests or their heads with their bare hands. Women's polluting menstruation kept them from participating in the holy act of bloodletting self-flagellation, representing the supremely holy act of martyrdom, which requires bodily and spiritual purity (Hegland 1998b). In spite of significant ritual contributions in terms of time, effort, capability, and passion, women were viewed as religiously underqualified, and their religious voices sequestered.

Recent Developments Influencing Gender and Islam Dynamics

Several changes in the Middle East have led to the emergence of dramatic Islamic gender transformations. One change is the resurgence of Islamic fundamentalism, or Islamism: more attention to religion and the overt involvement of religious figures, parties, forces, concepts, and behavior in political competition and conflict. Women, family, sexuality, and gender are crucial to Islam, and Islamism particularly spotlights women and their definition and role.

A second related change is the widespread mobilization of women in political/religious movements.[17] Women marched in the Iranian revolution's huge street demonstrations in equal numbers with men. All recent Islamist movements have called upon women to play crucial roles. Both within countries and against the West in general, essentialized Islamic women are constructed to be core cultural and religious markers.[18]

Chaste, modest, pious, secluded women and an Islamically organized family are considered the source of stability and religiosity for an Islamic country. Women must obey and conform, for the "ideal" society can be reached only by means of "ideal" Muslim women (Papanek 1994).[19] They are the main markers between the corrupt and dissolute West and the pure, righteous Islamic nation.

In Iran, the phrase *gharbzadegi,* "struck by the West" or "West-toxification," conveys the sense of westernization as cultural imperialism. Women were thought to be most susceptible to Western cultural imperialism. Supposedly, through women, Iranian society and culture could be penetrated and invaded (see Thaiss 1978). Ayatollah Khomeini and his supporters believed that the shah had allowed Western penetration of the nation through the westernizing corruption of women. By veiling and controlling women's sexuality, Iranian males could fend off this danger (Moghissi 1994; Najmabadi 1987, 1991, 1994; Paidar 1995; Thaiss 1978). Thus, women's dress and segregation served as the main marker of Iran's Islamic nature (Friedl 1997, 154).

Women are central to the Islamic agenda. Therefore, political/religious leaders give women attention, recruit them into movements, court their votes, use them for leadership and propaganda, inflame them to attack the opposition, bring them into public positions and offices, get them on the streets in mass demonstrations, pressure them into Muslim dress and behavior, urge them to correct their less-advanced sisters, and honor them for donating their sons for service and martyrdom. Islamists and governments are using women in religious movements as Islamic icons; as religious, political, and anti-imperialist symbols; and as recruiters and socializers. To make sure women fulfill these functions, they must be tightly controlled, socialized, and religiously educated. Islamists must therefore curtail women's freedom to chose or develop their own identities (V. Moghadam 1993, 1994a, 1994b; Papanek 1994, 42).

A third change has taken place that challenges religious leaders and officials. Women, developing their critical capabilities through education and experience, are thinking for themselves and entering religious discourse. Unintentionally, in encouraging women's Islamic education, Islamists have prepared women to question engendered Islam.

In addition, previous decades under modernizing, westernizing governments have influenced women's abilities, self-perceptions, and expectations in ways that are problematic for religious leaders who see women as resources to be applied toward their own goals. Many Middle Eastern women have gained schooling; jobs and careers; foreign travel and education; exposure to liberal, Marxist, and feminist concepts; interaction and community with other female social critics; and experience in dissident organizations. Many had entered the public sphere and interacted with a far greater range of individuals than the relatives and neighbors to which women were previously limited. In Iran, women's participation in the 1978–1979 revolution seems to have radicalized even some women from clerical families. As a result of all of these changes, when Islamist leaders pressure women to fit into the image of the ideal Muslim woman, women have resisted.

Women's Resisting Stances

Secular feminists from Islamic backgrounds. Secular feminists in Iran and Pakistan must censor themselves. Iranian and Pakistani women living in the West are freer to develop radically feminist stances. Some Iranian and Pakistani scholars who live in the West emphasize what women do to cope or to act for women's benefit under Islamists' pressures. Others emphasize the negative conditions for women prompted by Islamists. They may point out the gap between Islamic ideals about treatment of women and the reality of women's situation in Muslim societies. These women cite Qur'anic verses allowing multiple wives for men, husbands' responsibility to beat disobedient wives, inheritance and power inequities, the equating of two females to one male witness, *sigheh* (Shi'i temporary marriage), men's monopoly on divorce, girls' marriages as early as age nine—which, they assert, amount to child rape and sexual abuse—and patriarchal, misogynous Islamic traditions and history to argue that Islam is inherently antifemale.[20] In their opinion, gender equity can be pursued only in the absence of Islam or at the very least in secularized environments of complete religious freedom (Moghissi 1994; Mojab 1994; Paidar 1995; Royanian 1979).

Quiet, personal belief in Islam. Many Iranian women are not feminists or activists, but reject the Islamic Republic's version of Islam. Commonly, Iranian Muslims decide for themselves what they accept or dismiss about currently orthodox Shi'i Islam. Although they may overtly defer to religious authorities and dominant ideologies for political, social, or economic reasons, they may personally hold quite different religious worldviews.[21] A strong current of anticlericalism runs through Persian culture. Although at some level believing that clerics should be shown respect, Iranians are apt to make jokes about them; think them pompous, ridiculous, or out of sync with reality; or believe them to be grasping, manipulative, and self-serving. Clerics must earn regard through long years of consistently worthy talk and behavior.

Since clerics have taken over the government, Iranians' anticlerical streak has flourished. Even without the Islamic Republic government's record of violence and repression, people would naturally blame disappointments and governmental shortcomings on those in charge—now the Shi'i clerics. But forced, heavy-handed Islamization has greatly exacerbated many Iranians' distrust of organized Shi'i Islam. Even some previously devout women ceased praying and fasting during Ramadan, feeling that if what government clerics were preaching and practicing was Shi'i Islam, they wanted no part of it.[22] Some people quietly boycotted Moharram commemorations. Others in Iran do not involve themselves religiously, or they maintain personal beliefs to one level or another.

Women revising Islam. A relatively small group of Middle Eastern women are criticizing male-centered religious traditions and teaching and promoting their own interpretations of the holy sources. From the relative safety and freedom of their homes in exile, overseas Iranians and Pakistanis are commenting on Islam and its interpretations as preached and practiced by clerics and supporters in their homelands.

Some women defend Islam, arguing that women are (or should be) protected by Islam, while working for gender change from within the system. Feminist scholar Riffat Hassan, for example, is concerned about Muslim young people, who "haven't seen any evidence of Islam's compassion in the 'Islamization' that has gone on in many Muslim countries in the last two or three decades. Instead," she states, "the focus has been on putting women in a subordinate place and on importing so-called Islamic punishments" (1995a, 64). Hassan works in the area of reexamining theology, questioning how men can actually give the Hadith (passed-down and thus debatable traditions about the Prophet) weight equal to or even greater than that of the Qur'an, which Muslims believe God to have transmitted to the Prophet. There should be no question about the primacy of the Qur'an (which is more gender equitable), Hassan asserts, over the Hadith, the source of most misogynous Islamic rulings (Hassan 1993, 1995b).[23]

Secularists and reformists influencing Islamic gender constructions. The influences of secularists and reformists touch women living in Muslim countries. For example, in Islamabad, Pakistan, with a roomful of Pakistani women, I heard a lecture by Riffat Hassan sponsored by a Pakistani women's group.

Many Iranian women are living in the United States. Their parents fly back and forth to visit; Iranian-American women's attitudes are communicated back to Iran. A delegation of Iranian women attended the International Women's Conference in Beijing (Tohidi 1996b). Some Iranian women living abroad publish articles in Iranian women's magazines or travel to Iran, meeting with female Islamic activists. Sometimes Iranian women come to speak in the United States.

What women from Muslim backgrounds are doing and thinking about gender and Islam outside is relevant for women's situations inside their home countries. Their published and broadcast criticisms put "Islamic" governments, politicians, and individuals on the defensive. These governments may find themselves torn between needing women as resources to maintain patriarchal family and social structure and to demonstrate religiosity and Islamic identity vis-à-vis other Islamic nations and the West[24] on the one hand, and needing women's participation in education and work and defensively wishing to show how Islam promotes women's rights and opportunities on the other. Islam allows women to be modern and publicly involved while also protecting them from corruption and exploitation, they may argue.[25]

To defend Islamic treatment of women, almost unawares, Islamists have appropriated aspects of feminism and feminist movements while railing against feminism, which they tout as Western and corrupting of women, the family, and society. Islamic figures have co-opted the liberal, feminist assertion that women should have freedom, rights, education, employment, and political participation.

They are then susceptible to arguments that women's situation should be changed so as to live up to these precepts. Women can turn the appropriation process around. Some Iranian women co-opt the Islamic regime's assertions of respect and advantages for women, and use government and clerical claims to argue for women's benefits (Moghissi 1996; Paidar 1995).

In Iran, women engaged the fundamentalist religious leaders in debates during the 1980s and 1990s, challenging them to provide resources and social justice to women. Female religious leaders and parliamentarians have criticized regime authorities and pressured them to allow women's full development. In 1989, when Speaker of the Parliament Hashemi Rafsanjani urged men to marry several wives because of high male casualties in the Iran-Iraq War, the editorial board of the women's magazine *Zan-e Ruz* (Modern Woman) upbraided him, arguing that one man could not treat several women justly. Polygyny therefore brings women misery. Rafsanjani revised his comments in response (Haeri 1994). Nayereh Tohidi points to the example of Parliament member Maryam Gorji. Although previously not interested in pursuing women's rights, she began working on a feminist Qur'anic interpretation (V. Moghadam 1994a, 1994b; Tohidi 1996a).

Gender and Islam:
Women's Accommodating Resistance

Why accommodate? No independent women's movement is tolerated by the state in Iran. No atheist, agnostic, or secularist movements or publications are allowed. Feminism is condemned as a Western ideology that leads to the corruption of women and thus of society. Women in Iran and Pakistan who are interested in working for women's rights and for improving women's living conditions cannot publicly advocate rejecting Islam. If they should, they would be forced to operate incognito or escape the country. They are left only with the possibilities of keeping silent, voicing bitter comments to close associates or a compatible network, or somehow working for feminist causes (improvement in women's rights, quality of life, equality, and opportunities) within an Islamic framework.

Further, in Muslim countries where the government and population are heavily influenced by Islamists, fundamentalists, or others who support rigid gender beliefs, it is personally difficult for women to overtly attack gender rules or the Islamic framework on which they are based. Women generally do not wish to refute principal cultural and religious tenets in such situations, for they would jeopardize their strong connections to community, family, and religion. Islamists have been quite successful in framing affinity or affiliation with feminists and Western women as disloyalty to Islam and nation, thus effectively cutting Muslim women off from such women's movements and empowering strategies.

In Muslim countries that have seen a resurgence of Islam in public consciousness and political power, there have generally been two contradictory yet complementary trends regarding gender rules and limitations on women. Opportunities for women within the religious framework increase. At the same time, Islamists restrict women's opportunities outside of Islamic frameworks and attempt to control women within Islamic frameworks, leaving them with little choice but accommodation.

The tight control of Islamists, and the serious consequences of noncompliance. Fundamentalist pressures limit women's mobility, dress, education, and work. Fundamentalist attitudes strengthen male authority, tighten sexual control, and expose women to potential violence. Islamists attempt to homogenize women and constrain them into community, male, family, and national service.

Women's mobility is curtailed, as they should not go anywhere without a male relative as a chaperon. For example, Iranian women can face serious trouble with government authorities if they are apprehended in the presence of a male who is not a husband, father, brother, or son (Razavi 1993).

Women's work and educational opportunities have been restricted (F. Moghadam 1994). In Iran, women are prevented from becoming judges, edged or harassed out of public employment, and disallowed from many fields of study (Higgins and Shoar-Ghaffari 1994; Mojab 1995). Female government workers are forced to wear regulation veiling. Those who do not, or who fail to show sufficient knowledge of state Islam or devotion to correct beliefs, lose their jobs.

The importance that Islamists place on women's *hejab* (veiling) invites males to harass and harm inadequately sheathed women. In Iran after the revolution, groups of men calling themselves "Whippers of Naked Women" patrolled streets in Shiraz and elsewhere, attacking women whom they considered to have less than adequate *hejab*. During the postrevolutionary period, Revolutionary Guards stopped women who were insufficiently covered, wearing makeup or nail polish, or allowing a wisp of hair to slip out from under their head scarf and physically punished them on the spot or took them to prison. Individual men reprimand, slap, or refuse to serve women not wearing correct *hejab*. Bands of men may beat up women who are covered insufficiently or who are engaged in activities deemed inappropriate for women, such as bike riding (Sciolino 1997, 50). Women's bodies become a battleground: Their apparel, modesty, seclusion, behavior, and interaction with males become sites of contention with symbolic, political, and religious meaning.[26]

Fundamentalism and Islamism provide good excuses to more forcefully impose local culture and customs, such as female-derived honor and shame. In an Egyptian village, "the honor of men depends on the virtuous conduct of their female relatives" (Brink 1997, 205). As the seclusion, modesty, and male-controlled sexuality of women become principal fundamentalist and Islamist markers, males gain greater sanction to dominate their female family members and regulate their sexuality. Reportedly, in some fundamentalist areas, honor murders of females are rising.

Islamists seek to regain tighter control over women's sexuality and to conserve it for the benefit of the family and nation. In Iran, the female marriageable age was lowered from sixteen to nine. There is renewed emphasis on *mut'a* or *sigheh,* the Shi'i institution of temporary "marriage" (Haeri 1994). Men are allowed sexual access to as many women as they wish by entering into a verbal contract stipulating the duration of the liaison and the payment to be given to the woman. Islamic Republic officials encouraged temporary marriage among the youth to prevent Western corruption, in spite of the fact that virginity is highly valued in Iran and a *sigheh* marriage stigmatizes a female, seriously harming her chance of permanent marriage (Haeri 1994). Iranian women may not go abroad without the permission of their male guardians, for fear they might become "corrupted." Single young women are not allowed to study abroad.[27]

Islamic governments have repealed liberalized family laws, to women's detriment (Pakzad 1994). Some new legislation has harmed women (Afkhami and Friedl 1994). In Pakistan, the Hudud law requires women to produce three Muslim male witnesses to rape in order to bring charges against a rapist. Otherwise, if they charge rape, thus admitting sexual intercourse, women themselves will be lashed for illegal fornication! Thus, Pakistani women basically have no legal protection against rape (Ahmed 1994; Haeri 1995b; Mehdi 1990; Mumtaz and Shaheed 1987).

In general, fundamentalist Islamic movements restrict women's purpose to serving males, families, and the Muslim community. Women and their work are to be harnessed for maintaining "tradition," religiosity, and group identity. Male sexuality and rights to children are privileged. Women are the means to the biological and social reproduction of the Islamic community. In fundamentalist societies, women are pressured to conform to this course by fear of punishment within and outside the family and by the possibility of divorce, loss of children or economic support, or divine disapproval (Haeri 1993; Hardacre 1993, 139–143; Rugh 1993).

The benefits of accommodation. Simultaneously with further restricting women and threatening physical punishment to nonconformists, Islamized countries are providing more religiously framed opportunities for women. Risking punishment if they transgress, discouraged or prevented from many activities and occupations, and lacking or unaware of other possibilities, most women in Muslim countries have little choice but to work within an Islamic framework. In conjunction with Islamization, women are becoming more visible in some areas of public life.

Middle Eastern Muslim women are more often attending mosque rituals now, although they must maintain sex segregation.[28] In Shiraz, Iran, according to Zahra Kamalkhani (1993, 1997), newly built mosques feature outside balconies for menstruating women; they need not stay away to prevent polluting the edifice and other worshipers. Also in Iran, women's home-based religious gatherings are burgeoning. Azam Torab (1996) documents the upsurge of women's collective rituals. In the South Tehran neighborhood where Torab worked, so many of these *jalaseh,* or prayer meetings, were held that women could chose among several each day. The increase in women's religious gatherings provides plentiful opportunities to professional female religious speakers.

In postrevolutionary Iran, there is a "new religious ambience which claims to encourage active participation by highly educated and intellectual religious women" (Kamalkhani 1997, 88). Such women can sometimes even speak to audiences including men. In these cases the ban against allowing men to hear women's voices has been overruled. Leading woman religious figures may speak on the radio or use loudspeakers to broadcast their sermons at large women's gatherings. Cassettes of female preachers' religious recitations have been distributed, with the explanation that the religious mission's significance overrules the restriction on women's voices (Kamalkhani 1997).

Throughout the Middle East, women are studying and teaching the Qur'an. In Egypt, for example, women are now present in mosques, discussing the Qur'an with other women and presenting their own interpretations of Islamic sources. In Iran, women's religious education has increased dramatically. Now there are three female theological schools in Shiraz, Kamalkhani reports, preparing women preachers and sending students out to educate women.[29] Women have entered seminaries in Iran, formally strictly male turf. Several hundred females attend the seminary facilities in Qom.[30] Female graduates in religion can earn salaries teaching Qur'anic courses at the large number of women's religious schools springing up or preaching to women's gatherings. Women preachers often possess sufficient credentials to put forward religious interpretations *(tafsir)*. Many have written Islamic theses *(resaleh)* and gained high rank *(mujtahed)*, attracting large followings. Some even lead women's communal prayers, although women disagree about whether or not females can appropriate this male prerogative (Kamalkhani 1993, 1997). In Iran, Islamist women are writing for newspapers and women's magazines. In addition to serving as symbols of Islamic and national identity, strength, and unity, Muslim women can provide proof that Islam is modern and progressive. Women are gaining visibility in Iran.

During my research with Shi'i women in Peshawar during the summer 1991 Moharram, I noted an increase of women's rituals in conjunction with growing religious fundamentalism, a strengthening of Shi'i identity, and close collaboration among Shi'is from various ethnic backgrounds. Women enjoyed their expanding opportunities to participate in religious activities such as forming and maintaining social and ritual relationships among various Shi'i communities; instructing and guiding others; organizing, supervising, and hosting women's mourning rituals; pressuring others to attend religious activities and exhibit zeal; engaging in ritual performances and sectarian activism; exhorting modesty and piety; and borrowing and innovating to construct tradition (Hegland 1997). Through their expanding ritual involvement, females have gained pride, self-definition, and social recognition as well as opportunities to develop spiritual growth, networking skills, and ritual performance competence (Hegland 1997).

Women may use the enforced Islamic framework to their own advantage. Women from the conservative lower-middle classes find in Islamization's veiling and sex segregation the means to education, work, and public activity, without jeopardizing family and community support. Wearing a veil, it is easier for women to get out of the house with fewer negative ramifications. Veils form, in effect, mobile enclosures.[31] Islamic activities provide some women with additional opportunities, in situations where nonreligious opportunities may be severely restricted.

However, those positions and opportunities open to women under Islamist regimes are severely limited to only specific groups of women. When Islamic fundamentalism spreads to rural areas, women lose out. Village women's religious activities are generally limited to informal folk practices. In an Egyptian village, Judy Brink (1997) found fundamentalist young men pressuring their sisters to veil fully and stop engaging in "unIslamic," "superstitious" practices. Unable to study the Qur'an because of illiteracy, forbidden to attend the mosque, and not allowed to leave the home for religious discussions with other women, these village women have "been stripped of most of their religious rituals" (Brink 1997, 204).

Even in urban areas, expanded religious opportunities are available only for certain women. In Iran, enhanced religious power and position are open to literate women, mothers of martyrs, female relatives of highly placed male religious figures, young childless women, and older women whose grown children had left home (Friedl 1994). The pious *jalaseh*-attending women described by Torab were mainly mothers of grown children and grandmothers and therefore relatively free of childcare responsibilities. Success as a *jalaseh* preacher requires literacy, a dynamic and gracious personality, intelligence, religiosity, speaking ability, and permission from the male guardian for study and public speaking. The move to bring women speakers and gatherings under direct government control, by requiring speaker certification for example, will further limit which women can attain these positions (Torab 1996). Female candidates for office must be approved by a board. Generally, these candidates have been close relatives of male religious leaders. Only a tiny group of women (one journalist estimated the number to be no more than three dozen; Sciolino 1997, 48) are active in this field, using the clerics' own language and religious texts to judiciously pressure for changes benefiting women.

Peshawar Shi'i ritual eminence was likewise severely restricted to literate, wealthy, and child-free women. Famous *noheh* (mourning chant) performers were young, educated, unmarried women related to well-off Shi'i male leaders. Outstanding *majles* organizers, preachers, and ritual leaders were older women—widows, spinsters, childless women, or women whose children were grown (Hegland 1997).

If women do not act within the parameters dictated by Muslim males, governments, and societies, they may be snubbed, ostracized, harassed, dismissed from work or education, battered at home, attacked on the street, jailed, tortured, raped, or killed.[32] It is hardly surprising, then, that the great majority of women living in Muslim countries chose to pursue personal satisfaction through one form or another of "accommodating protest."[33]

Muslim women's accommodating strategies. With the recent scholarly emphasis on agency—how individuals act to serve their own interests—many researchers have examined the ways in which Muslim women, even those in Islamized nations, somehow manage to manipulate religious precepts and rituals to improve their situations without seriously risking their safety or their family, community, and religious connections. Generally, respect and protection is conditional upon women's obedience and silence (Kandiyoti 1987, 1988, 1991a, 1991b). Therefore, women do not usually resist openly. However, Muslim women often find subtle ways to critique misogynous religious attitudes. They evade phallocentric religious concepts and policies. They even use their confining religious and social frameworks to act as they wish and promote women's interests to one extent or another. Scholars are beginning to attend to "women's own efforts in shaping their religious and cultural lives" (Friedl 1997, 155), even in closely regulated conditions. Women may speak their dissent privately or in women's gatherings, disobey, veil inappropriately, develop personal Islamic interpretations, dissimulate and camouflage with pious behavior, vote, gain public office and pressure for change, and appropriate rituals and myths for their own needs. They may subvert religious meanings to better fit their own existential situations.

Women with relatively little power and few resources may be able only to think their critical observations or voice them privately to trusted associates. Excluded from meritorious religious rituals and judged for the sins committed due to their God-given inferiority, women in a Boir Ahmad village struggled to come to terms with their position in a male-dominated religion, anthropologist Erika Friedl reports. One poor, illiterate woman "declared very firmly to me that she thought that religion, as preached and practiced, was not made by God but by men in order to suppress women!" (1989, 133).

At a Shiraz women's *rozeh*, the female preacher warned that any woman who did not provide sex to her husband upon demand "would be hung by her breasts in hell," anthropologist Anne Betteridge records. In response to this misogynous religious teaching, one young woman commented to her neighbor, "If a man doesn't make love with his wife when she wants to, what do they hang him by?" (1989, 106).

After the 1979 Iranian revolution, when the mullah stationed at my village research site tried to prevent women's dancing at weddings, one young wife sarcastically commented, "If dancing is such a sin, why are men allowed to do it!" Iranian women disputed mainstream constructions of femininity and female sexuality by acting out suggestive songs at women's wedding parties (Safa-Isfahani 1980). Shahin Gerami found indications of critical gender subjectivity among Iranian women in spite of the deluge of messages from official sources about Islamist notions of femininity, backed by harsh repressive measures. Women rejected the regime's restriction of women to the home, and thus they rejected the prohibition against women's employment (Gerami 1994, 346).

Women at home-based religious gatherings might question the preacher, disagree with her or with other participants, or energetically express their own differing views. At one Shiraz Qur'an meeting, discussion centering on husbands' injustice became so heated that the preacher called for a *salavat* (jointly chanted salutation to the Prophet) to distract the women from their arguing. The women continued to fuss about Muslim men's right to polygyny (Kamalkhani 1997, 124).

Even women tightly controlled by family and community "Islamic" rules of subordination, obedience, and self-abnegation resist such domination through limited acts of disobedience. A woman may exert pressure on her husband, father, or brother by disobeying orders or refusing to provide services. But refusal to answer male demands violates Islamic morality and further proves women's sinfulness (Friedl 1994).

With Islamic societies stressing *hejab,* inevitably women turn veiling into subtle resistance. They veil to further their own goals.[34] Veiled women can more comfortably travel on buses and walk alone. If they attend classes and work while veiled, they are signaling their acquiescence to religious modesty requirements and public opinion while pursuing their own goals. Covered women can engage in a wider range of activities with less approbation and harassment.

In Iran, where the Islamic Republic requires veiling, even those women who are completely opposed to veiling must cover their hair and shape. When Iranian women overtly protested in the early 1980s, they were punished or jailed. Women learned they must accept veiling but resisted the forced modesty code in subtle ways (Moghissi 1994). Many cynically subvert forced modesty and use "good *hejab*" to gain official approval and thereby advancement and greater power. Others may follow the letter of the law while evading its basic purpose by turning veiling into fashionable ornamentation (Haeri 1993, 190–191; 1995a). They subtly defy *hejab* by allowing a lock of hair to slip out from under their scarves, using a bit of makeup, or wearing less than completely opaque stockings. Such individual acts of protest may bring punishment and condemnation for *bad hejab* (deficient covering) (Friedl 1994, 152–158; Haeri 1993, 1995a). However, women's slight deviations seem to have had some effect; strict enforcement of such subtle breaches of modesty has slackened.

Women may derive a sense of their overall importance from recitations about great historical Muslim women. Shi'i Muslim women can turn to such figures, such as Fatima's daughter Zaynab, who courageously joined her brother Imam Husein at Karbala, shepherded the Karbala survivors, and kept the Karbala story alive, to justify women's assertiveness and public roles.[35]

Some women in Iran exhibit pious behavior publicly to camouflage private misbehavior (Friedl 1994, 164). Women can manipulate the Islamic "code of piety" by meticulously and ostentatiously following politically correct dress, speech, and behavior when seeking university acceptance or career advancement.

In Iran, some women relatives of leading male figures are in charge of institutions and organizations. Some loyal, pro-regime women have run for office and been elected to Parliament (Esfandiari 1994). Female members of Parliament have cautiously attempted to improve conditions for women.

They have gained a four-month maternity leave, back housework wages for women divorced by their husbands, legalized abortion to save the mother's life, an equal opportunity law, and, instead of up to seventy-four lashes, only a jail term from ten days to two months for women who fail to cover head and body properly (Sciolino 1997, 49). Azam Taleqani, the outspoken daughter of the respected late Ayatollah Taleqani, has sharply reprimanded regime authorities for failing to consider women's human rights (Sanasarian 1992). Islamic elite women are proposing that women be eligible to be elected president and to work as judges. They have proposed establishing battered women's shelters, preventing automatic divorce at men's will, and protecting daughters from forced marriages.

In December 1996, women argued that the money that a groom agrees to give his wife in the event of divorce should be adjusted for inflation between the marriage and the divorce. A male member disagreed: "A woman who gets married at a young age is of high value to her husband, and as she becomes older, her value declines. So it is not right to adjust upward for inflation because she is worth less." The women were outraged. "He believes that women are created to be used by men, that they are the second sex which should be in man's service. This is against the Koran," a female member of Parliament retorted. The measure was eventually passed (Sciolino 1997, 50).

Women and others in Iran who are disaffected recently expressed their dissatisfaction with the political/religious status quo by voting. In the May 1997 elections, in spite of the Islamic Republic regime's support for hardliner Parliament Speaker Ali Akbar Nateq Nouri, 69 percent of the massive 91 percent voter turnout voted for moderate, scholarly cleric Mohammed Khatami. Women and youth support gave Khatami his landslide victory.

Most commonly, Shi'i women's resistance to received phallocentric, top-down religious teachings is an unannounced, sometimes unconscious reworking of these teachings, emphasizing salient aspects and downplaying less-welcome aspects or subtly transforming their meanings. The great majority of Middle Eastern women continue to derive spiritual and social satisfaction from their various Muslim beliefs and practices, even if these amount to little more than quiet faith in God and occasional ritual participation. Their Muslim practices give them religious assistance and community support in coping with life-cycle events, especially death. Performing the five prayers daily can be a quiet escape from endless household work and child attendance, a moment of meditation, some time for the woman's own spirituality. Particularly in the Shi'i tradition, people feel that women are especially emotionally attached to the Karbala martyrs and the Prophet's family. As contemporary women have suffered much themselves, they empathize with the sorrowing Karbala females. Because of women's weeping and compassion for the saints, the saints may have a soft spot in their hearts for the women and their problems, it is felt, and are less able to resist their entreaties.

Muslim women commonly appropriate religious rituals and occasions for their own purposes while simultaneously involving themselves in their spiritual and religious aspects. Women at my Iranian village research site engaged in exciting, fulfilling antigovernment demonstrations during the 1978–1979 revolutionary period, defending their outings as religious duty (Hegland 1983; 1990, 189). Especially after the revolution, when they lost other occasions for legitimate gatherings, women turned to religiously meritorious Thursday afternoon graveyard visitations for recreation and socializing (Friedl 1994, 163). Making pilgrimages to local shrines (tombs of holy figures) is a female-dominated religious activity (Betteridge 1993; Mernissi 1989; Narasamamba 1992; Tapper [Lindisfarne] 1990). Many women feel more comfortable praying through the intermediation of holy persons. Although men belittle women's shrine visitations, women construct their pilgrimage experiences positively, Nancy Tapper (Lindisfarne) argues. Through shrine visits and *mevlud* services, women have "a relationship with the supernatural which is unmediated by men" (1990, 250). Even educated women who do not readily admit to shrine visitation may participate (Narasamamba 1992).[36] Some shrines are built for women saints, are maintained by women, and are visited exclusively by women.

Urban women enjoy refreshments and conviviality at *sofreh*s, *rozeh*s, and Moharram mourning gatherings and may sponsor rituals to compete with rivals.[37] As Betteridge notes, "The ritual meal may also be an occasion for showing off finery, gossiping, bawdy storytelling, singing, and dancing" (1989, 105). Often bereft of temporal means, Shi'i women try to solve their problems through religious vows and then celebrate their resolution with *rozeh*s.

Muslim women have always sought to find in religious beliefs and practices meanings for their own lives. Specific societal developments, however, may allow women to subvert androcentric teachings and rituals in particular ways. In the following paragraphs, I present three recent case studies of how Shi'i women have responded to societal change, subverting interpretations or rituals to better address their own existential situations.

Boir Ahmad village women: subverting, manipulating, and constructing ideal femininities. Friedl documents how postrevolutionary Iranian women take advantage of religious ambiguities and contradictions, utilize alternative legitimate models of Muslim womanhood, and construct ideal feminine models from below to defend a wide range of permissible decisions, lifestyles, and personalities. Even within their society's fundamentalist framework, Boir Ahmad village women were revising morality and femininities to

study, pursue careers, avoid marriage or at least large families, and participate in locally organized recreational activities (Friedl 1997).

Ordinary women develop their own versions of "ideal womanhood"
within the context of everyday life, Friedl asserts. Rather than visible signs
of piety and meticulous ritual enactment, women stress qualities necessary
for harmonious interaction such as kindness, honesty, and generosity
(Friedl 1997). Friedl notes how women in the Islamic Republic of Iran
are frequently urged to follow the example of Fatima, the Prophet
Muhammad's daughter, in obedience, humility, and endurance—very useful to male authorities. However, Fatima's reported level of self-effacement
goes beyond most women's abilities in this regard. Further, those women
most able to fulfill family responsibilities are sharp, assertive, and shrewd.
Thus, the woman who is both "good" in a pious sense and competent in
a practical sense is a contradiction. Rather than accepting the regime's
teachings about historical Shi'i women, Friedl found, Iranian women construct their own images of Fatima and her daughter Zaynab to fit their own
lives—as empathetic holy figures who understand women's problems and
grief (Friedl 1997, 148–151).

A Tehran woman preacher: quietly contesting engendered theology. In
her 1992 and 1993 research on Iranian women's *jalaseh,* prayer meetings
where the Qur'an is read and its meaning discussed, Azam Torab (1996)
found that women may formulate their own interpretations of Islam, even
while formally adhering to mainstream precepts, and may pass their self-
developed views on to other women. Through field research with one
renowned female *jalaseh* speaker, Mrs. Omid, Torab analyzes "an ethnographic situation in which an individual accepts dominant cultural versions
of gender, yet also speaks and behaves in ways which contest them" (1996,
235). Omid's formal acceptance of men's monopoly over reason and
women's inherent emotionality contrasted with her Islamic gender ideology
modifications constructed from experience and social interaction. She
agreed wholeheartedly with Hazrat-e Ali's[38] statement on women as lacking both wisdom and faith. The speaker endorsed the dominant Islamic
view that men's and women's natures are inherently different, suiting them
for different responsibilities and domains. Further, she preached strict sexual segregation and women's complete *hejab.*

However, in her *jalaseh* "lived experience," Torab found, Omid offered
reformulations of these Islamic gender teachings. She expected women to
establish intentions for religious practices and good behavior. As intention
is thought to require both emotion and reason, clearly Omid saw women
as capable of rationality. Although she cited women's natural wish to "flirt
with men" as the reason for sexual segregation, she subverted this view in
her gatherings. It is men, she said, who are lustful. They are not able to
control themselves, and so women must be responsible for maintaining

morality through veiling and segregation. In their interactions with her, women attribute to her characteristics that are masculinized in dominant religious discourses. Because of her religious standing, they see her as possessing justice, rationality, divinely transmitted knowledge, spiritual blessing and healing power, and authority over women (Torab 1996).

"Rather than contest the dominant discourses," according to Torab, "the women appropriate and transcend them through their particular constructions of piety. . . . Through their ritual discussions and performances, the women can alter themselves and their circumstances, as well as those of others, in a positive way in this world and the next" (Torab 1996, 248).

Peshawar Shi'i women: forming and asserting alternative femininities through ritual practice. In my own 1989–1990 research in Peshawar (1995, 1997, 1998a, 1998b), I found another example of how Shi'i women can simultaneously hold a multiplicity of gender constructs. While accepting the religiously dominant view of women at one level, at another level, that of ritual practice, some Peshawar Shi'i women constructed themselves as competitive, assertive, aggressive, competent, and famous; as talented performers, generous hosts, powerful speakers, spiritual leaders, and able organizers. Partly because of Pakistan's troubled history with Hindu India as well as enmity and violence between the minority Pakistani Shi'is and the majority Pakistani Sunnis, Peshawar Shi'i women did not verbally express differences with androcentric Muslim theology. Particularly because of their sense of being under siege, the women felt certain attachments to patriarchal Shi'i spirituality, religious community, and family. Rather than voicing resistance, as did Mrs. Omid, the Tehran *jalaseh* speaker, these women employed their own bodies to develop and convey gender meanings through their ritual performances. Through their Shi'i ritual practices, they implicitly contested views of female religious dependence and unworthiness.

For example, Shi'i women routinely spent the more than two and a half months prescribed for mourning engaged in a strenuous round of home-based rituals, attending up to even eight a day. As ritual participation was segregated, women served as preachers, organizers, Qur'an readers, mourners, and prayer leaders. Certain women and girls excelled at performing mourning hymns and chants. Other women administered the ritual process, hosted ritual gatherings, or developed distinct flagellation styles. Women played significant roles in reaching out to other women, thus unifying the Peshawar Shi'i community. They disseminated information about violence against Shi'is and roused other women to grief and anger. Women developed leadership and managerial abilities, performance renown, social skills and networks, assertiveness, and self-confidence. While acting out Shi'i mourning rituals, and gaining religious and spiritual credit, these women addressed their own aims in religious practice, pursuing their own enjoyment, mobility, and spiritual comfort as well as socializing. Especially for the outstanding participants, the meanings and identities Peshawar women constructed through their ritual experiences seemed to affect their sense of self and social place more potently than phallocentric Shi'i ritual symbols, sermons, and gender beliefs (Hegland 1997, 1998a, 1998b).[39]

Conclusion

Until recently, neither Muslim males nor outsiders were much aware of how women molded practices and created meanings to better answer their own spiritual and temporal needs. Today, numerous researchers are investigating and publishing on women's religious rituals and worldviews. Many Muslim societies, governments, and individuals have recently focused on women's appearance, segregation, behavior, and family connections as the primary sign of Muslim identity, power, and resistance to the West. As efforts are made to pressure women into the roles needed to convey the desired religious and political meaning, women are increasingly sensitized and entering into the dialogue. Gender has become the major site of contention in Middle Eastern Islam, and women's religious voices are rising.

Escalating religious pressure on women has brought a backlash of resistance, from private dissenting thoughts to comprehensive scholarly rejection of Islam because of its perceived misogynous perspective. With the growth of global culture and, as a result, with many Muslim communities living away from their home countries, Muslim governments, movements, and leaders cannot escape international commentary and pressure. In the context of the ensuing controversies, Muslim women (and men) have put religious authorities on the defensive in some cases and, with the passage of national labor requirements, have managed to manipulate them into easing restrictions on women.

In arguing that an Islamic environment protects and supports women, Muslim leaders are implicitly agreeing with feminists that women's rights and quality of life are important. They are pressured to take steps to demonstrate Islam's benefits for women. In some ways, Iranian officials have been led, unwittingly, to continue the gender struggle on feminist ground. It is not only women in Muslim countries who are forced to struggle on terms defined by the opposition.

In many ways Muslim women are making their marks and impacting gender and religion. But ultimately, women living in Muslim societies can go only so far in co-opting, revising, and rejecting Islamic beliefs, practices, policies, and history. Islam has developed over long centuries of male control in patriarchal cultures. The religion is still largely based in heavily male-dominated and patriarchal nations. How much women will be able to revise Islamic beliefs and practices depends a great deal on developments in Islamic nations—their political, economic, social, and cultural conditions. Context powerfully constrains individuals' agency and worldview formation. People gather skills and predispositions for religious interpretation from their social and cultural environments. It is not reasonable to expect interpretations of Islam to become less phallocentric and misogynous if the corresponding social environments do not.

The religious freedom of women living in the Islamic Republic of Iran is severely constrained and that of women in other Muslim countries limited to various degrees. Nevertheless, their continuous if accommodating resistance to phallocentric Islamic interpretations cannot but bear some fruit.

Notes

1. Middle Eastern women scholars who study and write about Middle Eastern women are so numerous that it is impossible to list them here. A look at the bibliography at the end of this chapter confirms how active they are.

2. In her stunning analysis of Saudi women's writings, anthropologist Saddeka Arebi (1994) documents how female writers join the discourse on gender and Islam. They cautiously but effectively wield Islamic sources and beliefs to further women's interests and opportunities.

3. People of many religious heritages live in the Middle East: Armenians, Assyrians, Druzes, Jews, Baha'is, and Zoroastrians. But in order to maintain focus, I will discuss gender only in relation to Islam, the majority religion by far in the region.

4. For typical, more conservative Islamic views on women's place in marriage, family, and society, see Ahmad 1995 and Durkee 1995.

5. Shi'is and Sunnis (the latter form the majority in most Muslim countries) are the two main groups of Muslims. Like Catholic Christians, Shi'is believe in intercession between God and humanity—in this case through the Family of the Prophet, imams (successors to the Prophet), and *imamzadeh* (descendants of the imams). Similar to Protestant Christians, orthodox Sunnis do not accept intermediation or spiritual hierarchy, although many among the Sunni masses do.

6. I resided in Iran in 1966–1968, summer 1969, 1971–1972, summer 1977, and June 1978–December 1979; and in Peshawar, Pakistan, in August 1990–January 1991 and July 1991–September 1992. For research funding, I am grateful to the Social Science Research Council and the American Council of Learned Societies; the State University of New York at Binghamton; the American Association of University Women; the National Endowment for the Humanities; Franklin and Marshall College; Santa Clara University; and Fulbright. I am heavily indebted to the numerous Iranian and Pakistani women who have so warmly befriended and assisted me, enriching my life and making my research and writing possible. Thanks to Diane Jonte-Pace for thoughtful suggestions.

7. In this chapter I will not be privileging orthodox, clerical approaches to Islam. To the contrary, I will discuss Islam as it is popularly understood and practiced in specific settings. Information has been gathered by anthropological field research, mainly participant observation and in-depth interviewing.

8. In discussing the connections between gender and Islam, I have no option but to consider Islam as it is defined, practiced, and understood by specific individuals and groups: Islamic beliefs and practices are only available to me through the prism of specific Muslim contexts. Therefore, I will deal with the realities of how "Islamic" nationals, societies, communities, and individuals affect women and how women deal with these constraints, practices, and ideologies.

9. See Betteridge 1985, 1989, 1993; Hegland 1997, 1998b; and Kamalkhani 1993, 1997. In their study of Turkish village *mevlud*, poetic rituals centered on the Prophet Muhammad's life, Tapper (Lindisfarne) and Tapper argue that women's *mevlud* practices, although more "popular" and "unorthodox," actually carry great significance. Women's emotional rituals emphasizing miraculous events provide intimacy with the Prophet and allow him special holy status enabling intercession. "In their services, which almost always occur in the context of death, women create and confirm the promise of individual salvation which is offered to all Muslims. . . . death can be overcome by seeking Muhammad's intercession with God, the acknowledged source of all creation" (1987, 84, 85). Men and the local religious leaders deny the *mevlud's* significance. However, the authors assert, women's *mevlud* practices express central spiritual values shared by both men and women. In the face of the state-controlled Islamic hierarchy's denigration and banning of home-based religious gatherings, men, more active in public and state affairs, "become both guardians and enactors of the state-established orthodoxy," whereas "the women seem to have become the repositories of spiritual values to which both women and men subscribe but which, paradoxically, only women can experience with performative immediacy because of their inferior status vis-à-vis past and present religious establishments" (1987, 83, 86).

10. Betteridge 1989; Friedl 1989; Schubel 1993; Tapper (Lindisfarne) 1990; Tapper (Lindisfarne) and Tapper 1987; and Torab 1996.

11. Some earlier exceptions were Atkinson 1832; Beck 1980; Fernea 1989; Fernea and Fernea 1978; Friedl 1989; Nashat 1983; Tapper (Lindisfarne) 1978, 1983; Rice 1923; and Smith 1981.

12. Similarly, women's involvement with the *zar* cult of spirit possession in the Sudan is often seen as unorthodox and peripheral to Islam. See Boddy 1989; Hale 1996; and Kapchan 1996.

13. On the tenth ('Ashura in Arabic) of this Arab lunar month, Shi'i Muslims commemorate the A.D. 680 martyrdom of Imam Husein (grandson of the Prophet Muhammad and the Shi'i community's third imam, or leader, after the Prophet's death in A.D. 632). Imam Husein and some seventy of his male followers were killed on the Karbala plains, south of Baghdad in present-day Iraq, in their battle against the reigning caliph's army. After the very uneven battle, the victorious caliph's army took the womenfolk to the Damascus caliphate. According to tradition, the courageous lamentations and recounting of the Karbala tragedy by the captive Zaynab, sister of Imam Husein, initiated the Shi'i mourning commemorations of weeping, telling stories about the Karbala martyrs, and acting them out in passion plays. For a discussion of *sofrehs*, see Betteridge 1989 and Jamzadeh and Mills 1986.

14. "Aliabad" (pseudonym for my 1978–1979 Iranian research site), located half an hour from the outskirts of Shiraz, is a Fars village that had a population of some 3,000 at the time.

15. The Mohajir are migrants from India; the Qizilbash are Persianized Anatolians who had been Nadir Shah's soldiers during his late 1730s India campaign.

16. During the late 1980s and early 1990s, Shi'i leaders in Peshawar were attempting to unify Shi'is from various ethnic backgrounds, such as the Mohajir, Qizilbash, and Pashtuns (the majority ethnic group in Pakistan's North-West Frontier Province), to form a more effective interest/pressure group vis-à-vis the Pakistani government and country's majority Sunni population. Peshawar Shi'i women were active in reaching out to women from other ethnic groups and unifying them by making them feel welcome in Shi'i rituals and rousing their emotions after violence against Shi'is (Hegland 1997).

17. See Azari 1983; Badran 1994, 1995; Brink and Mencher 1997; Hale 1996; Hegland 1997, 1998a; Hendessi 1990; Kandiyoti 1991a, 1991b, 1996; V. Moghadam 1993, 1994a, 1994b; Moghissi 1994; Nashat 1983; Ong 1990; Paidar 1995; Peteet 1991; Reeves 1989; Tabari and Yeganeh 1982; and Zuhur 1992.

18. Sondra Hale has been studying "the manipulation of religious ideology toward a more 'native/authentic' culture for political mobilization in Sudan." There too, secular forces struggled with "cultural nationalist religious forces, who see a 'pure' and authentic Islam as Sudan's only defense and cultural salvation against an invading west" (1994, 149; 1996). See also V. Moghadam 1993, 1994a, 1994b; Moghissi 1994; Paidar 1995.

19. See also Bouatta and Cherifati-Merabtine 1994.

20. One young Iranian woman living in the United States sharply criticized Muhammad, specifically citing his sexual behavior—his many wives and his consummation of marriage with nine-year-old Aisha.

21. Shi'i theology accepts dissimulation to safeguard life and welfare.

22. Many Iranians in the United States have reported such cases to me among their families and relatives.

23. See Riffat Hassan's (1993, 1995a, 1995b, 1996) and Fatima Mernissi's (1991a, 1991b, 1992, 1993, 1995, 1996) later work for examples of feminist scholarship on Muslim theology and history. For others who have suggested Islamic interpretations more positive for women, see Afkhami 1995; Afkhami and Vaziri 1996; Engineer 1992; Ghadbian 1995; Kausar 1995; and Stowasser 1994.

24. Kandiyoti argues that ideas of "cultural imperialism" have "discouraged a systematic exploration of the local institutions and cultural practices, centrally implicated in the production of gender hierarchies and in forms of subordination based on gender" (1996, 18). Moghissi's Iranian case study (1994) documents how "traditional" culture and religion have been used to combat imperialism colonialism, thus placing the main emphasis on external threats and minimizing attention to internal problems. See also Haeri 1993, 1995a; Hale 1994, 1996; V. Moghadam 1993, 1994a, 1994b; Najmabadi 1987, 1991, 1994; and Paidar 1995.

25. In Hale's analysis, similarly, in the Sudan, "The modern Islamist woman is the *embodiment* of the Islamic nation and the reproducer of its culture." But she must also help with the work of nation building. "These expectations, then, often require that she earn wages, that she hold office, drive a car, get an education, educate the children, and the like. She becomes, then, the *modern Islamic Woman*" (Hale 1994, 162). See also Baffoun 1994.

26. After Gaafar Mohamed el-Nimeiri declared the Sudan to be an Islamic republic in 1983, "Self-appointed moral guardians harassed women in the streets about their conduct or dress" (Hale 1994, 149). In Algeria, fundamentalists have murdered a number of women for displaying less than satisfactory Islamic dress or comportment and beaten up female students for staying out late (Baffoun 1994). The Afghan Taleban are notorious for their repressive treatment of women.

27. See also Hale 1994 for similar restrictions in the Sudan.

28. Saba Mahmud's forthcoming dissertation (Department of Anthropology, Stanford University) focuses on Egyptian women's flourishing mosque involvement.

29. A couple of Mahtab-e Zahra women educators regularly visited my village research site to teach women about Islam.

30. In 1991, I met a young Indian Muslim woman who, with her husband, was on her way back to Qom to continue her religious education. I also talked with two young Peshawar Shi'i women who studied in Qom.

31. Interestingly, the Persian word for veil—chador—is the same as the word for tent.

32. All of this can happen to Western women as well. Ten percent of American professional men beat their wives, and the leading cause of violent death among American women is a murderous mate. American women must self-censor their appearance, behavior, and activities and when, where, and with whom they move around. Even then they may be raped. However, in general, Middle Eastern Muslim women's behavioral parameters are narrower and their "misconduct" punished more severely.

33. See MacLeod's (1991, 1992) use of this term. For examples of Muslim women's accommodating resistance additional to those presented below, see Abu-Lughod 1986, 1990; Afkhami 1995; Afshar 1993; Afshar and Paidar 1996; al-Khayyat 1990; Altorki 1986; Arebi 1994; Beck and Keddie 1978; Boddy 1989; Bodman and Tohidi 1997; El-Solh and Mabro 1994; Fernea 1989; Friedl 1989, 1991a, 1991b, 1994, 1997; Gocek and Balaghi 1994; Haeri 1989; Hale 1996; Jalal 1991; Jeffery 1989; Kandiyoti 1987, 1988, 1991a; Kapchan 1996; Keddie and Baron 1991; MacLeod 1991, 1992; Milani 1992; V. Moghadam 1993, 1994a, 1994b; Moghissi 1994; Nashat 1983; Ong 1990; Paidar 1995; Peteet 1991; Tapper (Lindisfarne) 1988–1989, 1991; Tohidi 1991, 1994, 1996a, 1996b; Wikan 1982; and Zuhur 1992.

There are no firm boundaries between those Muslim women who resist more overtly and those who practice accommodating resistance. Likewise, one cannot divide resisting women into discrete categories according to their level or stance of resistance; these categories are for purposes of more efficient discussion. In reality, women's stances will likely fit into more than one category.

34. See El Guindi 1981, 1983; Friedl 1994; Hoodfar 1991; MacLeod 1991, 1992; V. Moghadam 1994a, 1994b; and Zuhur 1992.

35. See D'Souza n.d.; Friedl 1993, 1997; Haeri 1993, 1995a; Mernissi 1992, 1993, 1996; Schubel 1993; Shariati 1980; and Spellberg 1994.

36. Fatima Mernissi recognized shrine visitation's value for women—providing emotional and psychological support, a space to complain, and an opportunity to analyze personal problems. But, she cautions, frequenting sanctuaries, "women invest all of their efforts and energies in trying to get a supernatural force to influ-

ence the oppressive structure on their behalf. This does not affect the formal power structure, the outside world" (1989, 111). Of course, when repression is too effective, direct opposition may be disastrous rather than productive.

37. Sunni women host and attend rituals welcoming back hajjis (pilgrims to Mecca), Qur'an reading rituals (each participant takes a separate bound chapter to recite to herself), and rituals honoring the Prophet Muhammad's birthday. In Pakistan, for example, I found women managing the complex hajj ceremonies. Peshawar Shi'i women held Qur'an reading sessions for many different occasions: receiving a degree, supporting a male relative's political candidacy, showing gratitude for a family member's recovery from illness, or welcoming a traveler home. Sunni Muslim women in Peshawar commemorated the Prophet Muhammad's birthday by singing hymns and reciting religious sources and praise poetry. I attended such gatherings, most individually sponsored but also one for the entire undergraduate and master's program student body at the University of Peshawar's College of Home Economics. For a description of Sarajevo women's *mevlud*s, see Sorabji 1994. Qureshi (1996) describes the rituals of Pakistani women living in Canada, such as the *milad* to praise the Prophet and *qur'ankhwani,* or Qur'an recitations. Werbner (1988) documents Pakistani labor migrants' "interhousehold women-centered spirituality" in England. Buitelaar (1993) discusses Moroccan women's religious participation during Ramadan and at other rituals. Young (1993) argues that gender restrictions were loosened during pilgrimage rituals at Mecca.

38. Hazrat-e Ali was the Prophet Muhammad's son-in-law, married to his daughter Fatima; he became the first Shi'i Imam, leader of the Shi'i community after the death of the Prophet in A.D. 632.

39. For a discussion of the shortcomings of accommodating resistance tactics, see Hegland 1995.

References

Abu-Lughod, Lila. 1986. *Veiled Sentiments: Honor and Poetry in a Bedouin Society.* Berkeley: University of California Press.

———. 1990. "The Romance of Resistance: Tracing Transformations of Power Through Bedouin Women." *American Ethnologist* 17: 41–55.

Afkhami, Mahnaz, ed. 1995. *Faith and Freedom: Women's Human Rights in the Muslim World.* Syracuse, N.Y.: Syracuse University Press.

Afkhami, Mahnaz, and Erika Friedl, eds. 1994. *In the Eye of the Storm: Women in Post-revolutionary Iran.* Syracuse, N.Y.: Syracuse University Press.

Afkhami, Mahnaz, and Haleh Vaziri, eds. 1996. *Claiming Our Rights: A Manual for Women's Human Rights Education in Muslim Societies.* Bethesda, Md.: Sisterhood Is Global Institute.

Afshar, Haleh. 1996. *Feminism and Islam: Legal and Literary Perspectives.* New York: New York University Press.

Afshar, Haleh, ed. 1993. *Women in the Middle East: Perceptions, Realities, and Struggles for Liberation.* London: Macmillan.

Afshar, Haleh, and Parvin Paidar. 1996. "Women and the Political Process in Twentieth Century Iran." *Development and Change* 27: 606.

Ahmad, Imtiaz. 1995. "The Role of the Family in Islamic Society." *Dialogue and Alliance* 9 (Spring-Summer): 40–48.

Ahmed, Leila. 1991. *Women and Gender in Islam: The Historical Roots of a Modern Debate.* New Haven: Yale University Press.

Ahmed, Nausheen. 1994. "Pakistan: Rape Laws Against Women." *WIN News* 20: 34.

Altorki, Soraya. 1986. *Women in Saudi Arabia: Ideology and Behavior Among the Elite.* New York: Columbia University Press.

Arebi, Saddeka. 1994. *Women and Words in Saudi Arabia: The Politics of Literary Discourse.* New York: Columbia University Press.

Atkinson, James. 1832. *Customs and Manners of the Women of Persia and Their Domestic Superstitions.* London: Oriental Translation Fund of Great Britain and Ireland.

Azari, Farah. 1983. *Women of Iran: The Conflict with Fundamentalist Islam.* London: Attaca Press.

Badran, Margot. 1994. "Gender Activism: Feminists and Islamists in Egypt." In *Identity Politics and Women: Cultural Reassertions and Feminisms in International Perspective,* ed. Valentine M. Moghadam, 202–227. Boulder: Westview Press.

_____. 1995. *Feminists, Islam, and Nation: Gender and the Making of Modern Egypt.* Princeton: Princeton University Press.

Baffoun, Alya. 1994. "Feminism and Muslim Fundamentalism: The Tunisian and Algerian Cases." In *Identity Politics and Women: Cultural Reassertions and Feminisms in International Perspective,* ed. Valentine M. Moghadam, 167–182. Boulder: Westview Press.

Bayat-Philipp, Mangol. 1978. "Women and Revolution in Iran, 1905–1911." In *Women in the Muslim World,* ed. Lois Beck and Nikki Keddie (Cambridge: Cambridge University Press).

Beck, Lois. 1980. "The Religious Lives of Muslim Women." In *Women in Contemporary Muslim Societies,* ed. Jane Smith. Lewisburg, Pa.: Bucknell University Press.

Beck, Lois, and Nikki Keddie, eds. 1978. *Women in the Muslim World.* Cambridge: Harvard University Press.

Betteridge, Anne. 1985. "Ziarat: Pilgrimage to the Shrines of Shiraz." Ph.D. dissertation, Department of Anthropology, University of Chicago.

_____. 1989. "The Controversial Vows of Urban Muslim Women in Iran." In *Unspoken Worlds: Women's Religious Lives,* ed. Nancy Auer Falk and Rita M. Gross, 102–111. Belmont, Calif.: Wadsworth Publishing Company.

_____. 1993. "Women and Shrines in Shiraz." In *Everyday Life in the Muslim Middle East,* ed. Donna Bowen and Evelyn Early, 239–247. Bloomington: Indiana University Press.

Boddy, Janice. 1989. *Wombs and Alien Spirits: Women, Men, and the Zar Cult in Northern Sudan.* Madison: University of Wisconsin Press.

Bodman, Herbert L., and Nayereh Tohidi, eds. 1997. *Diversity Within Unity: Gender Dynamics and Change in Muslim Societies.* Boulder: Lynne Rienner.

Bouatta, Cherifa, and Doria Cherifati-Merabtine. 1994. "The Social Representation of Women in Algeria's Islamist Movement." In *Identity Politics and Women:*

Cultural Reassertions and Feminisms in International Perspective, ed. Valentine M. Moghadam, 183–201. Boulder: Westview Press.

Brink, Judy. 1997. "Lost Rituals: Sunni Muslim Women in Rural Egypt." In *Mixed Blessings: Gender and Religious Fundamentalism Cross Culturally,* ed. Judy Brink and Joan Mencher, 199–208. New York: Routledge.

Brink, Judy, and Joan Mencher, eds. 1997. *Mixed Blessings: Gender and Religious Fundamentalism Cross Culturally.* New York: Routledge.

Bruck, G. Vom. n.d. "Down-playing Gender: Khatm Rituals in San'a." *Quaderni di Studi Arabi.*

Buitelaar, Marjo. 1993. *Fasting and Feasting in Morocco: Women's Participation in Ramadan.* Mediterranean Series. Providence, R.I.: Berg.

D'Souza, Diane. n.d. "The Figure of Zaynab in Shi'i Devotional Life." Unpublished paper.

Durkee, Noura. 1995. "Marriage for a Muslimah: Surrender to Him for *Him.*" *Dialogue and Alliance* 9 (Spring-Summer): 115–123.

El Guindi, Fadwa. 1981. "Veiling *Infitah* with Muslim Ethic: Egypt's Contemporary Islamic Movement." *Social Problems* 28, (April): 465–485.

_____. 1983. "Veiled Activism: Egyptian Women in the Contemporary Islamic Movement." *Femmes de al mediterranée, Peuples mediterranéens* 22, no. 23: 79–89.

El-Solh, Camillia Fawzi, and Judy Mabro, eds. 1994. *Muslim Women's Choices: Religious Belief and Social Realities.* Providence, R.I.: Berg.

Engineer, Asghar Ali. 1992. *The Rights of Women in Islam.* London: C. Hurst.

Esfandiari, Haleh. 1994. "The Majles and Women's Issues in the Islamic Republic of Iran." In *In the Eye of the Storm: Women in Post-revolutionary Iran,* ed. Mahnaz Afkhami and Erika Friedl, 61–79. Syracuse, N.Y.: Syracuse University Press.

Farman Farmaian, Sattareh, with Dona Munker. 1992. *Daughter of Persia: A Woman's Journey from Her Father's Harem Through the Islamic Revolution.* New York: Crown.

Ferdows, Adele. 1983. "Women and the Islamic Revolution." *International Journal of Middle East Studies* 15: 283–298.

Fernea, Elizabeth Warnock. 1989. *Guests of the Sheik: An Ethnography of an Iraqi Village.* New York: Anchor Books.

Fernea, Robert A., and Elizabeth Warnock Fernea. 1978. "Variations in Religious Observance Among Islamic Women." In *Scholars, Saints, and Sufis: Muslim Religious Institutions Since 1500,* ed. Nikki Keddie, 385–401. Berkeley: University of California Press.

Friedl, Erika. 1983. "State Ideology and Village Women." In *Women and Revolution in Iran,* ed. Guity Nashat, 217–230. Boulder: Westview Press.

_____. 1989. "Islam and Tribal Women in a Village in Iran." In *Unspoken Worlds: Women's Religious Lives,* ed. Nancy Auer Falk and Rita M. Gross, 125–133. Belmont, Calif.: Wadsworth Publishing Company.

_____. 1991a. *Women of Deh Koh: Lives in an Iranian Village.* New York: Penguin.

_____. 1991b. "The Dynamics of Women's Spheres of Action in Rural Iran." In *Women in Middle Eastern History: Shifting Boundaries in Sex and Gender,* ed. Nikki Keddie and Beth Baron, 195–214. New Haven: Yale University Press.

_____. 1993. "Legendary Heroines: Ideal Womanhood and Ideology in Iran." In *The Other Fifty Percent: Multicultural Perspectives on Gender Relations,* ed. Mari Womack and Judith Marti, 261–266. Prospect Heights, Ill.: Waveland Press.

_____. 1994. "Sources of Female Power in Iran." In *In the Eye of the Storm: Women in Post-revolutionary Iran,* ed. Mahnaz Afkhami and Erika Friedl, 151–167. Syracuse, N.Y.: Syracuse University Press.

_____. 1997. "Ideal Womanhood in Postrevolutionary Iran." In *Mixed Blessings: Gender and Religious Fundamentalism Cross Culturally,* ed. Judy Brink and Joan Mencher, 143–157. New York: Routledge.

Gerami, Shahin. 1994. "The Role, Place, and Power of Middle-Class Women in the Islamic Republic." In *Identity Politics and Women: Cultural Reassertions and Feminisms in International Perspective,* ed. Valentine M. Moghadam, 329–348. Boulder: Westview Press.

Ghadbian, Najib. 1995. "Islamists and Women in the Arab World: From Reaction to Reform?" *American Journal of Islamic Social Science* 12 (Spring): 19–35.

Gocek, Fatma Muge, and Shiva Balaghi, eds. 1994. *Reconstructing Gender in the Middle East: Tradition, Identity, and Power.* New York: Columbia University Press.

Haeri, Shahla. 1981. "Women, Law, and Social Change in Iran." In *Women in Contemporary Muslim Societies,* ed. Jane Smith, 209–234. Lewisburg, Pa.: Bucknell University Press.

_____. 1983. "The Institution of *Mut'a* Marriage in Iran: A Formal and Historical Perspective." In *Women and Revolution in Iran,* ed. Guity Nashat, 231–252. Boulder: Westview Press.

_____. 1989. *Law of Desire: Temporary Marriage in Shi'i Iran.* Syracuse, N.Y.: Syracuse University Press.

_____. 1993. "Obedience Versus Autonomy: Women and Fundamentalism in Iran and Pakistan." In *Fundamentalisms and Society: Reclaiming the Sciences, the Family, and Education.* The Fundamentalism Project, vol. 2., ed. Martin E. Marty and R. Scott Applyby, 181–213. Chicago: University of Chicago Press.

_____. 1994. "Temporary Marriage: An Islamic Discourse on Female Sexuality in Iran." In *In the Eye of the Storm: Women in Post-revolutionary Iran,* ed. Mahnaz Afkhami and Erika Friedl, 98–114. Syracuse, N.Y.: Syracuse University Press.

_____. 1995a. "Of Feminism and Fundamentalism in Iran and Pakistan." *Contention: Debates in Society, Culture, and Science* 4 (Spring): 129–149.

_____. 1995b. "The Politics of Dishonor: Rape and Power in Pakistan." In *Faith and Freedom: Women's Human Rights in the Muslim World,* ed. Mahnaz Afkhami, 161–174. Syracuse, N.Y.: Syracuse University Press.

Hale, Sondra. 1994. "Gender, Religious Identity, and Political Mobilization." In *Identity Politics and Women: Cultural Reassertions and Feminisms in International Perspective,* ed. Valentine M. Moghadam, 145–169. Boulder: Westview Press.

_____. 1996. *Gender Politics in Sudan: Islamism, Socialism, and the State.* Boulder: Westview Press.

Hardacre, Helen. 1993. "The Impact of Fundamentalisms on Women, the Family, and Interpersonal Relations." In *Fundamentalisms and Society: Reclaiming the Sciences, the Family, and Education.* The Fundamentalism Project, vol. 2., ed. Martin E. Marty and R. Scott Applyby, 129–150. Chicago: University of Chicago Press.

Hassan, Riffat. 1993. "The Issue of Gender Equality in the Context of Creation in Islam." *Chicago Theological Seminary Register* 83 (Winter-Spring): 3–15.

_____. 1995a. "Reform, Revivalism, and the Place of Women in Islam: An Interview with Riffat Hassan." *Second Opinion* 20 (April): 62–71.

_____. 1995b. "Women in Muslim Culture: Some Critical Theological Reflections." *Dialogue and Alliance* 9 (Spring-Summer): 124–137.

_____. 1996. "Western Denial of a Progressive, Pivotal Islam Must End." *The Witness* 79: 28.

Hegland, Mary Elaine. 1983. "Aliabad Women: Revolution As Religious Activity." In *Women and Revolution in Iran,* ed. Guity Nashat. Boulder: Westview Press.

_____. 1986. "Political Roles of Iranian Village Women." *Middle East Report* 16, (January-February).

_____. 1990. "Women and the Iranian Revolution: A Village Case Study." *Dialectical Anthropology* 15: 183–192.

_____. 1991. "Political Roles of Aliabad Women: The Public-Private Dichotomy Transcended." In *Women in Middle Eastern History: Shifting Boundaries in Sex and Gender,* ed. Nikki Keddie and Beth Baron, 215–230. New Haven: Yale University Press.

_____. 1995. "Shi'a Women of Northwest Pakistan and Agency Through Practice: Ritual, Resistance, Resilience. *PoLAR: Political and Legal Anthropology Review* 18: 65–79.

_____. 1997. "A Mixed Blessing: The *Majales,* Shi'a Women's Rituals of Mourning in Northwest Pakistan." In *Mixed Blessings: Gender and Religious Fundamentalism Cross Culturally,* ed. Judy Brink and Joan Mencher, 179–196. New York: Routledge.

_____. 1998a. "The Paradoxical Power in Women's Majles Rituals: Freedom and Fundamentalism, Community and Coercion." *Signs* (Autumn).

_____. 1998b. "Fundamentalism and Flagellation: (Trans)Forming Meaning, Identity, and Gender Through Pakistani Women's Rituals of Mourning." *American Ethnologist.*

Hendessi, Mandana. 1990. *Armed Angels: Women in Iran.* Report no. 16. London: Change.

Higgins, Patricia J., and Pirouz Shoar-Ghaffari. 1994. "Women's Education in the Islamic Republic of Iran." In *In the Eye of the Storm: Women in Post-revolutionary Iran,* ed. Mahnaz Afkhami and Erika Friedl, 19–43. Syracuse, N.Y.: Syracuse University Press.

Hoodfar, Homa. 1991. "Return to the Veil: Personal Strategy and Public Participation in Egypt." In *Working Women: International Perspectives on Labour and Gender Ideology,* ed. Redclift and Sinclair, 104–124. London and New York: Routledge.

Jalal, Ayesha. 1991. "The Convenience of Subservience: Women and the State of Pakistan." In *Women, Islam, and the State,* ed. Deniz Kandiyoti, 77–114. Philadelphia: Temple University Press.

Jamzadeh, Laal, and Margaret Mills. 1986. "Iranian 'Sofreh': From Collective to Female Ritual." In *Gender and Religion: On the Complexity of Symbols,* ed. C. W. Bynum, S. Harrell, and P. Richman. Boston: Beacon Press.

Jeffery, Patricia. 1989. *Frogs in a Well: Indian Women in Purdah.* London: Zed Press.

Kamalkhani, Zahra. 1993. "Women's Everyday Religious Discourse in Iran." In *Women in the Middle East: Perceptions, Realities, and Struggles for Liberation,* ed. Haleh Afshar, 85–95. London: Macmillan.

––––––. 1997. *Women's Islam: Religious Practice Among Women in Today's Iran.* London: Kegan Paul.

Kandiyoti, Deniz. 1987. "Emancipated But Unliberated? Reflections on the Turkish Case." *Feminist Studies* 13: 317–318.

––––––. 1988. "Bargaining with Patriarchy." *Gender and Society* 2: 274–290.

––––––. 1991b. "Islam and Patriarchy: A Comparative Perspective." In *Women in Middle Eastern History: Shifting Boundaries in Sex and Gender,* ed. Nikki Keddie and Beth Baron, 23–42. New Haven: Yale University Press.

––––––. 1996. *Gendering the Middle East: Emerging Perspectives.* Syracuse, N.Y.: Syracuse University Press.

Kandiyoti, Deniz, ed. 1991a. *Women, Islam, and the State.* Philadelphia: Temple University Press.

Kapchan, Deborah. 1996. *Gender on the Market: Moroccan Women and the Revoicing of Tradition.* Philadelphia: University of Pennsylvania Press.

Kausar, Zeenath. 1995. *Women in Feminism and Politics: New Directions Towards Islamization.* Selangor, Malaysia: Women's Affairs Secretariat, International Islamic University Malaysia.

Keddie, Nikki. 1991. Introduction to *Women in Middle Eastern History: Shifting Boundaries in Sex and Gender,* ed. Nikki Keddie and Beth Baron, 1–22. New Haven: Yale University Press.

Keddie, Nikki, and Beth Baron. 1991. *Women in Middle Eastern History: Shifting Boundaries in Sex and Gender.* New Haven: Yale University Press.

al-Khayyat, Sana. 1990. *Honor and Shame: Women in Modern Iraq.* London: Al-Saqi Books.

MacLeod, Arlene Elowe. 1991. *Accommodating Protest: Working Women, the New Veiling, and Change in Cairo.* New York: Columbia University Press.

––––––. 1992. "Hegemonic Relations and Gender Resistance: The New Veiling As Accommodating Protest in Cairo." *Signs* 17: 533–557.

Mehdi, Rubya. 1990. "The Offence of Rape in the Islamic Law of Pakistan." *International Journal of the Sociology of Law* 18: 19–29.

Mernissi, Fatima. 1975. *Beyond the Veil: Male-Female Dynamics in a Modern Muslim Society.* Cambridge, Mass.: Schenkman Publishing Company.

––––––. 1989. "Women, Saints, and Sanctuaries in Morocco." In *Unspoken Worlds: Women's Religious Lives,* ed. Nancy Auer Falk and Rita M. Gross, 112–121. Belmont, Calif.: Wadsworth Publishing Company.

––––––. 1991a. *The Veil and the Male Elite: A Feminist Interpretation of Women's Rights in Islam.* Trans. Mary Jo Lakeland. New York: Addison-Wesley.

_____. 1991b. *Women and Islam*. Oxford: Blackwell.

_____. 1992. *Islam and Democracy: Fear of the Modern World*. Trans. Mary Jo Lakeland. New York: Addison-Wesley.

_____. 1993. *The Forgotten Queens of Islam*. Minneapolis: University of Minnesota Press.

_____. 1995. *The Harem Within*. New York: Bantam.

_____. 1996. *Women's Rebellion and Islamic Memory*. London: Zed Press.

Milani, Farzaneh. 1992. *Veils and Words: The Emerging Voices of Iranian Women Writers*. Syracuse, N.Y.: Syracuse University Press.

Mir-Hosseini, Ziba. 1993. "Women, Marriage, and the Law in Post-revolutionary Iran." In *Women in the Middle East: Perceptions, Realities, and Struggles for Liberation*, ed. Haleh Afshar, 59–84. London: Macmillan.

_____. 1996a. "Women and Politics in Post-Khomeini Iran: Divorce, Veiling, and Emerging Feminist Voices. In *Women and Politics in the Third World*, ed. Haleh Afshar New York: Routledge.

_____. 1996b. "Stretching the Limits: A Feminist Reading of the Shari'a in Post-Khomeini Iran." In *Feminism and Islam: Legal and Literary Perspectives*, ed. May Yamani. Berkshire, England: Ithaca Press.

Moghadam, Fatemeh E. 1994. "Commoditization of Sexuality and Female Labor Participation in Islam: Implications for Iran, 1960–1990." In *In the Eye of the Storm: Women in Post-revolutionary Iran*, ed. Mahnaz Afkhami and Erika Friedl, 80–97. Syracuse, N.Y.: Syracuse University Press.

Moghadam, Valentine M., ed. 1993. *Modernizing Women: Gender and Social Change in the Middle East*. Boulder: Lynne Rienner.

_____. 1994a. *Identity Politics and Women: Cultural Reassertions and Feminisms in International Perspective*. Boulder: Westview Press.

_____. 1994b. *Gender and National Identity: Women and Politics in Muslim Societies*. London: Zed Press.

Moghissi, Haideh. 1994. *Populism and Feminism in Iran*. New York: St. Martin's Press.

Mojab, Shahrzad. 1994. "Islamic Feminism: Alternative or Contradiction?" *Fireweed*: 18–25.

_____. 1995. "Iran." In *Academic Freedom Three: Education and Human Rights*, ed. John Daniel, Nigel Hartley, Yves Lador, Manfred Nowak, and Frederiek de Vlaming, 140–159. London: Zed Press.

Mumtaz, Khawar, and Farida Shaheed. 1987. *Women of Pakistan: Two Steps Forward One Step Back?* London: Zed Press.

Najmabadi, Afsaneh. 1987. "Iran's Turn to Islam: From Modernism to a Moral Order." *Middle East Journal* 41 (Spring).

_____. 1991. "Hazards of Modernity and Morality: Women, State, and Ideology in Contemporary Iran." In *Women, Islam, and the State*, ed. Deniz Kandiyoti, 48–76. Philadelphia: Temple University Press.

_____. 1994. "Power, Morality, and the New Muslim Womanhood." In *The Politics of Social Transformation in Iran, Afghanistan, and Pakistan*, ed. Myron Weiner and Ali Banuazizi, 366–389. Syracuse, N.Y.: Syracuse University Press.

Narasamamba, K. V. S. L. 1992. "The Dargahs of Women Saints in East Godavari District." *Bulletin of the Henry Martyn Institute of Islamic Studies* (Hyderabad, India) 11: 81–86.

Nashat, Guity, ed. 1983. *Women and Revolution in Iran.* Boulder: Westview Press.

Ong, Aihwa. 1990. "State Versus Islam: Malay Families, Women's Bodies, and the Body Politic in Malaysia." *American Ethnologist* 17 (May): 258–276.

Paidar, Parvin. 1995. *Women and the Political Process in Twentieth-Century Iran.* Cambridge: Cambridge University Press.

Pakzad, Sima. 1994. "Appendix 1: The Legal Status of Women in the Family in Iran." In *In the Eye of the Storm: Women in Post-revolutionary Iran,* ed. Mahnaz Afkhami and Erika Friedl, 169–179. Syracuse, N.Y.: Syracuse University Press.

Papanek, Hanna. 1994. "The Ideal Woman and the Ideal Society: Control and Autonomy in the Construction of Identity." In *Identity Politics and Women: Cultural Reassertions and Feminisms in International Perspective,* ed. Valentine M. Moghadam, 42–75. Boulder: Westview Press.

Peteet, Julie. 1991. *Gender in Crisis: Women and the Palestinian Resistance Movement.* New York: Columbia University Press.

Peters, Emrys L. 1956. "A Muslim Passion Play: Key to a Lebanese Village." *Atlantic Monthly* 198: 176–180.

_____. 1972. "Shifts in Power in a Lebanese Village." In *Rural Politics and Social Change in the Middle East,* ed. Richard Antoun and Iliya Harik, 165–197. Bloomington: Indiana University Press.

Pinault, David. 1992. *The Shiites: Ritual and Popular Piety in a Muslim Community.* New York: St. Martin's Press.

Qureshi, Regula Burckhardt. 1996. "Transcending Space: Recitation and Community Among South Asian Muslims in Canada." In *Making Muslim Space in North America and Europe,* ed. Barbara Daly Metcalf, 46–64. Berkeley: University of California Press.

Razavi, Shahrashoub. 1993. "Women, Work, and Power in the Rafsanjan Basin of Iran." In *Women in the Middle East: Perceptions, Realities, and Struggles for Liberation,* ed. Haleh Afshar, 117–136. London: Macmillan.

Reeves, Minou. 1989. *Female Warriors of Allah: Women and the Islamic Revolution.* New York: E. P. Dutton.

Rice, Colliver. 1923. *Persian Women and Their Ways.* London: Seeley, Service and Co.

Royanian, Simin. 1979. "A History of Iranian Women's Struggles." *Review of Iranian Political Economy and History* 3.

Rugh, Andrea B. 1993. "Reshaping Personal Relations in Egypt." In *Fundamentalisms and Society: Reclaiming the Sciences, the Family, and Education.* The Fundamentalism Project, vol. 2., ed. Martin E. Marty and R. Scott Applyby, 151–179. Chicago: University of Chicago Press.

Safa-Isfahani, Kaveh. 1980. "Female Centered World Views in Iranian Culture: Symbolic Representations of Sexuality in Dramatic Games." *Signs* 6: 33–53.

Sanasarian, Eliz. 1982. *The Women's Rights Movement in Iran: Mutiny, Appeasement, and Repression from 1900 to Khomeini.* New York: Praeger.

_____. 1992. "The Politics of Gender and Development in the Islamic Republic of Iran." *Journal of Developing Societies* 8: 56–68.

Schubel, Vernon James. 1991. "The Muharram Majlis: The Role of a Ritual in the Preservation of Shi'a Identity." In *Muslim Families in North America,* ed. Earle

H. Waugh, Sharon McIrvin Abu Laban, and Regula Burckhardt Qureshi. Edmonton: University of Alberta Press.

_____. 1993. *Religious Performance in Contemporary Islam: Shi'i Devotional Rituals in South Asia.* Columbia: University of South Carolina Press.

Sciolino, Elaine. 1997. "The Chanel Under the Chador." *New York Times Magazine,* May 4, 46–51.

Shaheed, Farida. 1989. "Purdah and Poverty in Pakistan." In *Women, Poverty, and Ideology in Asia,* ed. Haleh Afshar and Bina Agarwal, 17–42. London: Macmillan.

_____. 1994. "Controlled or Autonomous: Identity and the Experience of the Network, Women Living Under Muslim Laws." *Signs* 19: 997–1019.

Shariati, Ali. 1980. *Fatima Is Fatima.* Trans. Laleh Bakhtiar. Tehran: Hamdami Foundation.

Smith, Jane, ed. 1981. *Women in Contemporary Muslim Societies.* Lewisburg, Pa.: Bucknell University Press.

Sorabji, Cornelia. 1994. "Mixed Motives: Islam, Nationalism, and Mevluds in an Unstable Yugoslavia." In *Muslim Women's Choices: Religious Belief and Social Reality,* ed. Camillia Fawzi El-Solh and Judy Mabro, 108–127. Providence, R.I.: Berg.

Spellberg, Denise. 1994. *Politics, Gender, and the Islamic Past: The Legacy of 'A'isha bint Abi Bakr.* New York: Columbia University Press.

Stowasser, Barbara. 1994. *Women in the Qur'an: Traditions and Interpretations.* Oxford: Oxford University Press.

Tabari, Azar, and Nahid Yeganeh, eds. 1982. *In the Shadow of Islam: The Women's Movement in Iran.* London: Zed Press.

Tapper (Lindisfarne), Nancy. 1978. "The Women's Subsociety Among the Shahsevan Nomads of Iran." In *Women in the Muslim World,* ed. Lois Beck and Nikki Keddie. Cambridge: Harvard University Press.

_____. 1983. "Gender and Religion in a Turkish Town: A Comparison of Two Types of Women's Gatherings." In *Women's Religious Experience,* ed. P. Holden. London: Croom Helm.

_____. 1988–1989. "Changing Marriage Ceremonial and Gender Roles in the Arab World: An Anthropological Perspective." *Arab Affairs* 8: 117–135.

_____. 1990. "Ziyaret: Gender, Movement, and Exchange in a Turkish Community." In *Muslim Travellers: Pilgrimage, Migration, and the Religious Imagination,* ed. Dale R. Eickelman and James Piscatori, 236–255. Berkeley: University of California Press.

_____. 1991. *Bartered Brides: Politics, Gender, and Marriage in an Afghan Tribal Society.* Cambridge: Cambridge University Press.

Tapper (Lindisfarne), Nancy, and Richard Tapper. 1987. "The Birth of the Prophet: Ritual and Gender in Turkish Islam." *Man (n.s.)* 22: 69–92.

Thaiss, Gustav. 1978. "The Conceptualization of Social Change Through Metaphor." *Journal of Asian and African Studies* 13: 1–13.

Tohidi, Nayereh. 1991. "Gender and Islamic Fundamentalism: Feminist Politics in Iran." In *Third World Women and the Politics of Feminism,* ed. Chandra Talpade Mohanty, Ann Russo, and Lourdes Torres, 251–267. Bloomington: Indiana University Press.

_____. 1994. "Modernity, Islamization, and Women in Iran." In *Gender and National Identity: Women and Politics in Muslim Societies,* ed. Valentine M. Moghadam, 110–147. London: Zed Press.

_____. 1996a. "Soviet in Public, Azeri in Private: Gender, Islam, and Nationality in Soviet and Post-Soviet Azerbaijan." *Women's Studies International Forum* 19, (January-April): 111–123.

_____. 1996b. "'Fundamentalist' Backlash and Muslim Women in the Beijing Conference: New Challenges for International Women's Movements." *Canadian Woman Studies, les cahiers de la femme* 16: 30–34.

Torab, Azam. 1996. "Piety As Gendered Agency: A Study of Jalaseh Ritual Discourse in an Urban Neighbourhood in Iran." *Journal of the Royal Anthropological Institute* 2: 235–251.

Werbner, Pnina. 1988 "'Sealing' the Koran: Offering and Sacrifice Among Pakistani Labour Migrants." *Cultural Dynamics* 1: 77–97.

Wikan, Unni. 1982. *Behind the Veil in Arabia: Women in Oman.* Baltimore: Johns Hopkins University Press.

Young, William C. 1993. "The Ka'ba, Gender, and the Rites of Pilgrimage." *International Journal of Middle East Studies* 25: 285–301.

Zuhur, Sherifa. 1992. *Revealing Reveiling: Islamist Gender Ideology in Contemporary Egypt.* Albany: State University of New York Press.

Index